NORTH AMERICAN SOCIETY FOR SPORT HISTORY 1972

Sport on Film and Video

The North American Society for Sport History Guide

Judith A. Davidson
Editor and Compiler
and
Daryl Adler
Compiler

The Scarecrow Press, Inc.
Metuchen, N.J., & London
1993

British Library Cataloguing-in-Publication data available.

Library of Congress Cataloging-in-Publication Data

Sport on film and video : the North American Society for Sport History guide / Judith A. Davidson, editor and compiler and Daryl Alder, compiler.
     p.   cm.
  ISBN 0-8108-2739-5
  1. Sports—History—Film catalogs. I. Davidson, Judith A., 1944- . II. Alder, Daryl. III. North American Society for Sport History.
GV576. S578 1993
796′ .029′4—dc20   93-27967

CONTENTS

INTRODUCTION

This project grew out of my constant search for films that were suitable for my sport history classes at the University of Iowa. In a moment of weakness at a meeting of the North American Society for Sport History, I volunteered to compile a list of sports films for NAASH members. It quickly became apparent to me that there were numerous films readily available which would serve a variety of educational purposes and which would be applicable beyond the boundaries of the classroom. Therefore, the films in this filmography range from general interest to specific historical, sociological, and psychological topics in sport. The age range covered by the films includes children to adults.

As the project began to take on mammoth proportions, I enlisted the help of Daryl Adler, then a Master's student in library science at the University of Iowa. We attempted to locate as many titles as possible by combining numerous film lists produced by corporations and sports organizations, and we attempted to keep up with new releases. Undoubtedly, some titles have been inadvertently omitted. I apologize for this and trust that whoever takes on the task of a second edition will rectify those omissions. Although the filmography is extensive, we did not include every possible film. I hope that you agree with our choices. A word about what is not included in this filmography; omitted were instructional films that show "how to do it," unless the film has value as a primary source, for example, women's three court basketball. There are simply too many of these films, and they did not match the intend of this filmography. Also omitted were commercial films. A filmography for those already exists: Jeffrey H. Wallenfeldt (ed.), *Sport Movies: A Guide to Nearly 500 Films Focusing on Sports* (Evanston, IL: CineBooks, 1989).

I hope that you get much use out of this filmography. What started out as a small project, turned out to be a major undertaking. Nevertheless, it was enjoyable and I hope it serves a useful purpose. Thanks and gratitude are due to the North American Society for Sport History, which funded this project. Richard Keller helped at the beginning with the subject index. The project could not have been completed without the good-natured assistance of Andy Bean. Andy did all the tedious data entry and corrections without complaining! He deserves the highest accolades and awards for his unending patience. Daryl Adler did the preliminary research and indexing. She deserves the lion's share of the credit for this project. I will take responsibility for any entries you feel should not have been included in the final indexing, for any which were left out, as well as for any other mistakes. I'll also assume the responsibility for the length of time it took to complete this project.

Judith A. Davidson
Central Connecticut State University
May 1993

HOW TO USE THIS FILMOGRAPHY

There are four separate indexes contained in this filmography: title, topic, name, and distributor. All films are listed at least twice, once alphabetically by title and at least once under a topic heading. Many films are listed under multiple topics, depending on content. For example, "Cat (A Woman Who Fought Back)," is indexed by topic under professional sport, boxing, and women and sport; and also in the name index under: Davis, Cathy. Using the topic index first will direct you to the titles of all films listed under the topic. Then, go back to the title index to find the film you want.

Each entry in the title index includes a brief description of the film and is followed by additional information, including the date the film was released, length of the film, type of projector required, color or black and white, age appeal (i.e., junior, high school, or adult), and a chronological placement of the subject of the film. NL indicates information was not available.

The final symbol(s) listed in capital letters is (are) the film's distributors. The distributors are listed alphabetically by symbol, then by name and address. We have tried to make this information as timely and as accurate as possible, but invariably there will be changes even as we go to press.

To obtain a film, contact the distributors listed, but leave adequate time to comply with varied procedures. In many instances, films are free of charge except for shipping. Because charges for rentals undoubtedly change over time, none are listed.

This is a straight-forward, simple guide to use; good luck and enjoyable viewing.

Example of title index:

BAER vs. LOUIS (1935)

This is the complete motion picture of the heavyweight boxing contest held at Yankee Stadium, New York on September 24, 1935.

1935; 22 min.; VHS; BW; JR, HS, A; Depression Era.

BHAWK

Explanation of Abbreviations Used

A = Adult
BHAWK = Distributor (For full address, refer to Distributor Index.)
BW = Black and White
E = Elementary School Age
HS = High School Age
JR = Junior High School Age
NL = Not Listed
VHS = Video Tape

TITLE INDEX

ABC STORY, THE

The hundreds of elements that go into making up the world's largest participation sports organization come to life in this thorough look at the inside and outside of the American Bowling Congress. Bowling Headquarters and how it operates is an important portion, as are segments about the ABC national tournament, the annual delegates' meeting, and a ride through New England with veteran field representative Bob Lynch going through his paces as the ABC's eyes and ears. A visit to Port Washington, WI shows how bowlers enjoy countless services and awards through their membership in the Congress. ABC's half-million-dollar awards program is another portion of the production.

NL; 25 min; 16 mm; NL; JR, HS, A; Post World War II.

ABC

ABIMES

The reconstruction of a spectacular accident: the fall of a mountain climber in the Alps. Exciting film.

1972; 16 min; 16 mm; color JR, HS, A; Post World War II.

FACSEA

ABLE DISABLED, THE

Shows in separate segments handicapped teenagers and young adults participating in a variety of activities, including organized sports, recreation, and wilderness living. Includes the segments Augustus, The Special Olympics, Picnic, and Outward Bound.

1980; 27 min; 16 mm, VHS, U-Matic; color; JR, HS, A; Post World War II.

LAWREN

ABOUT SPORTS IN GERMANY

Where there is sport, there are young, happy faces. Sometimes the camera will discover tensions and extreme concentration, especially in competitions. This film presents a variety of indoor and outdoor sports that are popular in Germany.

1963; 40 min; 16mm; NL; JR, HS, A; Post World War II.

MTPS

ABSENT LINK

The role of a certified trainer in the prevention, treatment, and rehabilitation of athletic injuries. The great need for a trainer and wide range of career opportunities available to young people in the field of athletic training are shown.

NL; 29 min; 16 mm; NL; JR, HS, A; Post World War II.

MTPS

ABSOLUTELY NONAUTHORITATIVE HISTORY OF AMERICAN SPORTS, THE

Chronologizes American sports, mixing animation and live action.

1984; 10 min; 16 mm; color; JR, HS, A; Premodern Sport; Making of Modern Sport; Modern Sport; Golden Age; Depression Era; Post World War II.

MTOLP

ABYSS

Documentary of R. Sorgato's expedition up the west peak of Lavaredo in the Dolomites, one of the most difficult alpine mountains to climb. Shows how Sorgato fell more than 140 feet over a sheer overhang of rock, and how, after being given up for dead, he managed to rescue himself.

1974; 17 min; 16 mm; color; HS, A; Post World War II.

PHENIX; PENNST

ACROSS CULTURES: A SERIES

Compares and contrasts the Japanese, the Tarajumara Indians of Mexico, and the Baoule tribe of the Ivory Coast of West Africa. Looks at their religion, customs, sports, and family needs. Includes these titles:

Baoule, The
Choices For the Future

Communication
Cultural Change
Cultural Exchange
Education
Environment, The
Japanese, The
Passing On Tradition
Providing For Family Needs
Religion
Sports, Society, and Self
Trahumara, The
1983; NL; VHS, U-MATIC; Color; JR HS, A; Ancient to Post World War II.
AITECH

ACTIVE ONES, THE

Film takes a look at the important part that bowling plays in the lives of modern American women. There is also a historical theme to the film, tracing bowling's history and depicting the role of women in the growth of the nation.
NL; 18 min; 16 mm; NL; JR, HS, A; Post World War II.
WIBC

ADVENTURE AT GREAT BEAR LAKE

Reveals the adventure of fishing for trophy-sized trout and greyling in the cold waters of Great Bear Lake in Northern Canada.
NL; 22 min; 16 mm; NL; A; Post World War II.
MCDO

ADVENTURE WITH MULE DEER

The story of deer hunting in the Jackson Hole, Wyoming, area. Includes scenes of geese and elk. With Fred T. Huntington, Gordon Eastman, and Les Turner.
NL; 25 min; 16 mm; NL; JR, HS, A; Post World War II.
RCBS

AERIAL DAREDEVILS

Exciting aviation daredevil thrills from the 1920s (silent).
NL; 10 min; 16 mm; NL; JR, HS, A; Golden Age.
BUDGET

AEROBIC EXERCISING

Aerobic exercising adds life to your living and years to your life. Any exercise that increases the body's intake of oxygen is aerobic: the increased oxygen benefits the entire body, with increased strength and endurance, a heightened feeling of well-being, loss of body fat, and lowered blood pressure. Empha-sizes the need for sensible preparation for any fitness program, as well as attention to safety.
1987; 14 min; 16 mm; color; JR, HS, A; Post World War II.
UWISC

AFL HIGHLIGHTS, 1965

NL; NL; 16 mm; NL; JR, HS, A; Post World War II.
MILLER

AFTER THE FIRST

A boy receives a rifle as a birthday gift, and he is taken by his father on his first hunting trip. The father sees the trip as the passing on of a tradition, an initiation. However, the boy's excitement at discovering the power of his gun is more than balanced out by his later realization of the cruelty and finality of death that it causes. This is a sensitive film that highlights the problem of traditional attitudes that do not always make it over the generation gap.
14 min; 16 mm, VHS; color; JR, HS, A; Post World War II.
FRACOC

AHEAD OF THE CROWD

Views athletes who have thoughts on the secrets of success. Details the winning strategies of these athletes and the motivating factor that lies behind successful people. Includes discussions with athletes such as Bob Griese of football, Stan Smith of tennis, Lou Brock of baseball, Laura Baugh of golf, and Mary Decker of track.
NL; 29 min; 16 mm; color; JR, HS, A; Post World War II.
MTPS

AIMING FOR THE GOLD

Witness U. S. Olympic shooting team skills in training as members aim for the gold. Events which require extraordinary discipline and perfection include free pistol, rapid-fire pistol, women's sport pistol, free rifle—3-position, women's standard rifle—3-position, running target (air rifle), women's and men's air rifle, and Olympic trap and skeet.
NL; 10 min; video, color; JR, HS, A; Post World War II.
NRA; KAROL

AKC . . . AND THE SPORT OF DOGS

Opening with a two-minute encapsulated history of the purebred dog, this program covers the diversity of competitive events held under the AKC rules. It is divided into three equal parts: dog shows, obedience, and field trials.

NL; 33 min; 16 mm; color; JR, HS, A, Post World War II.

MTPS

ALL-AMERICANS, THE

The American Road Race of champions, windup of a year's Sports Car Club of American road racing. This film features the OCF Racing Team—Tony De-Lorenzo and Gerry Thompson—driving the fastest Corvettes in the world.

NL; 12 min; 16 mm; JR, HS, A; Post World War II.

OWENSC

ALL-IRELAND FOOTBALL FINAL 1975

Kerry vs. Dublin

NL; 27 min; 16 mm; NL; JR, HS, A; Post World War II.

RSTF

ALL-IRELAND HURLING FINAL 1975

Kilkenny vs. Galway

NL; 27 min; 16 mm; NL; JR, HS, A; Post World War II.

RSTF

ALL PRO

A series of candid conversations with a group of top-notch, successful sports figures, this popular film provides viewers with numerous insights into what it takes to be an All Pro.

NL; 29 min; 16 mm, VHS; color; HS, A; Post World War II Sport.

CCCD

ALL-STAR GOLF

78 matches.

1959-60 series, 26 matches, 57 min. each.

1958-59 series, 26 matches, 57 min. each.

1957-58 series, 26 matches, 57 min. each.

1957-60; 57 min each; 16 mm; BW; JR, HS, A; Post World War II.

MILLER

ALL-STAR HIGHLIGHTS

A film on basketball games.

1973; 15 min; 16 mm; NL; JR, HS, A; Post World War II.

NBA

ALL THE STUFF THERE IS

Focuses upon developing positive student self-concepts through individual development of a variety of physical education skills. Emphasizes the importance of self-confidence and self-discipline as a basis for lifetime enjoyment of sports. Deals with elementary-age students.

1973; 14 min; 16 mm; color; E, JR, A; Post World War II.

AAHPER; UWISC

ALL THE WAY UP THERE

Tells the story of Bruce Burgess, a 24-year-old victim of cerebral palsy whose dream was to reach the top of New Zealand's Mt. Ruapehu.

1980; 27 min; 16 mm, VHS, U-Matic; color; JR, HS, A; Post World War II.

EBEC

ALMOST GIANTS (L'ENVERS DES MEDALLES—LES LIMITES DE L'IMPOSSIBLE)

In recent years, Canada has risen from virtual obscurity in women's gymnastics to become one of the top ten countries in the world, directly behind the United States and Eastern Europe. *Almost Giants* takes a behind-the-scenes look at the training process—from young hopefuls in individual clubs to the selection of competitors for a berth on the national team. Highlights include the team's training and preparation for, as well as participation in, the 1983 World Championships in Budapest, where the Canadian National Women's Gymnastic Team finished in the top twelve.

1984; 24.5 min; 16 mm; color; JR, HS, A; Post World War II.

NFBC

ALMOST PERFECT

This is a story of the 1973-1974 Milwaukee Bucks season that ended one game short of perfection. The drama of the NBA is captured in this film that offers a special tribute to one of the game's greatest, Oscar Robertson. Basketball fans will enjoy seeing Kareem Abdul Jabbar and his teammates take it all the way to the seventh game of the NBA finals with the Boston Celtics.

NL; 28 min; 16 mm; NL; JR, HS, A; Post World War II.

CINES

ALWAYS WITH STYLE

Highlights the 1966 professional football season featuring team and individual performances of the Baltimore Colts.

1967; 27 min; 16 mm; color; JR, HS, A; Post World War II.

NFL

AMERICAN ATHLETE, THE: THE JUNIOR OLYMPIC WAY

Every year, 3 million young athletes, ages 8-18, compete in the AAU/Sears Junior Olympics, the nation's largest multisport program. Narrated by Kurt Thomas and Jennifer Chandler, the film shows the culmination of months of training and discipline as athletes compete in this 16th national meet—the stepping stone to international competition and possible Olympic glory.

NL; 20 min; 16 mm, U-Matic; color; HS, A; Post World War II.

SEARS; MTPS

AMERICAN GREYHOUND: THE DOG

Traces the history of greyhound racing from ancient times to the present. Shows some of the contemporary breeding and training techniques used in greyhound racing in America today.

1975; 20 min; 16 mm; color; JR, HS, A; Ancient to Post World War II.

AGTOA

AMERICANS ON EVEREST

In this extraordinary film record of one man's mountain-climbing achievements, a team of American mountaineers is followed from the earliest training and testing on Mount Rainier, Washington, to the top of Everest. The narration, containing a remarkable amount of detail, and the photography combine to illustrate some of the suspense, excitement, hardship, failures, successes, and pride that the climbers felt.

1967; 55 min; 16 mm; NL; JR, HS, A; Post World War II.

PYRAMID; OSU

AMERICAN WILDERNESS, THE

Deals with man's needs for space to reflect, to retreat, and to come in contact with an unspoiled nature, presenting the American wilderness as an irreplaceable resource which must be preserved for future generations. Points out that, although a law to preserve these lands was passed in 1964, most wilderness areas, once destroyed, cannot be legislated back into existence. Scenic views include the Sierras, Yosemite, and the Cascades. Reported by Hugh Downs.

1971; 53 min; 16 mm; color; JR, HS, A; Post World War II.

NBC; FI; MICHMED

AMERICA'S CUP 1977

An overview of the 1977 America's Cup yacht races. Shows American and foreign trials for the cup, introduces various personalities involved, and gives highlights of the final races won by skipper Ted Turner in the American yacht *Courageous*.

1988; 12 min; 16 mm, VHS, U-Matic; color; JR, HS, A; Post World War II.

OFFSHR

AMERICA'S HORSE

An entertaining, in-depth look at the American quarter horse and why he is America's favorite horse. From breeding farms in Florida to a roundup in Texas, from showing in North Carolina to chariot racing in Idaho, and from rodeos to trail rides, *America's Horse* features the quarter horse in a variety of settings.

NL; 30 min; 16 mm; VHS, color; JR, HS, A; Post World War II.

AQHA

ANCIENT GAMES, THE

Former decathlon champions Bill Toomey and Rafer Johnson document the history of the ancient Greek games; explore Delphi, site of the Pythian Games—ranked second in importance only to the games held at Olympus—and discuss sports, physical education, competition, and Greek history, heritage, and culture.

1972; 28 min; 16 mm; color; JR, HS, A; Ancient Sport—Greece.

CORF

ANCIENT GREECE

Shows the Parthenon, the Academia, the Plain of Marathon, Delphi, and the Athenian countryside while pointing out the achievements of the ancient Greeks in philosophy, athletics, politics, and the arts.

1976; 10 min; 16 mm, VHS, U-Matic; color; JR, HS, A; Ancient Greece.

CORF

ANDRETTI

An inside look at the life of Mario Andretti, one of the superstars of automobile racing.

NL; 28 min; 16 mm; NL; JR, HS, A; Post World War II.
MCDO

ANGEL PERALTA (L'ART DE TORREER A CHEVAL)

The bullfight in which the toreador is on horseback is the most ancient form of the sport, and Angel Peralta is its most famous contemporary practitioner. Slow-motion and freeze-frame shots, together with classical music, emphasize the ritualistic, almost choreographic side of the ancient sport.
1973; 12 min; 16 mm; color; JR, HS, A; Post World War II.
UILL

ANGLER'S AUTUMN

This lyrical, nonnarrated portrait of the fisherman's solitary pleasures promotes respect for the river's intricate ecological balance.
NL; 11 min; 16 mm; color, JR, HS, A; Post World War II.
PYRAMID

ANIMAL OLYMPIANS

Intercuts scenes of humans participating in Olympic events with scenes of animals performing similar feats. Includes such scenes as a cheetah accelerating from 9 to 45 miles per hour in two seconds and a Jaguar going 70 miles per hour.
1981; 50 min; 16 mm; color; JR, HS, A; Post World War II.
BBC; FI; USC

ANIMAL PARTNERS

Shows three young people discussing their feelings about the animals they work with in preparation for sports competition.
1977; 13 min; 16 mm, VHS, U-Matic; color; JR, HS, A; Post World War II.
FI

ANOTHER YESTERDAY

Explores the theme of "How it Feels to Be Beat-Up" through the life of an Afro-American prize fighter. Shows the fighter getting up for road work at 6:00 A.M., working on the docks, training in the evening, and finally, fighting the big fight.
1963; 16 min; 16 mm; BW; JR, HS, A; Post World War II.
UPENN

ANTI-HERO, THE

Edited from the motion picture *The Loneliness of the Long Distance Runner,* starring Tom Courtenay. The film treats the theme of the struggle for identity and investigates the conflict of the alienated individual and society. Also examines the pressures to "play the game."
NL; 20 min; 16 mm, VHS; NL; JR, HS, A; Post World War II.
SF

ANY NUMBER CAN PLAY

Presents an in-depth look at the extensive sports program of the Indiana High School Athletic Association. Shows young boys and girls competing in track, swimming, baseball, basketball, football, and golf. Notes that many high school athletes often go on to become professional athletes.
1976; 26 min; 16 mm; color; HS, A; Post World War II .
IU

ARABIANS

At a horse ranch high in the Rockies, we see the breeding and care of purebred Arabian stallions.
1945; 10 min; 16 mm; NL; JR, HS, A; Post World War II.
BUDGET

ARCHERY

Introduces archery in American sign language, showing the fun of the sport as well as the importance of precaution and safety. Signed by Maria Torres. (silent)
1975; 2 min; 16 mm; color; E, JR, HS, A; Post World War II.
JOYCE

AROUND THE LEAGUE WITH THE MILWAUKEE BRAVES 1962

NL; 20-30 min; 16 mm; color; JR, HS, A; Post World War II.
BUDGET

ASTRO BLUE BONNET BOWL

1964 HIGHLIGHTS Tulsa 14, Mississippi 7
1965 HIGHLIGHTS Tennessee 27, Tulsa 6
1966 HIGHLIGHTS Texas 19, Mississippi 0
1967 HIGHLIGHTS Colorado 31, Miami 21
1968 HIGHLIGHTS SMU 28, Oklahoma 27
1969 HIGHLIGHTS Houston 36, Auburn 7
1970 HIGHLIGHTS Oklahoma 24, Alabama 24
1971 HIGHLIGHTS Colorado 27, Houston 17
1972 HIGHLIGHTS Tennessee 21, LSU 14

1973 HIGHLIGHTS Houston 47, Tulane 7
1974 HIGHLIGHTS North Carolina State 31, Houston 31
1964-74; 30 min each; 16 mm; NL; JR, HS, A; Post World War II.
ABB

AT 2 P.M. PRECISELY
Featuring the 1971 Wimbledon Championship final between John Newcombe and Stan Smith, the film also includes match play starring Laver, Court, Ashe, Gonzales, and Evert and Goolagong.
1971; 52 min; 16 mm; color; JR, HS, A; Post World War II.
USTEN

ATHLETES AND ADDICTION: IT'S NOT A GAME
This specially edited ABC Sports production offers viewers a realistic picture of addiction and treatment. The program shows why people, especially athletes, can succumb to the lures of substance abuse and relapse after recovery. The viewer gets an intimate glimpse of life in a treatment center as recovering addicts—including Edmonton Oiler hockey player Dave Hunter—talk about their struggles with substance abuse. Viewers will also follow the stories of several other professional sports figures who are fighting the battle with drugs and alcohol. Hosted by Jim McKay and Lynn Swann, the program presents informative interviews and insights into addiction and enables one to experience a 28-day treatment program.
1990; 55 min and 32 min; VHS; color; JR, HS, A; Post World War II.
ABCS; CORF; MTI

AUSTRALIAN REPORT
Surveys Australia in the mid-seventies, enjoying the benefits and coping with the disadvantages of its technological development. Discusses the growth of cities and shows the sports of the coastal fringe dwellers, as well as the work and play of those in new areas of vast mineral deposits. Economically, wool, cattle, and steel production are strong contributors.
1975; 20 min; 16 mm; color; JR, HS, A; Post World War II.
JOU; UCOLO

AUTO-RACE-ARAMA
Power-packed machines and talented drivers prove their mettle in USAC events: Indianapolis 500, Milwaukee's Miller 200 and Rex Mays Classic, Phoenix 150, and a sprint car sizzler.

NL; NL; 16 mm; NL; JR, HS, A; Post World War II.
MILLER

AUTO RACING
A combination of many forms of racing, from automobile, motorcycle, stock, and formula car, to specialized racing in rain and a very special auto race in slush and snow.
NL; 30 min; 16 mm; NL; JR, HS, A; Post World War II.
BUDGET

BABE RUTH
Biography of one of baseball's all-time greats.
1965; 25 min; 16 mm; BW; JR, HS, A; Golden Age, Depression Era and World War II.
SF; MICHMED

BAER vs. LOUIS (1935)
This is the complete motion picture of the heavyweight boxing contest held at Yankee Stadium, New York, on September 24, 1935.
1935; 22 min; VHS; BW; JR, HS, A; Depression Era.
BHAWK

BAHAMAS TUNA THRILLS
The huge, fighting tuna falls to the strength and perseverance of the sport fisherman.
NL; 28 min; 16 mm; NL; JR, HS, A, Post World War II.
CINES

BAJA 1000
The Baja 1000 race is held in Baja, California. It is a grueling 1000-mile course over every kind of terrain—mountains, desert, dirt roads, no roads, and a little bit of pavement, too. This is the last outlet for the frustrated racer who cannot afford the huge money outlay of Indy car racing or the sports car and stock car fields.
NL; 20 min; 16 mm; color; JR, HS, A; Post World War II.
BUDGET

BAJA: OFF-ROAD WITH BFG
The Baja: one of the meanest, toughest, most punishing rides in racing. A grueling, off-road contest between the most rugged of terrain and men and their machines. Join Frank "Scoop" Vessels and Gary Pace, as they come roaring home as winners. Includes preparation scenes, interviews, and behind-the-wheel action.

NL; 24 min; 16 mm; color; JR, HS, A; Post World War II.
MTPS

BAJA: ROAD TO MANHOOD

This film is set within the rugged countryside of Baja, in which 20 youngsters ages 12-16 challenged and conquered a 1200-mile journey to manhood. The trek lasted some two weeks, through heat and dust. Film shows the planning and work and endurance that the youngsters had to go through to make the adventure a success.

NL; 15 min; 16 mm; NL; JR, HS, A; Post World War II.
HONDA

BALLAD OF A TEAM

Making a team is one thing—becoming a team is another. Poetic words and music are used to show how a disparate group of 45 young men who come from all parts of America join together to become a team. This ballad follows the young men from their beginnings in the NFL through trials and tribulations and finally to that moment of victory when they realize that they have become a team in the truest sense of the word. This program is inspirational, with a touch of humor and a strong theme of unity.

1985; 10 min; 16 mm, VHS, U-Matic; color; JR, HS, A; Post World War II.
NFL; TMA

BALLOON SAFARI

Joan and Alan Root, famed wildlife cinematographers, take to a hot-air balloon as a quiet, slow-moving vehicle for filming the animals and people of Kenya. A colorful adventure narrated with amiable humor by David Niven. Spectacular climax with the first balloon flight over Mt. Kilimanjaro.

1981; 55 min; 16 mm; color; JR, HS, A; Post World War II.
BNCHMK; OSU

BANG THE DRUM SLOWLY: FRIENDSHIP AND COMPASSION

Set against the backdrop of big-league baseball, the film is an exploration of American values. Based on the novel by Mark Harris, the film adaptation is, on one level, the moving story of two ballplayers and their unlikely friendship. On a deeper level, it is an examination of the motivations and actions of big-league ballplayers, of men regarded as national heroes. Henry Wiggen is the New York Mammoth's ace pitcher, and Bruce Pearson is the second-rate catcher. When Henry learns that Bruce is dying of Hodgkin's disease, he begins to reexamine his values and friendship and compassion become more important than winning.

1979; 38 min; 16 mm; color; JR, HS, A; Post World War II.
LSU

BART STARR

Unlike the rest of the quarterbacks in the Hall of Fame, Bart Starr was not a natural athlete, but was rather a self-made man. His progress came slowly, but through an understanding of his own faults, Starr's story is worth telling to all young players who aspire to play quarterback.

1985; 8 min; VHS, U-Matic; color, JR, HS, A; Post World War II.
NFL; TMA

BASEBALL: THE NOW CAREER

Baseball offers exciting opportunities to young men with athletic ability. The story of the road to the big leagues, as seen through the eyes of several players, including Nolan Ryan and Reggie Jackson, who were Little League graduates, Johnny Bench and Tug McGraw.

NL; 26 min; 16 mm; NL; JR, HS, A; Post World War II.
LLBI

BASKETBALL: 1974 HIGHLIGHTS

Including NCAA college and university divisions, NAIA National Championship, Collegiate Commissioners Association Tourney, NBA and ABA championships, ACC coaches in-game action.

1974; NL; 16 mm; NL; JR, HS, A; Post World War II.
ASF

BASKETBALL STRATEGY FOR GIRLS

Shows various basketball plays on a magnetic board; then the plays are demonstrated on the basketball court by a group of college girls. Includes screening plays, figure "8" offense, and fast breaks. Illustrates guarding techniques—zone defense, triangle defense, player-to-player defense, and diagonal defense. Summarizes both offensive and defensive play in chart form. Useful as a primary source to demonstrate change in the women's game.

1955; 11 min; 16 mm; BW; HS, A; Post World War II.
MGHT; UTA

BASKETBALL TECHNIQUES FOR GIRLS

Shows a group of college girls demonstrating the basic skills in basketball—control of body movement, passing, shooting, turning, and starting. Illustrates such passing fundamentals as holding the ball, finger control, footwork, turning, types of passes, and catching. Illustrates movements with slow-motion techniques and summarizes each section with charts.

1955; 11 min; 16 mm; BW; HS, A; Post World War II.

MGHT; UTEX

BASKETBALL TODAY

Opens with a comical reenactment of the original version of the game and shows how refinement of the rules led to the exciting game we see today. Covers the following important areas of the rules: contact situations, goal tending, basket interference, fouls, and officiating mechanics.

1973; 28 min; 16 mm; BW; JR, HS, A; Making of Modern Sport, Modern Sport, Golden Age, Depression Era and World War II Sport, Post World War II.

UCOLO

BASS AND THE PROS

Television sportsman Jerry Chiappetta, of *My Pal, My Son* fame, takes a look at the fastest growing sport on water: tournament bass fishing. You will see what big-league bass tournaments are really like and get tips from some of the top money-making bass fishermen.

NL; 26 min; 16 mm; NL; JR, HS, A; Post World War II.

SOLANA

BASS ANGLERS '72 CLASSIC

Twenty-four of the world's top professional bass anglers compete for lunker bass and cash prizes at J. Percy Pries Reservoir in the annual Bass Angler's Sportsmen Society Classic.

NL; 27 min; NL; NL; JR, HS, A; Post World War II.

TELEFILM

BASS FISHING'S BEST

A film about fishing: a mystery site; a select group of bass anglers; a 3-day competitive "fish-off"; a Miller High Life Cup; and a $15,000 first-place check.

NL, 26 min; 16 mm; NL; JR, HS, A; Post World War II.

MILLER

BASS SOUTHERN STYLE

Beginning with short background on "Bass Country, U.S.A.," the film carries the viewer to the South's hottest fishing holes, including Toledo Bend, Lake

Amistad on the Texas-Mexico border, and the Santee-Cooper lake counties of South Carolina. The film covers the origin of the bass boat from a simple "johnboat" in the Louisiana bayous to its modern evolution in today's fishing world. The bass boat's capabilities are also depicted, and the viewer of the film will clearly understand why pro anglers call it the "purest fishing machine ever."

NL; 25 min; 16 mm; NL; JR, HS, A; Modern Sport to Post World War II.

SOLANA

BATTER UP

This enjoyable short takes you back to Ebbets Field in 1917 and brings you up to the date the film was made. Relive exploits of some of baseball's all-time giants: Babe Ruth, Lou Gehrig, Joe DiMaggio, and Carl Hubbel—who strikes out Ruth, Gehrig, and Jimmy Foxx in a row. You'll see a roster of presidents who carried on the tradition of throwing out the first ball—Wilson, Harding, Coolidge, Roosevelt, and Truman—and get glimpses of Will Rogers and baseball's first commissioner, Kenshaw Mountain Landis. Also included is footage of the first game played at night in New York (1941), as well as highlights of the 1948 Cleveland-Boston game.

NL; 10 min; 16 mm; NL; JR, HS, A; Modern Sport to Post World War II.

FILMIC

BATTLE OF THE AGES

Twenty-nine-year-old Pete Tountas and 60-year-old Buzz Fazio lock up in a thriller that goes down to the last ball of the 1968 ABC Masters.

NL; 15 min; 16 mm; NL; JR, HS, A; Post World War II.

ABC

BATTY WORLD OF BASEBALL WITH HARRY CAREY

NL; 29 min; 16 mm; color; JR, HS, A; Post World War II.

NBHF

BAY AT THE MOON

The baying of hound dogs is to many men "the sweetest music in the world," and this film shows men and dogs both having the time of their lives in pursuit of raccoon, rabbit, and mountain lion. No commercial narration . . . just the voices of the dogs, the talk of the hunters, and an unusual background of American folk music and songs. Sequences showing rabbits in the snow, raccoons being treed, and a mountain lion cornered in a canyon by cowboys are particularly interesting. Plenty of campfire views, Western atmosphere, and some fine evening-in-the-forest scenes with great action by the stars of the film—the hounds.

30 min; 16 mm, VHS, U-Matic, BETA; color; JR, HS, A; Post World War II.

KAROL

BEAR BEATS THE BEST, THE

Presents the 1975 PGA championship won by Jack Nicklaus, the "Bear."

NL; 27 min; 16 mm; color; JR, HS, A; Post World War II.

PGA

BEAUTY KNOWS NO PAIN

Shows the ordeal of training and testing to which coeds submit themselves in order to join the Kilgore (Texas) College Rangerettes and share in the glamor of the football field. Includes interviews with members and is partly narrated by the group's director. Some viewers will applaud the dedication, patriotism, charm, and obedience shown by these young women, while others will criticize their exploitation as sex objects and their indoctrination to "All-American" values. Many may miss the subtle satire throughout.

1973; 25 min; 16 mm; color; JR, HS, A; Post World War II.

BNCHMK; UCB

BE FIT AND LIVE

1974; 18 min; 16 mm; color; JR, HS, A; Post World War II.

PYRAMID; UILL

BEFORE YOU HUNT

This partly animated film emphasizes the vital role of the hunter in establishing game laws, promoting game management, and financing wildlife conservation. Hunter ethics and firearm safety are clearly explained.

NL; 28 min; 16 mm; NL; JR, HS, A; Post World War II.

MTPS

BEGINNING OF WINNING

The story centers around a Little League baseball team and the struggles they have with their coach, their parents, and their own inabilities, with a clear message about the need for good leadership and good sportsmanship.

1984; 30 min; VHS; color; JR, HS, A; Post World War II.

USOOE

BEGINNINGS

Highlights from the second National Sports Festival in Colorado Springs.

1980; 28 min; 16 mm; color; JR, HS, A; Post World War II.

USOC

BEGINNING RESPONSIBILITY

Explores several situations which involve a brother and sister in acts of sportsmanship and gives insights into motivation and suggestions for improvement. Includes suggestions such as continuing to try, encouraging others, laughing at oneself, listening to others, and standing up for what is right. Shows that consideration and compromise are foremost in sportsmanship. Contains sexual stereotyping.

1969; 10 min; 16 mm; color; JR, HS, A; Post World War II.

IU

BEING FEMALE AND BEING ATHLETIC

This program focuses on the special physiological needs of women in sports; needs due to thinner bones, less muscle, and more body fat than their male counterparts, to the possible effects of exercise on the menstrual cycle—of oligo or amenorrhea—of other hormonal changes typical in competitive female athletes, and of possible physical dangers to the breasts, uterus, and bone density. The program stresses the importance of frequent checkups and testing, and describes treatment for the typical problems that arise.

NL; 19 min; VHS; color; HS, A; Post World War II.

FOTH

BEST I CAN, THE

Looks at the lives of three former participants in the Special Olympics for the handicapped, showing the effect that participation has had on them and those close to them.

1978; 16 min; 16 mm; color; JR, HS, A; Post World War II.

COCA

BEST I CAN, THE

Gymnast Marcie practices gymnastics four hours daily. During the Junior Olympics competition, we see her slip from the balance beam, but she gets back up and goes on. Diver Lara spends much time working out before she even gets near the water. She demonstrates some dives, discusses competition, and talks about overcoming fears.

1975; 12 min; 16 mm; color; JR, HS, A, Post World War II.

FI; OSU

BEST OF 33

A film about 33 drivers who compete at the Indianapolis 500. Thirty-three cars qualify and make the field, but only one will be a winner. Indianapolis is the biggest auto racing event in the world from the standpoint of total purse, number of spectators, and from the immense investment in racing machinery. In this year of filming, speeds almost reached 200 mph, which may never happen again, due to anticipated rules changes.

NL; 30 min; 16 mm; color; JR, HS, A; Post World War II.

BUDGET

BEST OF ALL

Commentary by sportscaster Jimmy Crum, outlining campaign of the now retired free-for-all pacing star Best of All.

NL; 27 min; 16 mm; NL; JR, HS, A; Post World War II.

USTA

BEST OF BASEBALL

Shows the highlights of the Milwaukee Braves in 1960.

1960; 30 min; 16 mm; color, JR, HS, A; Post World War II.

NBC

BEST OF BASEBALL 1960, THE

The Milwaukee Braves in competition with the Pittsburgh Pirates, Los Angeles Dodgers, and many other teams.

NL; 20-30 min; 16 mm; color; JR, HS, A; Post World War II.

BUDGET

BEST OF FOOTBALL FOLLIES, THE

Funny, clever, and strange segments from *Football Follies*.

NL; 44 min; VHS; NL; JR, HS, A; Post World War II.

KAROL

BEST OF THE FOOTBALL FOLLIES

A compilation of the funniest, most clever, and strangest segments from the famed *Football Follies* series. Slapstick, cartoon voices, classical music spoofs, and movie trailer parodies. Also included is a segment showing NFL coaches wired for sound dur-

ing games and a factual feature on the worst teams in football history.

1985; 44 min; VHS, U-Matic; color; JR, HS, A; Post World War II.

NFL; TMA

BEST OF TIMES (1920-1924)

For many Americans, the early years of the 1920s are fondly remembered as "the golden era" . . . days of peace and prosperity when anything seemed possible. Traces the rise of Rudolf Valentino, John Barrymore, and the young Franklin Delano Roosevelt, then campaigning for the vice-presidency against Warren Harding. Coverage of the inauguration of the nation's first commercial radio station, KDKA in Pittsburgh, and the first World Series to be recorded on film.

1984; 24 min; 16 mm; color; JR, HS, A; Golden Age of Sport.

UWISC

BEST YOU CAN BE, THE

Highlights the Pan American Games of 1979, held in San Juan, Puerto Rico; features several athletes discussing their hard work and training as they work toward their goal of being an Olympic champion.

NL; 30 min; 16 mm; color; JR, HS, A; Post World War II.

USOC

BEYOND THE FINISH LINE

Presents several black Olympic champions who testify to the value of a drug-free life. Features comments by each champion on sports as a fulfilling personal experience in comparison to the use of drugs.

1974; 35 min; 16 mm; color; JR, HS, A; Post World War II.

CINES

BICYCLES ARE BEAUTIFUL

Bicyclists have the chance to test their knowledge of bicycle safety and rules of the road when they see this film. Narrated by Bill Cosby, this film includes a history of bicycling, a discussion of rules of the road, safety inspection of bicycles, and a safety test in which the audience participates.

NL; 27 min; 16 mm; NL; JR, HS, A; Modern to Post World War II.

MTPS

BICYCLING FOR PHYSICAL FITNESS, HEALTH, AND RECREATION

Defines the benefits of bicycling through practical examples and in basic physiological terms. Demonstrates the value of bicycle riding as exercise and recreation, both in terms of achieving and maintaining physical health. Shows how cycling can be incorporated efficiently into daily living.

1974; 14 min; 16 mm; color; JR, HS, A; Post World War II.

AIMS; UILL

BIG GAME AMERICA

This show shows how pro football's first 50 years reflected society as it evolved. The second half of the program features interviews and behind-the-scenes looks at Jim Marshall and Don Meredith as they prepared for a game. They were also miked for sound during the game.

NL; 51 min; 16 mm, VHS, U-Matic; NL; JR, HS, A; Depression Era and World War II to Post World War II.

NFL; TMA

BIG GAME, THE

As the basketball teams of Muncie Central and Anderson High in Indiana prepare to meet in an annual game of a long-standing rivalry, this film examines what this competition means to the community, the coaches, and the players themselves.

1982; 55 min; VHS, U-Matic; color; JR, HS, A; Post World War II.

FI

BIG GREEN LINE, THE

Lew Alcindor (Kareem Abdul-Jabbar) and Oscar Robertson lead the Milwaukee Bucks to National Basketball Association glory.

NL; 25 min; 16 mm; NL; JR, HS, A; Post World War II.

MILLER

BIG MOMENT IN SPORTS, THE: VOLUME I

Bud Palmer and Vin Scully narrate eight of the most exciting events in sports history—the Giant-Dodger baseball playoff in 1951; the War Admiral-Sea Biscuit match race of 1938; weightlifter Paul Anderson's Russian triumph; the 1955 Stanley Cup hockey playoff between the Montreal Canadians and the Detroit Red Wings; Lou Worsham's triumph in the Tam O'Shanter golf tournament in 1953; Pancho Gonzalez's victory over Ted Schroeder in the National Tennis Championship of 1949; the Navy-Notre Dame football game in 1945; and Roger Bannister's four-minute mile in 1954.

NL; 25 min; 16 mm, VHS; BW; JR, HS, A; Depression Era and Post World War II.

SF

BIG MOMENT IN SPORTS, THE: VOLUME II

Bud Palmer and Vic Scully narrate seven more of the most exciting events in sports history—the jinx against golfer Sam Snead in the U.S. open; Sugar Ray Robinson's 1951 riot-precipitating match with Gerhart Hecht in Berlin; the Nashua-Swaps match race of 1955; the story of basketball's Wilt Chamberlain; the New York Giant's last baseball game in the Polo Grounds, 1957; the end of the trail for Ebbets Field, former home of the Brooklyn Dodgers; and the case of the twelfth man on the football field in the game between Rice and Alabama.

NL; 28 min; 16 mm, VHS; BW; JR, HS, A; Post World War II.

SF

BIG MOMENT IN SPORTS, THE: VOLUME III

Eight more great events in sports history—Jim Brown of Cleveland scores four touchdowns against the Cardinals; glider riders realize a dream of man since prehistoric times; Canada defeats Russia for the World Amateur Hockey championships in Prague; highlights from the career of baseball immortal Ted Williams; big-league international soccer comes to New York; local boy Roger Ward makes good in record time in the Indianapolis 500; Austrian skier Toni Sailor shows championship form; the Detroit Lions upset the Baltimore Colts in one of the wildest finishes in pro football history.

NL; 25 min; 16 mm; VHS; BW; JR, HS, A; Post World War II.

SF

BIGGER, FASTER, STRONGER

Promotes power weight training programs to build bigger, faster, stronger athletes. Includes commentaries by coaches and players at high school, university, and professional levels.

1974; 24 min; 16 mm; color; HS, A; Post World War II.

BYU; UWISC

BIG ONE THAT GOT AWAY, THE

Presents a television special from the CTV program "Olympiad," which takes a sympathetic look at competitors who were close to winning Olympic gold medals but lost. Shows how their expectations of winning were dashed through various circumstances that disqualified them.

1976; 50 min; 16 mm; color; JR, HS, A; Post World War II.

CTV

BIG SURF

A tour of Hawaii and some of the surfing capitals of the world, done with narration poking fun at the dangers and mishaps of this exciting sport. Special guest star Bill Dana as Jose Jimenez completes this interesting sports reel.

NL; 10 min; 16 mm; color; JR, HS, A; Post World War II.

BUDGET

BILL "BOOM BOOM" BROWN

As a running back, receiver, and special-teams player, Bill Brown was a gutsy fighter and hard-nosed competitor. He knew only one way to play the game—all out.

1985; 7 min; VHS, U-Matic; color, JR, HS, A; Post World War II.

NFL; TMA

BILL COLE'S CHUTELESS JUMP

No one would attempt a free fall from a plane without a parachute, would they? Bill Cole did—and not by accident. In an incredible stunt, Bill Cole jumps from a plane without a parachute, receives and dons a parachute in mid-air, and lands. Cine-Golden Eagle Award.

1973; 15 min; 16 mm; color; JR, HS, A; Post World War II.

BUDGET

BILLIE JEAN KING

In the first full year of the Women's Tour, professional Billie Jean King becomes the first woman in any sport to win over $100,000. Though King wins far more competitions than she loses, included is a match in which she is overwhelmingly defeated by young Chris Evert. A strong-willed yet realistic personality is revealed in Billie Jean's discussion of this match, her unusually open conversation regarding her personal views on sports, and in talking of her work in advancing women's professional tennis.

1973; 22 min; 16 mm; color; JR, HS, A; Post World War II.

OKSU

BIOGRAPHY OF A ROOKIE

Baseball fans will enjoy *Biography of a Rookie*, the story of the career of Willie Davis of the Los Angeles Dodgers from his high-school days to the signing of his contract. The techniques of top professional baseball and Davis' dedication to training are emphasized.

NL; NL; 16 mm; NL; JR, HS, A; Post World War II.

SF

BIORHYTHM

Describes the cycle of intellectual, physical, and emotional patterns on which biorhythm is based. Tells how biorhythm is used by industrial and sporting concerns.

NL; 12 min; VHS, U-Matic; color; JR, HS, A; Post World War II.

JOU

B. J. AND EDDIE OUTWARD BOUND

Two young people pit their mental and physical endurance against the challenges of nature at the Outward Bound Hurricane Island School off the coast of Maine. Their rigorous schedule includes a daily mile run at daybreak, a plunge into the 42-degree ocean, and a three-day "solo," where each student is left alone on a deserted island with only the barest of necessities for survival. Confronting these challenges, the students develop self-confidence and an expanded capacity for achievement.

1974; 26 min; 16 mm; color; JR, HS, A; Post World War II.

NILLU

BLACK ATHLETE, THE

How important are sports to the young black community? Interviews with prominent black athletes and coaches offer contrasting points of view. O. J. Simpson, Harry Edwards, Muhammed Ali, Arthur Ashe, and others speak from their own experiences and observations.

By viewing the black athlete within the microcosm of sport, this film raises crucial questions about the status of black people in American culture as a whole.

The changing role of blacks in sports comes under James Michener's scrutiny in this first of three films based on his best-selling book, *Sports in America*. It features historic footage of such early black athletes as Jack Johnson, Joe Louis, and Jackie Robinson, and follows black participation in sports to the 1980s.

NL; 26 min; NL; color; JR, HS, A; Depression Era, World War II Sport, Post World War II.

EMLEN

BLACK ATHLETE, THE

This film realistically portrays the history of the black athlete in sports in the United States since 1936. It traces extraordinary feats and progress in the face of many obstacles and prejudices. Narrated by Jesse Owens, the history begins with Jesse's legendary four gold-medal performances in Berlin in the 1936 Olympic games.

NL; 38 min; 16 mm; NL; JR, HS, A; Depression Era to Post World War II.

MTPS

BLACK ATHLETE, THE

Traces the changing role of blacks in American sports. Features historic footage of Jack Johnson, Joe Louis, and Jackie Robinson, and includes interviews with many current black athletic stars. With James Michener.

1980; 58 min; 16 mm; color; JR, HS, A; Modern Sport, Depression Era, World War II, Post World War II.

PYRAMID

BLACK ICE

Shows the danger, the fierce spirit of competition, the tingling exhilaration of the roaring winds, glittering ice, and the breathtaking speed of ice boating.

1980; 11 min; 16 mm; color; JR, HS, A; Post World War II.

UWISC

BLACK OLYMPIANS

Traces the struggles of American blacks to be part of American athletics and society; shows the progress of black athletes from George Poage in 1904 through the 1984 Olympics. Major events in the history of black Olympians are covered—Jesse Owens, Wilma Rudolph, the black-power salute in Mexico City in 1968, and more. Black medalists are interviewed. Athletic achievements of blacks are placed in the context of their situation in American society.

NL; 28 min; 16 mm; color; JR, HS, A; Modern Sport, Golden Age of Sport, Depression Era and World War II, Post World War II.

CF

BLADES AND BRASS

A film without commentary illustrates Hemingway's definition of courage as grace under pressure. A good example of the incorporation of television techniques into film art, it uses constant shifts in tone through abrupt changes in style to create strong tension and viewer involvement. Filmed by the National Film Board of Canada during National Hockey League games. Winner of awards in Italy and Yugoslavia.

1967; 10 min; 16 mm; color; JR, HS, A; Post World War II.

IFB; NFBC

BLIND OUTDOOR LEISURE DEVELOPMENT

Active participation in all kinds of outdoor sports has brought enjoyment to blind people and a healthy way to spend their leisure time. This film portrays how BOLD, the Blind Outdoor Leisure Development Program, involves blind people in downhill skiing, cross-country skiing, ice skating, horseback riding, jogging, golfing, river rafting, and mountain climbing. John Denver narrates the film and participates in the downhill skiing sequences. A film of interest to the general public of all ages.

NL; 15 min; 16 mm, VHS, U-Matic, Beta; color; HS, A; Post World War II.

CRYSP

BLIND PARTICIPATE, THE

Shows blind athletes participating in skiing and gymnastics. Includes an animated segment explaining the many uses of Braille.

1980; 20 min; 16 mm; color; JR, HS, A; Post World War II.

LAWREN

BLUELINE

Set in Montreal, *Blueline* combines the talents of three of Canada's top young actors with a music score featuring popular rock performers, including David Bowie. The hero of the story is Jamie, an introverted teenager with a domineering father and a secret ambition to run in the Montreal International Marathon. Encouraged by his friend Myles and girlfriend Nicole, Jamie develops the self-confidence he needs to overcome a series of setbacks.

1985; 52.5 minutes; 16 mm; color; JR, HS, A; Post World War II.

NFBC

BLUE SAFARI

An exciting documentary-adventure featuring surfing greats Ricky Grigg (1969 world surfing champion) and Greg Noll (one of the foremost high-wave riders in the world). Along for beauty is Sue Peterson, Miss Teenage Fair of 1969, as daredevil board riders take on the big waves at Waimea Bay, the Bonzai Pipeline, and the big surf of California and Australia.

1967; 90 min; 16 mm; color; JR, HS, A; Post World War II.

BUDGET

BOATING FEVER

Shows all kinds of boats in action—outboards, inboards, sailboats, oceangoing yachts—even small kayaks shooting rapids.

NL; 18 min; 16 mm; NL; JR, HS, A; Post World War II.

KODAK

BOB LILLY

A Texas legend who was named All-Pro 11 times and inducted into the Hall of Fame in 1980, Tom Landry called him "the greatest player I ever coached." Filled with fascinating tips on how to play defensive line.

1985; 8 min; VHS, U-matic; color; JR, HS, A; Post World War II.

NFL; TMA

BOB PETIT

Features Bob Petit, twice NBA Most Valuable Player, talking about his playing career in the beginning of basketball's "Superstar Era."

NL; 20 min; 16 mm; color; JR, HS, A; Post World War II.

USC

BOB UECKER'S WACKY WORLD OF SPORTS

Full of sports bloopers. Mr. Baseball's offbeat sense of humor provides an entertaining show.

NL; 30 min; VHS; NL; JR, HS, A; Depression Era, World War II, Post World War II.

KAROL

BODY AND SOUL, PART 1: BODY

An examination of Afro-American contributions to sports in America, narrated by Harry Reasoner. Racial tensions on college and pro teams and the threat of an Olympic boycott in 1968 suggest that the sports world is not as integrated as most people think. Interviews shed light on a complex picture.

1968; 24 min; 16 mm; NL; JR, HS, A; Post World War II.

UCB

BORN TO FIGHT

The grace, skill, and precision of bull fighting on horseback is introduced in Portugal. Before the great spectacle is about to unfold in the arena, we are ushered back to a ranch where bulls are trained to fight. We not only view ranch life as a discipline of training, but are prepared for the eventual confrontation in the Lisbon bullring.

NL; 15 min; 16 mm; NL; JR, HS, A; Post World War II.

BUDGET

BORN TO PACE

Features Philadelphia sportscaster Jim Leaming tracing the birth and development of a standardbred colt at Hanover Shoe Farms in Pennsylvania.

NL; 26 min; 16 mm; NL; JR, HS, A; Post World War II.

USTA

BORN TO RUN

Running can offer benefits to everyone, from all walks of life and occupations. It's called the perfect way to restore and retain good health and to release human capacities and creativity.

NL; 25 min; 16 mm, VHS; color; JR, HS, A; Post World War II.

WOMBAT

BOW AND ARROW

The bow and arrow has been described as a "royal instrument of sport" and a "lethal instrument of war." This film presents a short history of a versatile tool and describes its functions through the ages, from the days of the great conqueror Genghis Khan, who overran China with this weapon, to the modern Olympics.

1979; 15 min; 16 mm, VHS, U-Matic, Beta; color; JR, HS, A; Ancient Sport, Medieval Sport, Renaissance Sport, Premodern, Making of Modern Sport, Modern Sport, Golden Age, Depression Era, World War II, Post World War II.

CAROUF; NFBC

BOWLING

Made during the training sessions of a group of dedicated bowlers in Welkenraedt, the film provides plenty of information on the game. Covers bowlers from Homer to Henry VIII of England to modern bowling. A French language film.

NL; 12 min; 16 mm; BW; JR, HS, A; Ancient Sport to Post World War II.

BELGIUM

BOWLING FOR VETERANS

Story of the BVL Fund and how organized bowling has helped meet needs of hospitalized veterans.

NL; 15 min; 16 mm; NL; A; Post World War II.

ABC

BOWLING'S MAGIC MOMENT

Inside look at the ABC tournament, the world's largest participation sports event. Film follows typical group of Booster division bowlers from their Hawarden, Iowa, homes and businesses through the 1965 ABC in St. Paul.

NL; 27 min, 16 mm; NL; HS, A; Post World War II.

ABC

BOWLING UNITES THE AMERICANS

Covers the 12th Annual Bowling tournament of the Americans which brings amateur bowling champions from two dozen nations and territories to Miami to combine competition and goodwill. A Spanish language film. Also available in English.

NL; 15 min; 16 mm; color; JR, HS, A; Post World War II.

MIMET

BOXER

A young baker is having his first amateur boxing match tonight. As time passes, his anxiety increases. Once in the ring, he must prove himself. A French language film with English subtitles.

1972; 16 min; 16 mm; color; JR, HS, A; Post World War II.

IFP; FACSEA

BOXING MATCH

This is an experimental film made by one of the first pioneers of the Belgian cinema. Focusing on a boxing match, the film concentrates in turn on the boxers, the referee, and the spectators.

Using negative frames, it highlights the all-too-often spurious, contrived, and falsified aspects of boxing and the industry that goes with it, at least of the big matches drawing huge audiences of people. The film attests to a genuine love of real boxing, contrasted with the greed and horse-trading of the organizers and the sadistic instincts of the general public.

1927; 10 min; 16 mm; BW; JR, HS, A; Golden Age.

BELGIUM

BOY'S GAMES: PUSHTU

Shows Pushtu boys playing an ancient game known throughout Asia. Demonstrates the toughness of these young men, as well as the value these tribal people place on physical superiority.

NL; 5 min; 16 mm; color; JR, HS, A; Ancient Sport to Post World War II.

IFF

BOYS WITH BATS

The film follows David Unowsky, who has visited 16 major-league ballparks in search of outdoor base-ball. He travels with a group of friends, taking a piece of Metropolitan Stadium (former home of the Minneapolis Twins) to Cooperstown, N. Y., for the induction ceremony of former Twins star Harmon Kilebrew into the Baseball Hall of Fame. At a Toronto game, Unowsky observes that even the players are beginning to look and play the same.

It also takes us to Baltimore, where Producer Deanna Kamiel talks with poet and national radio commentator Andrei Codrescu, a Rumanian exile. Baseball appeals to recent immigrants, Codrescu suggests, because it is simple to understand. It allows them to quickly integrate themselves into the culture and a shared passion. "Baseball becomes a landmark of their belonging and their becoming to belong," he says.

NL; 30 min; VHS, U-Matic; color; HS, A; Post World War II.

KTCATV

BRAVE BULLS, THE

All the atmosphere, splendor, and drama of the world of the bullfight has been captured in this version of the best-selling novel. A leading matador learns fear for the first time after being gored by a bull. A danger to those who risk their lives in the bull ring, the emotion of fear almost destroys the matador until he finally conquers his personal demons in a motion picture filled with fine performances and enhanced by on-location filming.

1951; 108 min; 16 mm; NL; JR, HS, A; Post World War II.

BUDGET

BREAKNECK SPORTS

A vintage compilation of sports around the world—sailing, water skiing, golf, horseracing with obstacles, bullfighting, horseracing in city streets, climbing pyramids in Egypt.

NL; 10 min; 16 mm; NL; JR, HS, A; Post World War II.

BUDGET

BRED TO WIN

Breeding of thoroughbred horses for racing in New Zealand.

NL; 28 min; 16 mm; NL; JR, HS, A; Post World War II.

NZGTO

BRIAN'S SONG

A true story of the deep friendship between two men, Gale Sayers, black halfback for the Chicago Bears, and his white teammate, Brian Piccolo. When the two arrive in Chicago for the Bear's training session, they are competitors for a single backfield slot. Later, Coach George Halas places them both in the first-team backfield and the boys play side-by-side. Soon Piccolo's career and life are threatened by cancer. Through the last painful months following Piccolo's first operation, Sayers strives to keep his friend's spirits up, but eventually even Gale has to face the facts of Brian's illness. At a football banquet, Sayers is presented the "most courageous player of the year" award. In his acceptance speech, he hands it over to Piccolo, whose courage in the face of cancer makes football-field bravery inconsequential. Brian Piccolo died at the age of 26. Stars James Caan, Billy Dee Williams, Jack Warden, Shelley Fabares, and Judy Pace.

1971; 74 min; 16 mm; color; JR, HS, A; Post World War II.

LCOA; UILL

BUFFALO BILL AND THE WILD WEST

A dramatic and nostalgic recreation of the life and times of William F. Cody (Buffalo Bill) of story, legend, and fact. Pony Express rider, buffalo hunter, Army scout, Indian fighter, and Indian friend, he has become part of the American experience.

NL; 24 min; 16 mm; NL; JR, HS, A; Making of Modern Sport.

MTPS

BUILDERS OF YOUTH

Shows the many roles of the high school athletic director in schools and in the service of his community. The six regional winners of the National Secondary School Athletic Director's award are featured, including the national winner, in a special 2.5-minute epilogue. The film is designed for use by athletic directors at the community level.

NL; 16 min; 16 mm; NL; JR, HS, A; Post World War II.

ASF

BULLFIGHT

A fascinating historical look at the art of bullfighting, with a complete explanation of the meaning of the sport. Featured are action shots of some of the great masters of the art.

1956; 76 min; 16 mm; NL; E, JR, HS, A; Ancient to Post World War II.

BUDGET

BULLFIGHTER AND THE LADY, THE

Robert Stack is the story's central character, Chuck Regan, who goes to Mexico and decides to become involved in the world of bullfighting. His mentor is a veteran idol of the bullring, who takes the novice under his wing and teaches him what he needs to know. A blunder in the ring results in a tragedy that turns the aficionados of the bullring against him and finally makes him fully realize his commitment to the sport that is unique. Director Boetticher took cast and crew to Mexico and shot footage in the bullring of actual bullfights, and at the bull-breeding farms.

1951; 87 min; 16 mm; NL; JR, HS, A; Post World War II.

BUDGET

BULLFIGHTS

Filmed in Spain, featuring such famed matadors as Don Alvaro Domecq, Paco Camino, Andres Vasquez, and Vincente Fernandez—"El Caracol." All the pageant and splendor of the corrida, narrated by Rodolfo Hoyos, Jr.

NL; 21 min; 16mm; color; JR, HS, A; Post World War II.

BUDGET

BULLY FOR HOCKEY

A promotional film for the sport of field hockey, which highlights the skills and thrills of a game in which Australian teams excel.

1980; 16 min; 16 mm; color; JR, HS, A; Post World War II.

FLMAUS

BULLPEN

Call them baseball's troubleshooters, rescue artists, or firemen. They are relief pitchers, and their home is in the bullpen. Their occupation is determined by necessity and is always based on trouble. Every pitch is a pressure pitch. Once they were old-timers finishing out a career, like Johnny Murphy, Hugh Casey, Joe Page, Joe Black, and Jim Konstanty. Then we get to recent great relievers like Hoyt Wilhelm, Ron Perranoski, Moe Drabowsky, Phil Regan, and Elroy Face. And the Mets' Tug McGraw tells us what it is like to occupy baseball's loneliest position.

NL; 23 min; 16 mm; NL; A; Post World War II.

WSTGLC

CALL OF THE CLAYBIRD, THE

Over ten variations of claybird shooting, ranging from the use of a handtrap at a relaxed family outing to the highly competitive Grand American that annually draws over 3,000 shooters. The stars are youngsters, parents, and grandparents who share a common interest in a sport that guarantees fun for all.

NL; 10 min; 16 mm; NL; JR, HS, A; Post World War II.
WINWES

CALL OF THE MOUNTAINS, THE

The difficult and dangerous task of three mountain climbers, a Frenchman, an Italian, and a German, climbing the northern side of the "Grosse Zinne" in the Dolomites.
1964; 14 min; 16 mm; NL; JR, HS, A; Post World War II.
MTPS

CAVALCADE OF ARCHERY

Featuring Howard Hill, "World's Greatest Archer," opening with a scene where Mr. Hill portrays the legendary William Tell in an archery tournament. Returning to the 20th century, Hill displays his prowess in some plain and fancy shooting.
NL; 10 min; 16 mm; NL; JR, HS, A; Post World War II.
BUDGET

CANADA'S SALMON COAST

Looks at sport fishing in Rovers Inlet, British Columbia. Comments on the life cycle of the salmon and the history of this area's commercial fishing industry.
1976; 28 min; 16 mm; color; JR, HS, A; Post World War II.
OMCL

CANADIAN SKI MARATHON, THE

The longest international cross-country ski tour in the world and the largest event of this type in North America challenges skiers of all ages and abilities with 100 miles of wilderness trail.
The film catches glimpses of such participants as Finland's former world champion Arto Tiainen, Canada's oldest skier, Jack Rabbit Johannsen, and the first women to ski the full distance carrying 12-pound packs.
NL; 12 min; 16 mm; color; JR, HS, A; Post World War II.
MORRALL

CANOE COUNTRY ADVENTURE, A

This is a story of the Canadian northwoods, as seen through the eyes of the narrator, a twelve-year-old boy. Donald, his parents, his three sisters, and his dog explore the wilderness country by canoe. They learn how to handle canoes, the meaning of portage, and view the step-by-step process used by Indians in building birch-bark canoes. They fish for northern

pike, go swimming and hiking, and enjoy the magic of an evening campfire. Donald's father is a wildlife photographer, and he finds many opportunities to photograph warblers, loons, grouse, moose, deer, and porcupines.
1980; 19 min; 16 mm; color; E, JR, HS, A; Post World War II.
UILL

CAREER IN PHYSICAL EDUCATION

Highlights the interesting aspects of a career in physical education. Makes a case for increased physical education and points out the need for trained educators in the field.
1960; 27 min; 16 mm; color; HS, A; Post World War II.
BYU

CAREERS: LEISURE INDUSTRIES

A close-up of one of America's rapidly expanding new businesses made possible by the increased availability of leisure time. A recreation director, camping trailer builder, and motor bike rental dealer are a few of the many people shown capitalizing on this lucrative market. States that most people get into leisure industries because they enjoy the activity and are now attempting to make it enjoyable for others.
1970; 9 min; 16 mm; color; JR, HS, A; Post World War II.
UILL

CAROL JOHNSTON

Carol Johnston is truly exceptional. She overcame the limiting effects of being born with an incomplete left arm to become a champion gymnast. In this film, Carol is shown coping with the problems of college life, performing in nationally televised competitions, and dealing with a knee injury which occurred during filming.
1980; 15 min; 16 mm; color; E, JR, HS, A; Post World War II.
BYU

CARRY THE FIRE

A moving look at the running of the 9000-mile, Olympic Torch Relay. Pride, passion, and patriotism are evident in the millions of Americans who participated in and watched the carrying of the fire. Culminates in the lighting of the torch at the Los Angeles Coliseum.
NL; 28 min; 16 mm, VHS, U-Matic; color; Post World War II.
MTPS

CASEY AT THE BAT

No American poem has been so accepted by the heartland of America and entertained so many as *Casey at the Bat*.

This film uses language and style that set the learning process firmly in motion, exposing many students to rather adult words. The use of such words gives the poem its style.

The visual treatment of the poem is twofold. A first reading is done over a scene showing a group of young boys playing baseball. The juxtaposition of "Mighty Casey," portrayed by a young ball player, adds to the humor of the piece. The poem is then read again, with the actual words superimposed over a beautiful slow-motion sequence from a major league game. (Specify Paramount version.)

1972; 12 min; 16 mm; color; E, JR, HS, A; Post World War II.
KRASKER

CAST OF THREE

A canoe fishing trip through the wilderness area of Minnesota, catching walleye and northern pike and smallmouth bass with a father and son. Trout and bass fishing in North Carolina, surrounded by the mountains and cypress trees. In Wyoming, cutthroat, golden, and brook trout are taken in the beautiful streams and lakes.

NL; 61 or 26 min.; 16 mm; NL; JR, HS, A; Post World War II.
PICAD

CAT (A WOMAN WHO FOUGHT BACK)

A portrait of Cathy Davis, a young woman who chose to pursue a career in professional boxing, even though it meant contesting legal and conventional wisdom that said boxing was no way for a lady to make a living. Cat majored in speech in college, where boxing replaced fencing as her favorite sport. She was confident of her ability because she trained hard. When the comment was made that she didn't look like a boxer, she quipped: "That's because I never get hit." On June 1, 1978, she won the right to box professionally in New York. Although Cat felt that every boxer takes the responsibility of getting hurt in the ring, the satisfaction and financial independence she gained from the sport kept her hard at work.

1978; 27 min; 16 mm; color; JR, HS, A; Post World War II.
CHAMP; FI; UILL

CATCH THE JOY

A beautiful and humorous pictorial representation of the thrill found in sand sports. Shots of sand skiing, sand surfing, sand sledding, and dune buggying are shown with a variety of camera techniques.

1970; 14 min; 16 mm; color; JR, HS, A; Post World War II.
PYRAMID; BYU

CELEBRATION

Two events celebrated the 100th anniversary of the automobile: the Laguna Beach Seca Automobile Races and the Pebble Beach Concours d'Elegance at Monterey Peninsula, California. This film documents the historic gathering of vintage Mercedes-Benz racers and priceless museum cars in a once-in-a-lifetime happening. Featured are racing legends such as Stirling Moss, Juan Fangio, and Phil Hill.

NL; 28 min; 16 mm; JR, HS, A; Post World War II.
MTPS

CELEBRATION DAYS

The Aqua-Follies in Minneapolis, 1946, with some of the all-time great Olympic swimming champions. Highlights from the Follies two-mile-long parade and the beauty pageant crowning the Queen of the Lake to celebrate the Minneapolis Aquatennial.

1946; 20 min; 16 mm; color; JR, HS, A; Post World War II.
BUDGET

CENTER SNAP

To the average football fan, the simplest and most taken-for-granted aspect of the game is the center snap. It's so simple that we hardly ever consider it important. But it is, after all, a part of the game which is practiced many times every day and without which no play could ever begin! It also has a history which might surprise even the most astute scholars of sport—a history which includes some of the weirdest, wildest and wackiest happenings ever to occur in pro football.

NL; 5 min; 16 mm, VHS, U-Matic; color; JR, HS, A; Modern to Post World War II.
NFL; TMA

CHALK-STREAM TROUT, THE

Shows how some Englishmen, who take their trout fishing very seriously, have produced a "master race" of hardy brown and rainbow trout. Documents the involved procedures in breeding trout, stimulating growth of the alevin, sorting out the fittest, and carefully and systematically stocking the chalk streams. Includes detailed sequences showing stripping of the hen trout, fertilization by the cock fish, hatching, rearing, and feeding the fry, and clearing the river of incompatible fish. In the final sequence, actor Dr. James Robertson Justice demonstrates his favorite pastime—fly-fishing.

1974; 36 min; 16 mm; color; HS, A; Post World War II.

UILL

CHALLENGE

In this excellent documentary featuring the grace and grit of the Davis Cup competition in 1969 between Rumania and the United States, Ilie Nastase, Ion Tiriac, Stan Smith, Bob Lutz, and Arthur Ashe are protagonists in a gripping, slow-motion presentation.

1969; 26 min; 16 mm; color; JR, HS, A; Post World War II.

USTEN

CHALLENGE OF MOUNT EVEREST

The third Indian expedition to Mt. Everest, sponsored by the Indian Mountaineering Foundation. The film presents the hazardous adventure of the team and their ultimate success in 1965 in conquering the highest peak in the world.

NL; 20 min; 16 mm; NL; JR, HS, A; Post World War II.

EMBIND

CHALLENGE OVER THE ATLANTIC

Fifty years after Lindbergh's historic trans-Atlantic flight in the *Spirit of St. Louis,* three American businessmen follow the same route in a balloon. This film demonstrates the positive results of thorough preparation, teamwork, courage, and the desire to succeed.

NL; 14 min; 16 mm; color; JR, HS, A; Post World War II.

ABCS; VANTAGE; PYRAMID

CHALLENGE, THE

It's man against the elements in this classic drama filmed partially in the Alpine region amid the legendary Matterhorn and neighboring peaks. The time is the mid-19th century, and this is the real-life story of Edward Whymper and Swiss guide Jean-Antoine Carrel. Three members of Whymper's team die in a fall, and suspicions start to grow that the Englishman cut the rope on his companions. The courage of Carrel eventually vindicates his friend's honor and proves to the world that Whymper's conquest of the Matterhorn was achieved honorably.

1938; 90 min; 16 mm; BW; JR, HS, A; Premodern, Making of Modern Sport.

BUDGET

CHAMPIONS OF AMERICAN SPORT

Noted sportswriter Red Smith narrates this history of American sport as personified by its champions. The cast includes Lou Gehrig, Jesse Owens, Babe Ruth, Joe Louis, George Halas, Billie Jean King, Ted Williams, Johnny Unitas, Arthur Ashe, Babe Didrickson, Muhammed Ali, and many others.

NL; 28 min; 16 mm; color; JR, HS, A; Golden Age, Depression Era, World War II, Post World War II.

CCCD

CHAMPIONSHIP CHALLENGE

The thrills of the Formula sports-car field, with such international driving celebrities as Jody Schecter from Australia and Mark Donohue, Brett Lunger, and Tony Adamowitz of the United States. Filmed at the Mid-Ohio Sports Club Raceway.

NL; 20 min; 16 mm; color; JR, HS, A; Post World War II.

BUDGET

CHAMPIONS, THE

40th World Shooting Championships, Phoenix, Arizona.

NL; 13 min; 16 mm; NL; JR, HS, A; Post World War II.

NRA

CHAMPIONSHIP, THE

Portrays four girls involved in a soccer championship. Shows lessons in sportsmanship.

NL; 24 min; U-Matic, VHS; color; JR, HS, A; Post World War II.

MULTPP

CHASE THE WIND

Presents an historical account of man's efforts to set the world's land speed record.

1974; 25 min; 16 mm; color; JR, HS, A; Post World War II.

STP

CHASING THE LIMITS

The one goal of motor racing is winning, but it is also an experiment in technology—a performance test without a laboratory to set limits. Burgess Meredith narrates an exciting endurance racing drama that takes viewers to Daytona, Miami, England, Le-Mans, Germany, and Japan to test B. F. Goodrich's experimental T/A radials in grueling long-distance competition.

24 min; 16 mm; color; JR, HS, A; Post World War II.

MTPS

CHAUTAUQUA EXPERIENCE, THE

In the beautiful town of Chautauqua, New York, people of all ages and backgrounds come together for a variety of experiences and events. They can participate in or observe and enjoy painting, music, sculpture, opera, ballet, crafts, lectures, and many sports. Fine entertainment and great photography make this a film for everyone.

30 min; 16 mm, VHS; HS, A; Post World War II.
MTPS

CHECKERED SECOND, A

The Canadian-American Challenge Cup series, with the monstrous group-seven sports cars and their 494-cubic-inch engines, is one of the most exciting series of road races in the world. This Can-Am race at Laguna Beach, California, is a battle between Peter Revson, driving a Team McLaren car, and Jackie Stewart, driving a Works Lola. Stewart gets the checkered flag, but "Champagne Peter" pulls into victory lane, and is finally declared the winner, in one of the most unusual finishes in the history of Can-Am racing.

NL; 21 min; 16 mm; NL; JR, HS, A; Post World War II.
GTARC

CHICAGO BEARS HIGHLIGHTS

Three films, covering 1957, 1958, and 1963. Latter includes championship game. Order by year.

NL; NL; 16 mm; NL; JR, HS, A; Post World War II.
MILLER

CHILDREN AND SPORT

In this film, James Michener surveys the world of the young athlete to discover how sports activities affect children. He takes a close look at both individual and team sports, talks with parents, coaches, physicians, and today's young superstars, and weighs the pros and cons of winning versus learning to meet challenges. A comprehensive overview of children's sports in America today.

NL; 26 min; color; JR, HS, A; Post World War II.
EMLEN

CHILDREN'S CHANTS AND GAMES

Visually lively look at the folklore of young Americans as manifested in playground chants and games. Shows the richness of the black, Asian, Latin, and European game traditions, and illustrates the similarities of the games in the various cultures. Observes games based on counting, ball bouncing, jumping rope, hand movements, counting out, London Bridge-type "catching," and big circles.

NL; 15 min; 16 mm; color; E, JR, HS, A; Post World War II.
UCB; PHENIX

CHILD'S PLAY

Play is a prime instrument in the development of a child's personality and in the creation of a sound, well-adjusted individual. This film shows how mental, social, emotional, and physical growth are linked to forms of play, and how these forms change as the child grows older. Shows how play allows children to work out their feelings and frustrations and sets the stage for creative ideas and fantasy. It provides continuing opportunities for youngsters to adapt to the world and readies them for contemporary society. The form of a child's play can be shaped in the schools, where play is used to teach specific skills. Parents especially, the film points out, should interact with their children, introducing new and challenging playthings, because the best way for their children to learn is through play. The experiences a child is given in early years enhance the progression toward maturity.

1978; 20 min; 16 mm; color; HS, A; Post World War II.
MGHT; LSU

CHINESE CHILDREN'S GAMES

This shows the games played by children in the Republic of China on Taiwan today. Games and folk usages include firecrackers, wooden swords, lion dances, and lanterns played during the Lunar New Year Season; shuttlecock, jump rope, windmill tops, and kites flown in a kind of sport; perfume sachets and colorful bags favored by girls; mathematical games as "nene connecting links," a puzzle that challenges ingenuity, and tangram, a large square divided by lines into seven parts which can be used to compose innumerable diagrams and patterns.

1982; 29 min; VHS; color; JR, HS, A; Post World War II.
OKSU

CIRCLE OF RACING

A multirace film feature covering sprints, midgets, drag racers, and stock cars. The only film ever produced of the first Ontario 500. The action from so many various types of racing makes the film move fast. One of the few films with racing action from the Laguna Seca Course in Monterey, California.

NL; 30 min; 16 mm; color; JR, HS, A; Post World War II.
BUDGET

CIRCUS KIDS

In the age-old tradition of performers, young Traci learns that effort, reliability, and teamwork are absolute essentials in her career with the traveling circus, which is "home" to her and her family.

NL; 16 min; 16 mm; color; E, JR, HS, A; Post World War II.

EBEC

CIRCUS : SERRINA BECOMES AN ACROBAT

Shows a junior high school girl, Serrina, during her first summer of training as a trapeze performer. Traces her progress through a rigorous program of constant exercise and practice, supervised by experienced acrobats. Emphasizes the diligence and patience needed to develop special skills.

1972; 11 min; 16 mm; color; JR, HS, A; Post World War II.

UILL

CLEAN SWEEP

Ontario, Indy, Pocono—three 500-mile "jewels" in the Triple Crown of USAC championship racing—are highlighted in this action-packed film. From qualifying runs and fast-paced pit action to the initial race day call of "Gentlemen, start your engines," the camera captures classic duels between such racing giants as A. J. Foyt, the Unser brothers, Gary Bettenhausen, Johnny Rutherford, Wally Dallenbach, and others traveling the grueling 2.5 mile oval circuits to the national championship. Johnny Rutherford drives his fast McLaren into the winner's circle at Indy and Pocono, following Bobby Unser's Ontario 500 victory. Unser claims the USAC National Driving Championship on points.

NL; 27 min; 16 mm; NL; JR, HS, A; Post World War II.

GTARC

CLEVELAND BROWNS FOOTBALL FILMS

1968 Highlights
1968 Browns vs. Colts (game film—regular season)
1968 Browns vs. Giants (game film—regular season)
1969 Highlights
1969 Browns vs. Bears (game film—regular season)
1970 Interim Highlights (first half of season)
1970 Browns vs. Cincinnati (game film—regular season)
1970 Highlights
1971 Interim Highlights (first half of season)
1971 Highlights ("Comeback in Cleveland")

1971 Browns vs. Cincinnati (game film—regular season)
1972 Highlights ("The Team That Wouldn't Quit")
1973 Highlights (no mailing)
1973 Browns vs. Steelers (game film—regular season)
1973 Browns vs. Broncos (game film—regular season)

NL; 35 min; 16 mm; NL; JR, HS, A; Post World War II.

BROWNS

CLIMB

Intended to be both a realistic adventure of mountain climbing and a metaphorical ascent in which individual limits are tested and personal values explored. Excellent photography of a two-day ascent up a sheer rock wall in Yosemite Valley.

1974; 22 min; 16 mm; color; JR, HS, A; Post World War II.

CF; LSU

CLIMB FOR THE TOP

A dramatic, suspenseful analogy that emphasizes the contributions required of each team member to reach the final goal, in this case the summit of Mt. McKinley. A team of mountaineers prepares for the expedition and, after a plane trip and a train ride, they finally reach the mountain and begin their slow climb up the treacherous slopes. They are confronted by the rigors of high altitude, the cruelty of a storm that pins them in their tents for seven days, and the dangers of soft snow that threatens to slide away beneath them. On the last day, each person has to use every bit of strength and resolution just to keep going until finally, the team stands on the summit.

1977; 16 min; 16 mm; color; JR, HS, A; Post World War II.

UILL

COACHES

Depicts the techniques, style, and personality of four of Canada's national coaches—Bill Neville, men's volleyball; Moo Park, women's volleyball; Sheila Wilcox, equestrians; and Jack Donahue, men's basketball—as they prepare their teams for the pre-Olympics. Each uses a different approach, as shown in scenes of games, practice sessions, and postgame critiques. Neville pushes his athletes to the limits of their physical and emotional endurance; Park commands his players' respect for his quiet competence; Wilcox, an ex-champion and victim of a crippling accident while competing, teaches with a brute force; Donahue is a cajoler and master of the big hype—and is also remarkably successful.

1976; 57 min; 16 mm; color; A; Post World War II.
UCB; NFBC

COACHES '61 ALL-AMERICAN TEAM

Top college players in action.
NL; 28 min; 16 mm; NL; JR, HS, A; Post World
War II.
CINES

COACHES '62 ALL-AMERICAN TEAM

All-American performances.
NL; 28 min; 16 mm; NL; JR, HS, A; Post World
War II.
CINES

COACHES '63 ALL-AMERICAN TEAM

College Stars on the gridiron.
NL; 28 min; 16 mm; NL; JR, HS, A; Post World
War II.
CINES

COACHES '64 ALL-AMERICAN TEAM

Spotlight on the top college players.
NL; 28 min; 16 mm; NL; JR, HS, A; Post World
War II.
CINES

COACHES '65 ALL-AMERICAN TEAM

Best College gridmen of 1965.
NL; 28 min; 16mm; NL; JR, HS, A; Post World
War II.
CINES

COACHES '66 ALL-AMERICAN TEAM

Best college players of 1966.
NL; 28 min; 16 mm; NL; JR, HS, A; Post World
War II.
CINES

COACHING

Presents a practical approach to effective coaching. Illustrates five necessary steps to successful
coaching and shows some of the barriers to learning
that may occur.
1983; 25 min; 16 mm; color; A; Post World War II.
MGHT; UCB

COHO CALLING

Three noted fishing enthusiasts and their quest
for the coho . . . from casting and trolling in the lake
to following the coho up the Manistee River in their
dramatic spawning run. Included is a brief history of
the coho, conservation efforts, and the tremendous
influx of fishermen, and its effect on the area and
industry.
NL; 27 min; 16 mm; NL; JR, HS, A; Post World
War II.
DUPONT

COLD RUSH, THE

Madcap history of how not to ski.
NL; 28 min.; 16 mm; NL; JR, HS, A; Post World
War II.
CINES

COLGATE—DINAH SHORE WINNERS CIRCLE

(1972 AND 1973)

NL; NL; 16 mm; NL; JR, HS, A; Post World War
II.
LPGA

COLGATE FAR EAST TOURNAMENT (1974)

NL; NL; 16 mm; NL; JR, HS, A; Post World War
II.
LPGA

COLTS FRONT FOUR

An offbeat, funny look back at the fabulous 50s,
when a little nuttiness was essential for succeeding—
and surviving—in the NFL. You'll meet Art Donovan,
Eugene "Big Daddy" Lipscomb, Don Joyce, and Gino
Marchetti, all of whom happened to be outstanding
players as well as colorful characters.
NL; 7 min; VHS, U-Matic; NL; JR, HS, A; Post
World War II.
NFL; TMA

COMBAT SPORT, THE : BOXING YESTERDAY AND TODAY

Is boxing moral? This provocative film examines
this complex question in a historical context. It traces
the evolution of the sport over 6,000 years—from
ancient Greece, through bare-knuckle boxing in 17th
and 18th century England, to present-day boxing in
the United States. This film skillfully interweaves
this historic inquiry with scenes from the training of
an aspiring young boxer and probing interviews with
world champion fighters. *The Combat Sport* challenges the viewing audience with questions concern-
ing human nature and society. Do we have violent
instincts, and, if so, how should they be controlled?
This film is certain to provoke lively discussion about

issues that have significance far beyond the boxing arena.

1990; 57 min; VHS; color; HS, A; Ancient to Post World War II.

WRP

COMEBACKER: THE BOB WELCH STORY

The story of Los Angeles Dodger pitcher Bob Welch and his recovery from alcoholism. Having been a teenage drinker, Welch is seen at 21, an alcoholic. Friends get him to a treatment center where he progresses from denial to acceptance of his addiction. Welch openly discusses his motivations and his feelings about himself.

1981; 22 min; 16 mm; color; JR, HS, A; Post World War II.

CF; MICHMED

COME FISHING

Fishing for a 200-kilo Nile Perch in the world's largest inland lake (Lake Victoria); in the Nile River, and in lakes and rivers around the country.

NL; 20 min; 16 mm; NL; JR, HS, A; Post World War II.

EMBUGA

COME FISHING IN BRITAIN

This film shows the variety of angling holidays—from rough fishing in the rivers, to salmon and trout fishing, to an exciting sequence of shark fishing off the Cornish coast.

NL, 13 min; 16 mm; NL; JR, HS, A; Post World War II.

AUDPLAN

COME RIDING IN NEW BRITAIN

The horse is still a familiar figure in Britain. Not only is there year-round racing, but a visitor can hire a horse to go riding in London parks or to hunt in the Cotswolds.

NL; 13 min; 16 mm; NL; JR, HS, A; Post World War II.

AUDPLAN

COMPETITION

This program focuses on the competitive American character and the drive to win on the athletic field, in business, or within the family. Is our aim to become better, or to become better than someone else, so that the success of one person means the failure of another? This "Phil Donahue Show" is especially adapted for the classroom.

NL; 28 min; VHS; color; HS, A; Post World War II.

FOTH

CONCERTO GROSSO

A gymnastic performance of 16,000 soldiers during this Spartakiade sports event.

NL; NL; 16 mm; NL; JR, HS, A; Post World War II.

CZECHEM

CONTEMPORARY SKIING

The scenic ski slopes of Sun Valley, Idaho, provide the background for instruction on the basics of skiing to exciting downhill racing.

NL; 16 min; 16 mm; NL; JR, HS, A; Post World War II.

BUDGET

CONSEQUENCES

The exhilaration, excitement, and beauty of adventure sports are contrasted with the potential consequences—accidents, spinal cord injury, and permanent paralysis. Breathtaking scenes of hanggliding, surfing, diving, auto racing, climbing, skiing, and other sports are intercut with comments from spinal-cord victims. They have experienced the thrill of these sports and discuss why they were injured and the changes in their lives since.

NL; 10 min; 16 mm, VHS, U-Matic, Beta; color; HS, A; Post World War II.

CRYSP

CONTRACT FOR LIFE: THE S.A.D.D. STORY

In 1981, two members of the same high school hockey team were killed in separate automobile accidents in which liquor was involved. Spurred by the tragedy, the boys' coach and friends formed Students Against Driving Drunk, which now has several thousand chapters around the United States. A moving and inspirational look at how dedicated adults and teenagers working together can make a difference.

NL; 31 min; 16 mm, VHS; color; JR, HS, A; Post World War II.

CF

CORK DRAWS THE SPORTSMEN

County Cork is a major industrial area and an important cultural center, but as a paradise for sportsmen, it draws hundreds of thousands of visitors each year. Kinsale is a popular deep-sea fishing center, and big-game fishing parties catch trout, salmon, and sharks. It is a great place for horses, yachting, and speed-boating, and as a site of Carrolls International Tournament, it is a golfer's delight.

NL; 22 min; 16 mm; NL; JR, HS, A; Post World War II.

TRIBUNE

CORRIDA INTERDITE

Though viewed by many Americans as barbaric, bullfighting is considered very much a sport in Spanish culture. *Corrida Interdite* captures the dreamlike essence and ritualistic quality of the bullfight. Spectacular slow-motion sequences reveal the beauty of the picador ritual without glossing over the deadly nature of the conflict.

NL; 10 min; 16 mm, VHS; color; HS, A; Post World War II.

FI

COSTA RICAN TAILWALKERS

A 7-day fishing expedition at Carlos Barrantes' Parismina Tarpon Rancho by four noted fishing enthusiasts and their quest for giant tarpon—casting, fly fishing, and trolling in the rivers, bays, lagoons, and offshore. Also, light-tackle fishing for wapudie, mahura, and snook.

NL; 27 min; 16 mm; NL; JR, HS, A; Post World War II.

DUPONT

COTTON BOWL CLASSIC

    1975 - Penn State 41, Baylor 20
    1974 - Nebraska 19, Texas 3
    1973 - Texas 17, Alabama 13
    1972 - Penn State 30, Texas 6
    1971 - Notre Dame 24, Texas 11
    1970 - Texas 21, Notre Dame 17
    1969 - Texas 36, Tennessee 13
    1968 - Texas A&M 20, Alabama 16
    1967 - Georgia 24, SMU 9
    1966 - LSU 14, Arkansas 7
    1965 - Arkansas 10, Nebraska 7
    1964 - Texas 28, Navy 6
    1963 - LSU 13, Texas 0
    1962 - Texas 12, Ole Miss 3
    1961 - Duke 7, Arkansas 6
    1960 - Syracuse 23, Texas 14
    1959 - Air Force 0, TCU 0
    1958 - Navy 20, Rice 7
    1957 - TCU 28, Syracuse 27
    1956 - Ole Miss 14, TCU 13
    1955 - Ga. Tech 14, Arkansas 6
    1954, 1952, and 1951—silent films

NL; 20-30 mins each; 16 mm; NL; JR, HS, A; Post World War II.

CBIS

COUNTDOWN TO A DREAM

The Milwaukee Bucks win the 1971 National Basketball Association championship.

NL; NL; 16 mm; NL; JR, HS, A; Post World War II.

MILLER

COURAGE

Defining courage as "being able to do what we know is right even if we are afraid," this film is the story of two brothers, one of whom wants to ski in the Olympics but is afraid of the final, most dangerous slope, and the other, who encourages him and whose injury finally supplies the necessary motivation to brave the danger. Spectacularly filmed in the June Mountain ski area of California.

1972; 17 min; 16 mm; color; JR, HS, A; Post World War II.

LSU

COURAGE TO SUCCEED, THE

Describes the extraordinary goals marathon swimmer Diana Nyad set for herself and the almost superhuman effort she made to reach these goals.

1977; 28 min; 16 mm; color; JR, HS, A; Post World War II.

UWISC

COWGIRLS

The cowgirls in this documentary are modern-day women aged six to sixty who ride, rope, and tough out the elements just as well as their more famous cowboy counterparts. The film spans three generations, telling the inspirational real-life stories of women who are living their own dreams.

1986; 29 min; 16 mm, VHS; color; JR, HS, A; Post World War II.

DIRECT

CREE HUNTERS OF MISTASSINI

Shows how Indian hunters and trappers of the Mistassini area of northern Quebec live with the land in a way that reflects their complex and subtle religious beliefs as well as ecological principles. Records the setting up of a winter camp where three families (a total of 16 people) share the long, hard winter months. Shows scenes of Indian life in the bush, the hunt and its rituals, division of labor, preparation of food and animal skins, maintenance of the lodge, and the judicious mixture of communal living and family privacy.

1974; 59 min; 16 mm; color; HS, A; Ancient Sport, Post World War II.

UILL; NFBC

CREW MORE THAN SPORT

The Boston University crew team is shown practicing and competing. The film captures the remarkable teamwork and camaraderie among rowers.

NL; 10 min; 16 mm; color; JR, HS, A; Post World War II.

BUDGET

CRICKET AUSTRALIAN STYLE

Cricket in Australia, from schoolboy games to international matches. Includes scenes from the 1974 Australia versus New Zealand test series. Presents comments about the game by former Australian captain Ian Chappell.

1974; 28 min; 16 mm; color; JR, HS, A; Post World War II.

FLMAUS; FI

CROSSBAR

Inspiring drama about a young man with only one leg who successfully makes the Olympic team in high jumping. Sensitive, humanistic production that shows how determination and self-motivation can overcome enormous obstacles.

1980; 33 min; 16 mm; color; JR, HS, A; Post World War II.

UCB

CROSS COUNTRY

The various kinds of motor sports have won themselves an ever-growing body of spectators who wonder what kind of life those sportsmen lead, what their training methods are, what rules they impose on themselves, and so on.

This film, which deals with cross-country motorcycle racing, shows us a year in the life of Joel Robert, a world-renowned Belgian champion.

1970; 14 min; 16 mm, 35 mm; color; JR, HS, A; Post World War II.

BELGIUM

CROSS-COUNTRY CYCLE RACING

A film that shows all the difficulties due to the nature of the terrain and the weather, as well as the comical aspects of the sport. The producer also shows us the frequently unsporting reactions of the onlookers. The ironic commentary is often very funny.

Those taking part are Eric De Vlaeminck, seven times world champion in this sport, and Eddy Merckx during the only cross-country cycle race in which he competed that year. A French and Dutch language film.

1973; 13 min; 16 mm; color; JR, HS, A; Post World War II.

BELGIUM

CROSS COUNTRY HIGH

Eddie dreams of winning the Junior Olympics cross-country meet at his elementary school, but Eddie has problems. Overshadowed by his peers and feeling rejected at home, he is easily influenced by older boys who challenge him to try a bottle of wine. Believing that alcohol can solve all his problems, Eddie depends more and more on the liquor he takes from his father's cabinet. On the day of the big race, he is too out of condition to face the challenge, falls farther and farther behind, and is finally forced out with cramps.

1975; 14 min; 16 mm; color; JR, HS, A, Post World War II.

UILL

CROSS COUNTRY RUNNER

The cross-country runner runs because it is the thing to do; there is no stopping, because nothing must interfere with the race. As the film closes, the race is still going on, and it is evident that it will do so forever.

1961; 14 min; 16 mm; NL; HS, A; Post World War II.

UCB

CROSS COUNTRY SKIING

Shows, through the eyes of a 12-year-old Vermont boy, the fun and adventure of cross-country skiing, which differs from ordinary skiing in both equipment and technique. Notes that anyone who can walk can enjoy this sport, and shows people skiing up hills, climbing over fences, and skiing across open land. Follows the boy and his friends as they prepare for a relay with United States coach and former Olympic skier John Caldwell.

1970; 30 min; 16 mm; color; JR, HS, A; Post World War II.

UCB

CROSSOVER

Shows the Thunderbirds off on a goodwill tour of South America to thrill thousands with spectacular aerial demonstrations.

1963; 15 min; 16 mm; color; E, JR, HS, A; Post World War II.

USAF; USNAC

CSSR : ZEME SPORTU

Czechoslovakia, a country of sports.

NL; NL; 16 mm; NL; JR, HS, A; Post World War II.

CZECHEM

CUE MASTERS

Features Jimmy Caras, 1967 U. S. Open Champion, demonstrating a variety of trick and fancy shots on a pocket billiard table.

NL; 10 min; 16 mm; NL; JR, HS, A; Post World War II.

BRNSWK

CUE TRICKS

World Pocket Billiard Champ demonstrates precision trick shots with instructions on how to achieve them.

NL; 28 min; 16 mm; NL; JR, HS, A; Post World War II.

CINES

CUM LAUDE, CUM LONELY

Moving drama of a teenager's struggle to win acceptance from his father. Steve is interested in intellectual and aesthetic pursuits; his father wants him to be the athlete that the father dreamed of being. An unexpected series of events brings the father close to his son, however, and the two achieve a hesitant understanding. Rather melodramatic story, well acted and thematically strong.

1976; 27 min; 16 mm; color; JR, HS, A; Post World War II.

UCB

CUTTING EDGE, THE

Yuichiro Miura (the man who skied down Everest) journeys to an 8,000-foot mountain in the midst of Antarctica's frozen wastes to experience the thrill of skiing where no one has skied before.

NL; 18 min; 16 mm; color; JR, HS, A; Post World War II.

PYRAMID

CYCLING: STILL THE GREATEST

Scenes from the 1976 Olympics and the 1978 Commonwealth Games capture all the thrills and excitement of cycling. Featured are some of the world's best cyclists and their coaches, in training and in competition. This fast-growing sport is attracting the attention of cyclists and spectators alike. Made from footage shot during the filming of *Going the Distance*.

1980; 28 min; 16 mm, VHS; NL; JR, HS, A; Post World War II.

NFBC

CYCLING UNDER YOUR OWN POWER

Explores the many ways to cycle for pleasure: short group rides, family outings, cycle camping, and racing. Sponsored by the American Youth Hostels, this production invites bicycle owners to become adventurous.

1983; 20 min; 16 mm; NL; JR, HS, A; Post World War II.

OSU

DAN ABRAMOWICZ

Abramowicz succeeded because he always said "I'll try," never, "I can't." His determination and concentration on the game of football, along with his resourcefulness, more than made up for his lack of size.

1985; 7 min; VHS, U-Matic; color; JR, HS, A; Post World War II.

NFL; TMA

DANCER TO WIN

This production shows the breaking of a yearling at Stanley Dancer's farm and some typical scenes from Dancer's busy schedule on and off the race track. It includes Dancer inspecting yearlings at Hanover Shoe Farms and in action at Liberty Bell Park.

1970; 10 min; 16 mm; NL; JR, HS, A; Post World War II.

USTA

DANGEROUS WHEELS AND RUDDERS

Mile-a-minute action in some rare footage of racing in cars, boats, planes, and motorcycles, some dating back to 1906! Exciting stunts performed by daredevils in some of the fastest-moving scenes ever recorded. Double-wingers, supercharged speed boats, and historical disasters.

NL; 20 min; 16 mm; NL; JR, HS, A; Modern to Post World War II.

BUDGET

DANNY

Beautifully photographed drama about a 13-year-old girl's fight to save an over-the-hill show horse, and about her own painful but triumphant lessons in growing up, accepting responsibility, and learning to love.

1981; 90 min; 16 mm; color; JR, HS, A; Post World War II.

UCB; WOMBAT

DARE THE WILDEST RIVER

Experienced oarsmen share their knowledge of the Colorado River's roaring, dangerous rapids as they maneuver their motorless rafts through Arizona's Grand Canyon.

NL; 19 min; 16 mm; color; JR, HS, A; Post World War II.
PYRAMID

DARE TO CLIMB

Shows acrobatic flyer Joe Hughes explaining what it takes to reach success in his field. Emphasizes the importance of confidence, discipline, and determination.
NL; 20 min; VHS, U-Matic; color; JR, HS, A; Post World War II.
SFTI

DAVID "DEACON" JONES

The flamboyant "Deacon" Jones delivers a colorful sermon on his pass-rushing philosophy and proclaims himself the "best football player, second to none." In these 7 minutes of big hits and belly laughs, he convincingly backs up his boasts.
1985; 7 min; VHS, U-Matic; color; JR, HS, A; Post World War II.
NFL; TMA

DAWN FLIGHT

A dramatic visual poem about a young pilot's achievement of self-confidence and self-awareness. In his mastery of glider control, displayed throughout the film in the treetop chases and maneuvers through narrow canyons, he is haunted by a mysterious superpilot in a red sailplane. After an incredible aerial dogfight, the flier finally draws abreast of the other glider and for the first time sees who its pilot is. Filmed over the Napa Valley, north of San Francisco.
1975; 21 min; 16 mm, VHS, U-Matic; color; JR, HS, A; Post World War II.
UILL, PYRAMID

DAY MANOLETE WAS KILLED, THE

Vivid account of the day in August, 1947, when Manolete came out of retirement to answer the challenge of young Luis Dominguin. Reconstructed completely with still photographs by Manolete's friend—novelist, matador, and moviemaker Barnaby Conrad—Manolete is seen in his hotel room as he dresses for the fight. He talks of his fear, yet when he goes out into the crowd he plays the role of the courageous matador. As one of his assistants said, "The crowd kept demanding more and more of him, and more was his life. So he gave it to them."
1957; 19 min; 16 mm; NL; JR, HS, A; Post World War II.
FI; UCB

DAY THE DERBY ALMOST DIED, THE

Investigates the scandal over an altered soapbox car which occurred at the 1973 Soapbox Derby at Akron, Ohio. Shows how the incident shook the confidence of both the public and the Derby promoters in the competition's fairness.
1974; 24 min; 16 mm; color; JR, HS, A; Post World War II.
CIHIB

DAY WE BEAT THE RUSSIANS, THE

Three Depression kids from Regina used to practice hockey with homemade sticks and road apples. In 1955, their team, the Penticton Vees, won the World Hockey Championship Cup in Krefeld, West Germany. This documentary is the story of the Warwick Brothers, their rise from humble beginnings in Canada to their peak in Europe, and their subsequent decline. Interviews with the three brothers and rare footage of the championship game tell a story of hockey and human drama.
1983; 27.5 min; 16 mm; color; JR, HS, A; Post World War II.
NFBC

DAYTONA RACING

Shows professional rider Dick Mann aboard his CB-750, winning the 1970 Daytona 200 in record time. This was the initial outing for the CB-750 in racing gear, and the results speak for themselves.
NL; 18 min; 16 mm; NL; JR, HS, A; Post World War II.
HONDA

DEAD RIVER ROUGH CUT: A WOODS MOVIE

Looks at the wilderness life-style of two men who have rejected modern society for the freedom of the forest. The woodsmen share a cabin in the backwoods of northern Maine, isolated but independent. Two oxen are kept to help them haul wood. Outlines the tasks and enjoyments that change with the seasons. The men talk about themselves, their willingness to give up conveniences and female companionship for the emotional rewards they derive from living, hunting, trapping, and fishing year-round in a natural environment.
1976; 28 min; 16 mm; color; JR, HS, A; Post World War II.
UILL

DEATH IN THE ARENA

Rare glimpses of Manolete at the height of his career, beginning with a few episodes taken from various bullfights, which demonstrate his skill and mastery as the "supreme" matador, to his untimely death in the bullring.

NL; 10 min; 16 mm; NL; JR, HS, A; Depression Era, Post World War II.

BUDGET

DEATH OF A SANDWICHMAN

A serious, accusing inquiry into the underworld of bicycle racing, occasioned by the funeral of world champion J. P. Monsere, who met an accidental death during a race. During the funeral ceremony, by means of a series of interviews, the producers analyze the world of professional cycle-racing: how it is organized by sporting managers and impresarios, how the racers advertise commercial products, the conditions in which they compete, what security they can expect from the social standpoint, and finally how certain politicians make use of their successes and failures as a means of securing votes. A Dutch language film with French and English subtitles.

1972; 35 min; 16 mm; BW; JR, HS, A; Post World War II.

BELGIUM

DECATHLON, THE

Presents a television special from the CTV program "Olympiad," which highlights dramatic moments in the history of the Olympic decathlon contests.

1976; 50 min; 16 mm; color; JR, HS, A; Modern Sport to Post World War II.

CTV

DESCENT

Alone, downhill skier David Murray practices on an icy slope, again and again. Then it's the big event itself. An exciting, fast-paced film that dramatizes the human need to begin again, to persevere, and rise above disappointment.

1975; 10 min; 16 mm, VHS, U-Matic, Beta; color; JR, HS, A; Post World War II.

NFBC; WOMBAT

DESEGREGATED DECADE, THE

Dr. St. Clair surveys the progress during the ten-year period which began in 1945 with the decision of the NAACP to launch an all-out attack on racial segregation in every aspect of American life. He discusses the contribution of President Truman and W. E. B. Dubois, the impact of Supreme Court decisions, the breakdown of racial barriers in sports, and the desegregation of the armed forces.

1969; 30 min; 16 mm; BW; JR, HS, A; Post World War II.

HRAW

DESERT MARINERS

So you think sailing is just for the water? Well, here's another type of sailing—land sailing, a 400-year-old sport that has been revived on America's deserts and beaches. Traveling at speeds up to 100 mph, daredevil land sailors, in their three-wheel craft, race over an ocean of sand.

1975; 7 min; 16 mm; color; JR, HS, A; Post World War II.

BUDGET

DEUTCHES TURNFEST BERLIN 1968

Participants of all ages from many countries meet for the 1968 German Gymnastics Festival in Berlin, not so much for competition, but for the fun of it.

NL; 17 min; 16 mm; NL; NL; Post World War II.

MTPS

DICK BUTKUS

An action-packed special on the greatest defender who ever lived—Butkus. The mere sound of his name calls to mind the mythic qualities of a larger-than-life figure: tough, mean, hard as an anvil. For eight years, he dominated opponents to a degree unknown before him and unmatched since. Bear players measured opponents' toughness by how they got up—if they got up—after being hit by Butkus. Although the Bears were never winners during his career, he never gave up on a play and made the phrase "sound effort" the badge of his professional conduct. Fifteen minutes of rock 'em, sock 'em action for football fans who appreciate the art of a hard tackle as much as a touchdown. (Note: program contains strong language.)

1985; 15 min; VHS, U-matic; color; JR, HS, A; Post World War II.

TMA

DIFFERENT KIND OF WINNING, A (CAPTIONED)

Helps viewers appreciate the art of sportsmanship. Relates the story of a young girl who let a championship go to another for humanitarian reasons.

1980; 27 min; 16 mm, VHS, U-Matic; color; JR, HS, A; Post World War II.

LCOA

DIVIDED GAME, THE

Documents the historical and traditional split between the two major versions of football played widely in Britain by amateur and professional teams: "Rugby" and "Association." Uses newsreel and historical film to trace the history of the game from its rowdy beginnings as intervillage roughhousing, through the middle ages and its subsequent adoption as a game, to its present highly commercialized status.

NL; 28 min; 16 mm; color, JR, HS, A; Renaissance to Post World War II.

UILL

DOC: THE OLDEST MAN IN THE SEA

Highlights of 57-year-old James "Doc" Counsilman's record-breaking swim of the English Channel are interwoven with flashbacks showing Doc in training for the event and at work coaching his university swimming team. Comments from Doc, Indiana University swimming coach since 1958 and two-time Olympic coach, reflect upon prior attempts by others to swim the Channel, his belief in the health and recreational value of swimming for older people, and his life as a coach and researcher. Captures the enthusiastic encouragement and support given by Doc's wife, his coach, and other boat passengers during all stages of his swim.

1980; 30 min; 16 mm, VHS; color, JR, HS, A; Post World War II.

IU

DOGS: BORN FOR ACTION

This exceptional film presents sequences about bird dogs, hunting dogs, show dogs, and racing dogs.

28 min; 16 mm; color; JR, HS, A; Post World War II.

MTPS

"DON'T KNOCK THE OX"

Presents highlights of one of the few remaining links with our pioneer past, International Oxpull in Bridgewater, Nova Scotia. Loggers, homesteaders, and cattlemen flock to the South Shore Exhibition to enjoy the parades and the carnival-like festivities, and above all, to watch the mammoth oxen as they pull sleds carrying up to 12,000 pounds in competition. Between the urging and cheering of the spectators are scenes of how oxen build muscles for this kind of effort: dragging a stone boat, pulling logs from a woodlot or farm implements over the land.

1970; 13 min; 16 mm; color; JR, HS, A; Post World War II.

NFBC; FI; UILL

DON'T QUIT

Dick Cavett narrates an inspirational poem entitled "Don't Quit." He reads to action footage shot in the snow, mud, and sunshine to illustrate the frustrating problems and heartwarming triumphs that show the emotional highs and lows of a pro football player in the NFL.

NL; 2 min; 16 mm, VHS, U-Matic; color; JR, HS, A; Post World War II.

NFL; TMA

DOVE SHOOTING IN COLOMBIA

NL; NL; 16 mm; NL; JR, HS, A; Post World War II.

BRANIFF

DOWN FOR THE COUNT: AN INSIDE LOOK AT BOXING

Is boxing worth saving? In this provocative look at the controversial sport, we see both sides of the question. People who are in it and love it say it is no more dangerous than any other sport. For many kids without options, it is a valuable activity. On the other side are deaths in the ring, brain damage, and blindness. An uncompromising view of a sport under attack.

NL; 46 min; VHS; color; JR, HS, A; Post World War II.

CF

DO YOU BELIEVE IN MIRACLES?

This emotionally charged program, based on one of the most exciting moments in Olympic sports history—the taking of the gold by the United States Olympic hockey team—illustrates the importance of teamwork, motivation, and leadership in goal attainment. The points made effectively demonstrate how important determination and drive are for achievement in any profession. Commentary by players, coaches, and narrator Jim McKay underlines the need for planning, tenacity, and self-confidence in order to come out a winner.

NL; 24 min; 16 mm, VHS, color; JR, HS, A; Post World War II.

ABCS; UWISC

DO YOU LIKE SNOW?

Breathtaking somersaults on skis, the slalom, ski leaps over cars, precision crisscrossing, breakneck bobsledding, curling, skating, humor on snow and ice. Lift rides to the peaks of the beautiful St. Moritz Mountains.

NL; 30 min; 16 mm; color; JR, HS, A; Post World War II.

BUDGET

DOVE, THE

The story of a 17-year-old boy sailing around the world alone on his 23-foot sloop, *Dove*, develops the meanings of growing up, of making mature decisions, understanding one's emotions, and finding love. It is the autobiography of Robin Graham, who spent the years 1965-1970 pursuing his dream and learning much about himself in the process.

1981; 40 min; 16 mm; color; JR, HS, A; Post World War II.

AIMS; UWISC

DO YOUR OWN THING

Fat Albert and the kids get an early taste of girl's lib, when Penny shows the gang that she is more than a match for the kids at sports. Fat Albert feels that cooking is the one area in which he can surpass Penny. Concludes with Albert winning first prize for his Easter egg chocolate marshmallow cake and the kids learning that you can "do your own thing," whether you are a boy or a girl.

1975; 13 min; 16 mm, VHS, U-Matic; color; E, JR, HS, A; Post World War II.

MGHT

DRINKERS OF THE WIND

This presentation of the versatility of the Arabian horse weaves together a montage of scenes depicting its endurance, beauty, gentleness, and diverse capabilities. Arabian working horses on a cattle ranch are contrasted with a suspense-filled Arabian Horse Show. The excitement of racing and the grueling ordeal of an endurance ride will interest viewers.

NL; 20 min; 16 mm, VHS; color; JR, HS, A; Post World War II.

MTPS

DRUGS: DON'T BE FOOLED

Captures the reality of the drug and alcohol scene. Shows how athletes are using and abusing amphetamines and other drugs, how long-term marijuana use may affect fetus development, how alcohol is involved in 26,000 highway accident deaths each year, and how use of depressants has reached pandemic proportions. Documents the fact that drugs have certain known effects and consequences, so viewers should act accordingly.

NL; 27 min; VHS, U-Matic; color; JR, HS, A; Post World War II.

AMEDFL

DUDH KOSI: RELENTLESS RIVER OF EVEREST

Seven of Britain's top whitewater paddlers challenge the dangerous and difficult rapids and obstacles of the Dudh Kosi River, which plummets down the slopes of Mt. Everest. They negotiate waterfalls, stoppers, ten-foot waves, and thousands of submerged boulders at speeds often greater than 30 mph before reaching their destination 12,000 feet below.

1977; 27 min; 16 mm, VHS; color; JR, HS, A; Post World War II.

IU

DUEL IN THE WIND: IN DEFENSE OF THE AMERICA'S CUP

The America's Cup is the symbol of yachting supremacy. For over 100 years, twenty challenges by racing yachts from England, Scotland, Ireland, Canada, and Australia have been turned back by defenders of the America's Cup. In 1970, off Newport R.I., United States skippers vying for the right to defend the Cup were Charles Morgan of the *Heritage,* Bob McCullough of the *Valiant,* and *Intrepid*'s Bill Ficker. The film shows the planning, building, and launching of the yachts and the process that transforms an experienced skipper and skilled sailors into a coordinated racing team. For the first time in the history of the Cup trials, onboard cameras and recorders show the nervous faces of the skippers and listen to actual cockpit debates in strategy. The action is followed right through the final Cup series, including the famous protest incident between *Gretel* (Australian finalist) and the *Intrepid,* when the two 12-meter racers collided at the starting line.

1970; 70 min; 16 mm; color; JR, HS, A; Post World War II.

BUDGET

EARL MORRALL

No player ever had to swallow so much pride or listen to so much nay-saying to get where he wanted to go than Earl Morrall. A moving profile of an athlete who never lost faith in himself.

1985; 7 min; VHS, U-Matic; color; JR, HS, A; Post World War II.

NFL; TMA

EAST AFRICAN ROAD RALLY: THE CONTINUING CHALLENGE

The East African Safari is more than a rally—it is a torture test of driver and car that traverses 3,800 miles of desert, jungle, veldt, and the toughest international driving competition.

NL; 28 min; 16 mm; NL; JR, HS, A; Post World War II.

ASF

EAST COMES WEST, THE

The consistent domination of Eastern European athletes in international competition has prompted all nations to reexamine the priorities, methods, and capacities of their sports systems. This film focuses on several coaches and athletes from Soviet-bloc countries who are now living in Canada. Their experiences in both socialist and Canadian systems will help audiences more fully appreciate the political, social, and cultural influences at work in international sports competition.

1984; 24.5 min; 16 mm; color; A; Post World War II.

NFBC

EDDIE LEBARON

A story illustrating how a lack of size is not always a serious handicap. The vital ingredients to success were LeBaron's sense of command, quick, accurate arm, desire, and poise. LeBaron parlayed his size and endless caring into a remarkable pro career.

1985; 6 min; VHS, U-Matic; color; JR, HS, A; Post World War II.

NFL; TMA

EDDY MERCKX AND JOEL ROBERT

First we see Eddy Merckx, the racing cyclist, displaying all his strength and endurance. He scored 52 victories during the year 1971 alone.

The sequence on Merckx shows us what a champion's life is like, with its iron discipline, its extremely strict diet, hard training in order to remain in peak condition, the preparation for his races, how the equipment and other members of the team are selected, the necessity for giving interviews, the risks he has to face, and all the dangers bound up with being "the man who must be beaten."

Joel Robert was five times world champion in the 250-cubic-centimeter class by the end of 1971. By that time, he had scored over 230 victories. He also had to subject himself to an intensive course of physical training and all the servitudes that Eddy Merckx had to face.

1972; 35 min; 16 mm; color; JR, HS, A; Post World War II.

BELGIUM

EDGE, THE

The Edge is that edge between great joy and possible disaster as each sport is experienced to the outer limits. The film features skiing in the Rocky Mountains, reef-diving with sharks off Mexico, surfing the thirty-foot waves at Waimea Bay, Hawaii, climbing the big walls in Yosemite, hang gliding in the Bugaboos of British Columbia, kayaking the Grand Canyon, and ice-climbing the Diamond Couloir on Mt. Kenya.

NL; 96 min; 16 mm, VHS, Beta; color; JR, HS, A; Post World War II.

CRYSP

EIGER, THE

The Eiger Mountain in the Swiss Alps has such treacherous slopes, especially the "killer wall," a 6000-foot near-vertical escarpment on the mountain's north face, that more than one-third of all climbers who have essayed the peak have died in the attempt. Undaunted by this prospect, and determined not only to scale the "killer wall" successfully but to film its conquest, four young Welshmen resolve to assault the Eiger. Shown throughout are treacherous slopes, ice fields and chimneys, turbulent weather, incredible feats of physical agility, the paraphernalia and techniques of modern mountain climbing, and a terrifying succession of challenges imposed by the mountain. Also depicts the utter interdependence which four individuals develop during the climb and the glory of their conquest.

1972; 24 min; 16 mm; color; JR, HS, A; Post World War II.

FI; UILL

ELEMENTS OF GOLD

Highlights of the 1984 Summer Olympic Games in Los Angeles.

1985; 61 min; 16 mm; color; JR, HS, A; Post World War II.

USOC

ELGIN BAYLOR

Highlights Elgin Baylor's basketball career. Shows footage from the occasion where Baylor scored a career high of 71 points in a single game.

20 min; 16 mm; color; JR, HS, A; Post World War II.

COUNFI; USC

ELIMINATORS

The Eliminators are not enforcers for the Mafia, but those drag-racing machines that make it to the final elimination. The film describes the different classes of drag vehicles, illustrates competition in each of the classes, and covers the final runoff on a national drag event.

NL; 30 min; 16 mm; color; JR, HS, A; Post World War II.

BUDGET

EQUAL CHANCE THROUGH TITLE IX, AN

Explains the intent of Title IX of the 1972 Education Amendments and aims at helping schools and communities implement equal opportunity physical education and sports programs.

1977; 22 min; 16 mm; color; HS, A; Post World War II.

AAHPER

EVEL KNIEVEL

The wild story of "the last of the daredevils," Evel Knievel, the man whose motorcycle exploits have made him a modern legend. From his childhood up to his most dangerous stunt (at the time of the film), jumping over 19 cars, *Evel Knievel* emerges as a film Judith Crist called "Fast, funny and incredible . . ." Footage of the real Knievel's stunts are skillfully interwoven with fine performances.

1971; 90 min; 16 mm; color; JR, HS, A; Post World War II.

BUDGET

EVEREST UNMASKED: THE FIRST ASCENT WITHOUT OXYGEN

A remarkable record of an adventure in mountaineering, showing the dramatic first ascent of Mt. Everest without an artificial supply of oxygen.

1978; 28 min; 16 mm; VHS; U-Matic; color; JR, HS; A; Post World War II.

IU

EVERY CHILD A WINNER

Presents a philosophy of physical education as a series of activities to develop a child's self-confidence and self-image through success. Endorses the notion that every child wins when doing his or her best. Emphasizes physical skill refinement for life enrichment and lifetime sports activities. Views physical education as a means to develop perceptual goal setting and problem solving for self-expression and growth of the self-image.

1974; 14 min; 16 mm; color; HS, A; Post World War II.

AAHPER; UWISC

EVERYTHING ABOUT BICYCLES

An animated adaptation of the National Safety Council's bicycle safety handbook. Includes an account of the history of the bicycle and a look at the future of bicycling.

1976; 14 min; 16 mm, VHS, U-Matic; color; JR, HS, A; Modern Sport to Post World War II.

PYRAMID

EVERYTHING OR SOMETHING

A film about sport—not the kind of sport that leads to great victories or the shattering of records, but sport for pleasure and healthy recreation, sport to keep the body in good condition so as to enjoy life more fully. To popularize the idea of physical fitness and give everyone a chance to improve his or her standards, the Netherlands Sport Federation introduced "proficiency tests." Anyone coming up to the required level received a certificate. But the most important thing is that one should be physically fit and able to take the tasks of everyday life in one's stride.

NL; 15 min; 16 mm; BW; JR, HS, A; Post World War II.

RNE

EXCELLENCE AND ISOLATION: CAROL MANN

This film is a full account of Carol Mann's emotional and revealing speech before the delegates of the New Agenda Conference in November of 1983. Ms. Mann discusses the difficulty women athletes experience in developing and nurturing quality relationships while competing at the elite level of sport. Isolation is often a cruel reality for elite women athletes.

NL; 15 min; 16 mm; color; HS, A; Post World War II.

WSF

EXIT THE DRAGON, ENTER THE TIGER

Did Bruce Lee die as reported, or was there foul play involved? That's the question that haunted martial arts enthusiasts all over the world when the superstar suddenly died. This is almost the basis upon which the plot of *Exit the Dragon . . .* hinges. An action-filled martial arts thriller, starring Bruce Li, a disciple of the late Lee. Teaming up with a reporter in Singapore, Li soon finds himself running headlong into very obvious (and physical) opposition from Lung Fei, a.k.a. The Baron, a feared gangster and top man in the Orient's dread triad syndicate. Despite warnings to forget his quest, as well as several attempts on his life, our hero defies all opposition as he attempts to find, and eventual rescue, the woman who can shed light on the mystery of his mentor's death.

1976; 84 min; 16 mm; color; JR, HS, A; Post World War II.

BUDGET

EXPRESSION SESSION II

During the winter months, when the largest waves break along the North Shore of Oahu, many surfing events are scheduled, and everyone hopes that the surf and weather conditions will be good on the scheduled days. When Expression Session II, second of a series of surfing art form exhibitions was held, the waves were perfect. The best surfers in the world, including Jeff Hakeman, Barry Kanaiaupuini, Gerry Lopez, and Rory Russell, met to express their own surfing creativity.

1975; 15 min; 16 mm; color; JR, HS, A; Post World War II.

BUDGET

FAIR FOR ALL

Shows harness racing at county fairs today. Designed as a USTA guide to fairs on how to make the most of their racing programs, this film primer gives do's and don'ts and shows some highly successful formulas that can upgrade county-fair racing at all levels.

NL; 20 min; 16 mm; NL; JR, HS, A; Post World War II.

USTA

FAIR PLAY

Explains how to acquire an awareness of fair play and learn to interact with this knowledge in the development of adult social values of sportsmanship and courtesy.

1970; 8 min; VHS, U-Matic; color; JR, HS, A; Post World War II.

SF

FAIR RACE, A

The popular sport of cycling in Belgium began long ago, when races were organized in the towns and villages. They have led to regular events in which the "budding hopes" participate alongside veteran cycle racers who attract a great crowd of onlookers.

Usually sponsored by commercial firms, the races are made increasingly difficult. The course usually takes the competitors over rough-cobbled streets of towns and villages which are barred to traffic for the occasion. There are often more than two hundred contenders, followed by a caravan of seconds and trainers, plus the race managers and officials.

These races often take place in conjunction with a local fair, thus enabling spectators to follow the race while enjoying all the amusements of the fairground. A Dutch language film.

1975; 10 min; 16 mm; color; JR, HS, A; Post World War II.

BELGIUM

FALCONRY

The art of hunting with birds of prey.

1966; 14 min; 16 mm; NL; JR, HS, A; Post World War II.

MTPS

FALL LINE

The high-risk sport of extreme skiing involves following the steepest line of descent between two points on a slope. The skier's course down the nearly vertical slopes is an affirmation of courage, skill, and determination to succeed despite danger and near disaster. Filmed on the upper regions of Wyoming's Grand Tetons, once considered too hazardous to climb.

1981; 12 min; 16 mm; color; JR, HS, A; Post World War II.

PYRAMID; UCB; WSU

FALKONEREN OGDEN VILDE FALK (THE FALCON AND THE WILD FALCON)

Tells of the falcon in its natural surroundings and of hunting with trained falcons, a sport of kings and princes, which has existed for centuries. Includes shots from Greenland, England, Morocco, and the Arabian Desert. A Danish language film.

1968; 15 min; 16 mm; BW; JR, HS, A; Ancient to Post World War II.

STATNS

FAMOUS FIGHTS NO. 1

Marciano-Moore; Pep-Sadler; Giardello-Cartier.

NL; 28 min; 16 mm; NL; JR, HS, A; Post World War II.

CINES

FAMOUS FIGHTS NO. 2

Satterfield-Brothers; Robinson-Turpin; Marciano-Walcott.

NL; 28 min; 16 mm; NL; JR, HS, A; Post World War II.

CINES

FAMOUS FIGHTS NO. 3

Basillo-DeMarco; Robinson-Basillo.

NL; 28 min; 16 mm; NL; JR, HS, A; Post World War II.

CINES

FAMOUS FIGHTS NO. 4

Patterson-Troy; Olson-Hairston; Marciano-Louis.

NL; 28 min; 16 mm; NL; JR, HS, A; Post World War II.

CINES

FAMOUS FIGHTS NO. 5

DeMarco-Sadler; Moore-Johnson; Marciano-Charles.

NL; 28 min; 16 mm; NL; JR, HS, A; Post World War II.

CINES

FAMOUS FIGHTS NO. 6

Includes contests between Joe Louis and Max Baer; Sugar Ray Robinson and Carmen Basillio.

NL; 28 min; 16 mm; NL; JR, HS, A; Depression Era and World War II, Post World War II.
CINES

FAMOUS FIGHTS NO. 7

Features memorable battles matching Louis and Walcott; Robinson and Turpin.
NL; 28 min; 16 mm; NL; JR, HS, A; Depression Era and World War II, Post World War II.
CINES

FAMOUS FIGHTS NO. 8

One of the great collections of historic fights: Louis vs. Schmeling; Ross vs. Armstrong; Zale vs. Graziano; Tunney vs. Gibbons; Tunney vs. Heeney.
NL; 28 min; 16 mm; NL; JR, HS, A; Golden Age, Depression Era and WW II, Post World War II.
CINES

FAMOUS FIGHTS NO. 9

Features a vintage fight between Jack Johnson and Stan Ketchel, plus: Muhamed Ali vs. "Big Cat" Williams; Louis vs. Farr; Louis vs. Baer; Carnera vs. Louhran; Carnera vs. Schmeling.
NL; 28 min; 16 mm; NL; JR, HS, A; Modern Sport, Golden Age, Depression Era and WW I.
CINES

FAMOUS FIGHTS NO. 10

Eight classic ring confrontations give this film a fast pace. Included are these memorable bouts: Schmeling-Walker (1932); Louis-Godoy (1940); Canzoneri-Ambers (1935); Ross-Mclarnin (1935); Gavilan-Cartier; Pep-Perez; Basilio-DeMarco; Basilio-DeMarco; and Robinson-Olsen.
NL; NL; 16 mm; NL; JR, HS, A; Depression Era and WW II, Post World War II.
CINES

FAMOUS FIGHTS NO. 11

Some of the biggest and best bouts in boxing history are included in this film. Boxing fans will enjoy these famous matches: Willard-Moran (1916); Carnera-Sharkey (1933); Baer-Schmeling (1933); Valdez-Jackson; Moore-Johnson; Slade-Patterson; Louis-Marciano; and Gibbons-Tunney.
NL; NL; 16 mm; NL; JR, HS, A; Modern to Post World War II.
CINES

FAMOUS FIGHTS NO. 12

This film features the premier black boxers in some of their toughest duels. Included are these famous fights: Johnson-Ketchel; Clay-Williams; Moore-Johnson; Slade-Patterson; Louis-Schmeling; Robinson-Olson; Louis-Baer; Louis-Farr; and Louis-Godoy.
NL; 28 min; 16 mm; NL; JR, HS, A; Modern to Post World War II.
CINES

FANTASTIC PLASTIC MACHINE, THE

The world of surfing is the subject of this excellent documentary that follows a group of surfers on their own odyssey. Members of the well-known Windensea Surf Club make a historic journey across the South Pacific to Australia, where they plan to compete with some of Australia's finest surfers.
1969; 90 min; 16 mm; color; JR, HS, A; Post World War II.
BUDGET

FAST BREAK

You don't have to be a basketball fan to enjoy *Fast Break,* but it would certainly help. In this zany comedy, a delicatessen clerk gets a job of coaching a college team of all-time losers. He persuades the college president that he can put the sleepy small-town school on the map by organizing a high-powered squad of hoopsters. His dream team is made up of a preacher, a jailbird, a muscleman, and the best guy on the team, a girl.
1979; 107 min; 16 mm; color; JR, HS, A; Post World War II.
BUDGET

FAST HORSE IN A BULL MARKET

Breeding and selling racehorses as big-money sport.
NL; 30 min; 16 mm; color; HS, A; Post World War II.
UCB

FEARLESS FIGHTERS

Every plot development created for the Chinese martial arts movie gets an inning here. You have four heroes—two men, two women (one of whom has the ability to leap across tall lakes at a single bound . . . while looking like the Flying Nun!), who display their kung-fu skill and swordsmanship. Then there's the "Lightning Whipper," an 80-year-old man who wipes out a horde of bandits. The villains are definitely not your usual run-of-the-mill heavies. There's the assassin who uses solar mirrors to create death rays of light; the Soul Pickers, a pair of cut-throats who'll pluck at your nerve ends; the Devil Ripper, whose claw-like gauntlets make him a real cut-up! Last, but not least, we have the Killer, a one-man army who becomes more than one person . . . a real split personality! Flat or Cinemascope. Please specify.

1973; 83 min; 16 mm; color; JR, HS, A; Post World War II.

BUDGET

FEATHERED WARRIOR

The illegal sport of cockfighting is documented in this film. A cockfighter who has won over 65 percent of his fights outlines the rules of the game, describes the skills and techniques needed to win, and talks about why people enjoy the sport. A slow-motion sequence shows the sweeping motion of the birds as each attempts to cut to victory.

1973; 12 min; 16 mm, VHS; color; HS, A; Post World War II.

APPAEL

FESTIVAL OF BULLS

Every year the natives, tourists, and the aficionados gather to celebrate the festival of the bulls. Only in Pamplona, Spain, during the feast of St. Fermin, can you be an amateur bullfighter (at your own risk) or a spectator, by taking on the charging bulls as they wind their way through narrow streets to the bullring.

NL; 10 min; 16 mm; color; JR, HS, A; Post World War II.

BUDGET

FIESTA BOWL

1971 Fiesta Bowl highlight film (Arizona State vs. Florida State)

1972 Fiesta Bowl highlight film (Arizona State vs. Missouri)

1973 Fiesta Bowl highlight film (Arizona State vs. Pittsburgh)

NL; NL; 16 mm; NL; JR, HS, A; Post World War II.

FIESTA

FIFTY YEARS OF BASEBALL MEMORIES

Presents baseball's history through some of its greatest players. Features stars such as Babe Ruth, Lou Gehrig, Ty Cobb, Tris Speaker, Mel Ott, Joe DiMaggio, Warren Spahn, and Mickey Mantle during some of their most exciting plays. Shows highlights of World Series games dating back to 1933.

1963; NL; 16 mm; BW; JR, HS, A; Golden Age, Depression Era, World War II, Post World War II.

NBHF

FIGHTERS OF 100 FATHOMS

Anglers head out from Panama City Beach marina to go after the really big ones in the Gulf of Mexico.

NL; 15 min; 16 mm; NL; JR, HS, A; Post World War II.

FLADC

FIGHTING BACK

Examines the effects on women of socialization, which conditions them not to be aggressive or to use physical violence to defend themselves. Shows a female martial-arts teacher instructing a class in self-defense, New York police giving advice on how to handle attackers, and members of New York Women Against Rape discussing the psychological effects of being raped. The martial-arts teacher notes that women must stop thinking of themselves as victims and must be willing to hurt an attacker.

1974; 24 min; 16 mm; color; HS, A; Post World War II.

UCB

FIGHTING BACK

The Cabbagetown Boxing Club in Toronto has produced many Olympic and world-class boxers. This film is the story of Asif Dar, an underweight immigrant who learned boxing in order to defend himself from neighborhood bullies. The film traces the relationship between Asif Dar, who came to the club as a youngster, and his instructor, Ken Hamilton, a longtime foe of the violence traditionally associated with boxing.

1984; 24.5 min.; 16 mm; color; JR, HS, A; Post World War II.

NFBC

FIGHTING BRAVES OF 1959

The Milwaukee Braves clash for the world championship, only to find disappointment at the end of the season.

NL; 20-30 min; 16 mm; color; JR, HS, A; Post World War II.

BUDGET; NBC

FILION

Covers business, personal, and track life of leading driver Herv Filion.

1973; 10 min; 16 mm; NL; JR, HS, A; Post World War II.

USTA

FILIPINO SPORTS PARADE

Howard Hill, champion archer, joins the Second Philippines Regiment in a "lechon," or native barbecue. During the festivities they engage in native sports, judo, sipa (played with the feet), yoyo spinning, and the use of the bolo, a knife. (Note: Please specify B&W or color version.)

NL; 10 min; 16 mm; BW or color; JR, HS, A; Post World War II.

BUDGET

FIRE IN THE COOL WORLD

Shows efforts of the Mantua community in Philadelphia to better their neighborhood by cleaning the streets, establishing athletics programs, rebuilding homes, and giving college scholarships.

1975; 27 min; 16 mm; color; HS, A; Post World War II.

SF

FIREAWAY

The story of a boy and his trotter.

NL; 19 min; 16 mm; NL; JR, HS, A; Post World War II.

USTA

FIRST ANNUAL GREAT SMOKY MOUNTAINS GATLINBURG HIGHLAND GAMES, THE

Depicts traditional dances, ballads, and bagpipe band at the first highland games held in Gatlinburg, Tennessee. Narration is in a conversational style, which sets the tone for this informal Scottish clan gathering. Contrasts the athletic contests, which date to the 11th century, with the rugged countryside and tourist attractions.

1983; 26 min; VHS, U-Matic; color; JR, HS, A; Medieval to Post World War II.

SANMRP

FIRST ASCENT

Follows two daring young women in their attempt to free-climb a sheer 1,000-foot rock wall in Colorado, using only their hands and feet, with no mechanical aids. Inspiring account of achievement, determination, teamwork, and courage.

1982; 12 min; 16 mm; color; JR, HS, A; Post World War II.

PYRAMID; UCB; WSU

FIRST GAME, FIRST SET

For those interested in the glories of tennis past, this unusual film traces the origins of lawn tennis from the vicarage lawn to the present class of world sport. Beginning with a detailed description of "real tennis," the modern game's oldest and most important ancestor, the film includes the birth of the Wimbledon Championship, with many shots of early great players.

1974; 20 min; 16 mm; color; JR, HS, A; Premodern to Post World War II.

USTEN

FIRST 10 YEARS, THE (1970 VIKING HIGHLIGHT FILM)

Highlights the Minnesota Vikings, 1969 and 1970 Central Division Champions in the National Football League, during their "building" years under explosive coach Norm Van Brocklin and scrambling quarterback Fran Tarkenton, their bruising rise to Central Division supremacy under tough but taciturn Bud Grant.

NL; NL; 16 mm; NL; JR, HS, A; Post World War II.

HAMMS

FISHING AT THE STONE WEIR: PARTS 1 AND 2

Documents, without narration, one part of the Netsilik Eskimo's nomadic cycle. The Netsilik, who live in the almost inaccessible northeast part of Canada's Northwest Territories, establish camps according to hunting and weather conditions. The film follows a man and his family as they travel from their spring seal-hunting camp on the shores of Pelly Bay to an inland river camp where they fish for migrating salmon at a stone weir. A feast follows the fishing; the men tell spirit-stories of animals and form their symbolic shapes out of caribou sinew. Finally, the family takes the salmon catch—an indispensable winter food store—and prepares to move on for caribou hunting at a fall camp farther inland.

1964; 58 min; 16 mm; color; JR, HS, A; Post World War II.

NFBC; UCB

FISHING FEVER

Florida's Deadwood Lake is over a thousand years old, full of legends of ghosts and goblins. Film shows crocodiles, snook, and largemouth bass. Follow the fishermen as they go down to Marco Bay and the Mango Jungle, catching fish that leap 12 to 20 feet in the air.

NL; 27 min; 16 mm; NL; JR, HS, A; Post World War II.

PICAD

FISHING IN SCOTLAND

Salmon, grayling, pike, and trout abound in the lochs and rivers of Scotland. Here the angler can enjoy a pleasant holiday, surrounded by some of the most beautiful and varied countryside in the world.
NL; 21 min; 16 mm; NL; JR, HS, A; Post World War II.
AUDPLAN

FISHING IN SPAIN

Salmon and trout rivers in the northern regions of Spain; underwater fishing in the Mediterranean.
NL; 15 min; 16 mm; NL; JR, HS, A; Post World War II.
ASF

FISHING IN THE EVERGLADES

Covers the background and history of the Everglades National Park as well as information on its wildlife and scenic beauty. A main feature of the film is a fishing trip by four fishermen traveling by houseboat through the Everglades.
NL; 30 min; 16 mm; NL; JR, HS, A; Post World War II.
DUPONT

FITZROY

Mount Fitzroy rises 10,000 feet above the plains of Patagonia in southern Argentina. It is one of the world's most famous mountains because of its great beauty and difficulty. Four mountain climbers drove from California to the tip of South America and after six months, 15,000 miles, and 31 days of living in an ice cave, they succeeded in making the third ascent by a new route.
NL; 28 min; 16 mm, VHS, U-Matic, Beta; color; JR, HS, A; Post World War II.
CRYSP

FIVE MILES BELOW ZERO

Stars Forrest Tucker. When Tucker competed in the International 500-mile Snowmobile Race from Winnipeg to St. Paul in 1972, he found out that it took a special breed of sportsman to win or survive.
NL; 28 min; 16 mm; NL; JR, HS, A; Post World War II.
HAMMS

FLABBY AMERICAN, THE

Stresses the importance of physical fitness and regular exercise as a means of achieving such fitness.
1963; 20 min; 16 mm; BW; JR, HS, A; Post World War II.
USC

FLASHETTES, THE

Documents an inner-city girls' track club, showing how being a part of this community project affects the self-confidence, self-image, and career aspirations of the girls involved.
1977; 20 min; 16 mm; color; JR, HS, A; Post World War II.
NEWDAY

FLIGHT OF THE DOUBLE EAGLE II, THE

On August 11, 1978, three men—Ben Abrusso, Max Anderson, and Larry Newman—made the first successful trans-Atlantic balloon crossing. *Flight of the Double Eagle II* documents this achievement, detailing the training and preparation which preceded the mission and tracking the balloon from launch at Presque Isle, Maine, to touchdown at Miseray, France, only 50 miles short of Lindberg's site at LeBourget, France.
1978; 24 min; 16 mm; color; JR, HS, A; Post World War II.
BUDGET

FLIGHT OF THE GOSSAMER CONDOR

Traces the development of the world-record-holding man-powered aircraft, the *Gossamer Condor*. Summarizes a few early attempts at man-powered flight, but concentrates on engineer Paul MacCready and his development of hang-glider-based design composed of aluminum tubing, piano wire, mylar tape, and bicycle parts. Depicts MacCready's pioneering struggle with the field of slow-flight aerodynamics. Culminates with MacCready's winning of the Royal Aeronautical Society's Kremer Competition Prize for man-powered flight.
1978; 27 min; 16 mm; color; JR, HS, A; Post World War II.
CF; UWISC

FLOATING FREE

Frisbee discs that float effortlessly through space, dance in mid-air, and find their targets with remarkable accuracy fill the screen in this film. The film spotlights the best performances of the 1977 World Frisbee Championships—fast-paced team competitions, virtuoso free-style performances, even trained dogs making impossible catches.
1978; 11 min; 16 mm; color; JR, HS, A; Post World War II.
PYRAMID; OSU

FLOW OF MOVEMENT IN RHYTHMICAL GYMNASTICS, THE

Explores rhythmical gymnastics in group performance and individual movements. Routines are presented by Finnish gymnasts of the University of Helsinki.

NL; 20 min; 16 mm; color; JR, HS, A; Post World War II.

UIOWA

FOCUS ON THE 30s

Uses archival photographs, sound recordings, and film footage to explore world events, sports, entertainment, life-styles, and scientific and technological advancements of the 1930s.

1980; 58 min; 16 mm, VHS, U-Matic; color; JR, HS, A; Depression Era.

ABCS; MTI

FOCUS ON THE 50s

Uses archival photographs, sound recordings, and film footage to explore world events, sports, life-styles, and scientific achievements of the 1950s.

1980; 58 min; 16 mm, VHS, U-Matic; color; JR, HS, A; Post World War II.

ABCS; MTI

FOOTBALL AS IT IS PLAYED TODAY

Uses time-lapse photography and a background of folk music to portray the day's events on a football Saturday at Ohio State University. Points out the ritual of people at mass sporting events.

1962; 6 min; 16 mm; color; JR, HS, A; Post World War II.

OSU; USC

FOOTBALL FOLLIES

The most popular sports film ever made. Satire, slapstick, and excellent integration of action and music.

NL; 22 min; VHS; JR, HS, A; Post World War II.

KAROL

FOOTBALL IN AMERICA

Eye-opening expose of the excessive violence and illegal hitting techniques that are currently a part of professional, college, high school, and even grade school football. Focuses on the crippling results of football injuries to show the high price former players are now paying for their moments of glory.

1982; 27 min; 16 mm; color; JR, HS, A; Post World War II.

PYRAMID; UCB

FOOTBALL'S PRO-BOWL CLASSICS

Many of football's superheroes are seen here in these classic Pro-Bowl games of the past:

1959 Pro-Bowl Classic

1960 Pro-Bowl Classic

1961 Pro-Bowl Classic

NL; 20-25 min each; 16 mm; color; JR, HS, A; Post World War II.

BUDGET

FOR ALL TO ENJOY

Depicts recreational areas, used by millions of people for outdoor recreation, around Corps of Engineers reservoirs in the Pacific. The multiple-purpose water resources projects are open to the public for boating, swimming, fishing, sight-seeing, and other water-oriented recreation.

NL; 30 min; 16 mm; JR, HS, A; Post World War II.

MTPS

FOR THE LOVE OF A HORSE

The joys of a young girl learning to ride horses are depicted in this film.

NL; 14 min; 16 mm; color; E, JR, HS, A; Post World War II.

FIARTS

FOUR DAY WEEK

By the year 2000, experts predict a standard 30-hour week and a three-day weekend. Many sociologists and psychologists feel that so much free time might well become a major social problem.

1968; 26 min; 16 mm; color; HS, A; Post World War II.

NILLU

FOUR-5-6 Plus

Tells the story of how Craig Breedlove became the first man in history to drive a car faster than 600 miles per hour at the famous Bonneville Salt Flats, Utah.

NL; 14 min; 16 mm; color; JR, HS, A; Post World War II.

GTARC

FRANK GIFFORD

Gifford was one of the first of the NFL glamor figures, yet beneath the glitter was a hard competitor who worked to excel at all aspects of the game.

1985; 6 min; VHS, U-Matic, color; JR, HS, A; Post World War II.

NFL; TMA

FRANK GIFFORD

Explains how Frank Gifford personified the complete football player during the glory years of the New York Giants. Covers his heroics as an All-American at the University of Southern California, his 12-year pro career, and his experiences as a sport broadcaster.

NL; 20 min; 16 mm; color; JR, HS, A; Post World War II.

COUNFI; USC

FRAN TARKENTON

Fran Tarkenton was the most unpredictable and imaginative quarterback to ever play pro football. Tarkenton defied old-time purists by playing every down as if it were a lifeboat drill. But while Fran won games and fans by scrambling with the football, he completed more passes for more yards and more touchdowns than any other quarterback in NFL history.

1985; 8 min; VHS, U-Matic; color, JR, HS, A; Post World War II.

NFL; TMA

FRENCH KICK

This film shows the performance of Annie Famose and four of America's best "hotdog" skiers during a week at some of France's ski resorts. For the Americans, it was their first trip to Europe, and for the French it was the first look at "hotdog" skiing.

1978; 13 min; VHS, U-Matic; color; JR, HS, A; Post World War II.

FACSEA

FREE RIDE

Cutting from one sport to another in a kaleidoscope of color and movement, this exciting film captures the pace and mood of surfing, skiing, sailing, and all of the free-ride sports.

NL; 10 min; 16 mm; color; JR, HS, A; Post World War II.

PYRAMID

FRIENDSHIP FIRST, COMPETITION SECOND

The film's title was coined by the Chinese for the visit of the American ping-pong team. The hosts, fairly certain that the home team would win, tactfully chose to emphasize hospitality over competition. The slogan caught on, and now expresses the spirit of all sport there. While the Chinese have enthusiastically adopted many western sports, they have not abandoned their traditional entertainments. Their acrobats, jugglers, and gymnasts are among the world's best, and we see, also, the traditional sword fights.

1973; 25 min; 16 mm; color; JR, HS, A; Post World War II.

UWASH

FRIENDSHIP UNDER SAIL

Vivid and entertaining psychological study of a group of friends who purchase, refurbish, and outfit a large oceangoing schooner and then sail it around the world. Explores the psychological reasons the group could work effectively and avoid major conflicts while cramped together in close quarters under frequently adverse conditions. A fascinating examination of human behavior and a delightful story of sailing adventure.

1982; 29 min; VHS, U-Matic; color; HS, A; Post World War II.

UCB

FROM THE OCEAN TO THE SKY

Sir Edmund Hilary and a team of adventurers journey by jet-boat and on foot up the 1,500-mile length of India's sacred River Ganges. They travel a thousand miles through the heartland of India, coming at last to the deep Himalayan gorges where the holy Ganges becomes one of the wildest rivers on earth. An ascent of a Himalayan peak culminates their journey.

1979; 50 min; 16 mm, VHS, U-Matic; color; HS, A; Post World War II.

FSU; PMI

FROM THE VERSATILITY TESTS TO THE OLYMPIC GAMES

The film shows the most difficult of riding competitions, also called the "Crown of Horsemanship," including showing, racing, cross-country racing, and hunting. Versatility tests in Lumuhlen, Germany, and the hunting event at the Olympics in Rome.

1960; 20 min; 16 mm; BW; JR, HS, A; Post World War II.

MTPS

FROZEN IN TIME : THE 1984 WINTER OLYMPIC GAMES

A fast-paced panorama of the world's best winter athletes. All of the Olympic events and ceremonies in Sarajevo, Yugoslavia are featured. Includes the dazzling speed of gold medalist Bill Johnson and the artistry of ice dancers Torvil and Dean.

1984; 31 min; 16 mm, VHS, U-Matic; color; JR, HS, A; Post World War II.

USOC; CCCD

FUGUE FOR ELEVEN CHAMPIONS

A ten-year-old boy busies himself in a shed, gets on his bicycle, and rides off to the football stadium of Standard, the Liege football team. Alone on the terraces, in the changing rooms, on the pitch, he dreams of his idols, the footballers. He sees himself sharing their triumphs, but when night falls, his parents begin looking for him. They find the little runaway peacefully sleeping in the stadium. A French language film with Dutch subtitles.

1971; 15 min; 35 mm; color; JR, HS, A; Post World War II.

BELGIUM

FUN GAP, THE

Accidents, old age, or inborn defects need not stop people from tackling new experiences and having more fun. Everyone is inspired further, once impossible-looking barriers are overcome. For the good of the whole community, the zest and humanity of the disabled needs drawing out. Everyone can help close the "fun gap." This film shows New Zealanders doing just that. Subtitled version available.

1981; 25 min; 16 min; JR, HS, A; Post World War II.

NFU

FUN OF YOUR LIFE, THE

Narrated by Charlton Heston. Produced by the President's Council on Physical Fitness and Sports. President Ford appears in the film, which highlights the fun of keeping fit in a medley of sports.

NL; 19 min; 16 mm; NL; JR, HS, A; Post World War II.

MTPS

FUN ON THE LANES

An in-depth look at the organization, fun, and excitement of the American Junior Bowling Congress.

NL; 17 min; 16 mm; NL; JR, HS, A; Post World War II.

ABC

GALE SAYERS

Features Gale Sayers relating some of the great moments in his career. Shows exploits on the field highlighted with a montage of film footage set to music. Covers the relationship shared by Sayers and Brian Piccolo.

NL; 20 min; 16 mm; color; JR, HS, A; Post World War II.

COUNFI; USC

GAMES 74

In the summer of 1974, the Xth British Commonwealth Games came to New Zealand, and athletes from 39 countries, as well as visitors from home and abroad converged on the city of Christchurch. As

Games 74 records some of the events won and lost, it recaptures something of the sense of immediacy and sharing that made this event more than just another international athletic meet.

1974; 105 min; 16 mm; JR, HS, A; Post World War II.

NFU

GAMES AND FESTIVALS: GREECE

An on-location look at the sites of major athletic festivals that made up "the circuit" in ancient Greece: Olympia, Delphi, Isthmia, and Nemea. Examines the writings, sculpture, vases, and other artifacts which had as their theme the athletic games. From the *Ancient Greece* series.

1979; 26 min; 16 mm; color; JR, HS, A; Ancient Sport-Greece.

MEDIAG; PENNST

GAMES OF THE XXI OLYMPIAD

Official film of the 1976 Montreal Olympics is more than just a gallery of medal winners—it serves as a record of the human significance of the games. Olga Korbut agonizes as Nadia Comaneci replaces her as queen of gymnastics, Bruce Jenner's wife delights in her husband's decathlon victory, and the injured Sylvio Leonard watches as another sprinter wins the race.

1977; 117 min; 16 mm; color; JR, HS, A; Post World War II.

NFBC; FI; PENNST

G'DAY SPORT

Introduces the Australian lust for racing, which makes them race anything from horses to frogs, crabs, cockroaches, and camels.

1979; 28 min; 16 mm, VHS, U-Matic; color; JR, HS, A; Post World War II.

FLMAUS; FI

GENTLE FALCON, THE

For over 4,000 years, sportsmen have been training wild hawks, or falcons, to hunt game birds such as grouse, quail, heron, and pheasant. Today, in Great Britain, a small group of falconers is keeping alive the ancient tradition. Slow-motion footage taken through powerful telescopic lenses permits the viewer to see maneuvers of actual falcon strikes. Includes detailed sequences on preparing hawks for the day's sport, hooding, care of plumage, bathing, the weigh-ins, snipping off an overgrown beak("coping"), and mending a broken tail-feather("imping"). Concludes with a plea for saving the peregrine falcon from extinction.

1974; 40 min; 16 mm; color; JR, HS, A; Ancient, Medieval, Renaissance, Premodern, Making of Modern, Modern, Golden Age, Depression Era, World War II, Post World War II.

UILL

GENTLEMEN, START YOUR ENGINES

An exciting look into the preparation and training for the Indy 500 auto race from the assembly of the vehicles to the speed skills in the pit stops. We review some past disasters and disappointments as the preparing drivers attempt to avoid these pitfalls.

NL; 20 min; 16 mm; color; JR, HS, A; Post World War II.

BUDGET

GEORGE BLANDA

Renowned as the oldest player in NFL history, with 26 active years, Blanda proved that at age 43 he was not "over the hill"—he was king of it.

1985; 8 min; VHS, U-Matic; color; JR, HS, A; Post World War II.

NFL; TMA

GERMAN DEMOCRATIC REPUBLIC: TAPE 2

Interviews Ambassador Peter Florin on the anniversary of the German Democratic Republic. Includes a film clip on "Sports Festival."

NL; 28 min; U-Matic; color; JR, HS, A; Post World War II.

PERRYM

GET IT TOGETHER

Portrays the life of Jeff Minnebraker, once a vigorous athlete, who lost the use of his legs in a crippling car accident. Despite pain, rage, and self-pity, he achieved a happy life, a fulfilling career, and a meaningful role in society.

1976; 20 min; 16 mm, VHS, U-Matic; color; JR, HS, A; Post World War II.

PYRAMID; UILL

GIANT HUNTERS

Underwater fishermen, armed with spears, go after the huge grouper in Mexican waters.

NL; 28 min; 16 mm; NL; JR, HS, A; Post World War II.

CINES

GIFT OF GRAB, THE

A look at the breathtaking skill and bravery of NFL pass receivers. A visual poem where risk is refined into beauty.

1985; 7 min; VHS, U-Matic; color; JR, HS, A; Post World War II.

NFL; TMA

GIRLS' SPORTS: ON THE RIGHT TRACK

Summarizes the changes in girls' sports. A short history of track and field, with archival footage of Babe Didrikson and Wilma Rudolph, portrays the limitations placed on women in the past. Documentary experiences of three high school girls (a cross-country runner, a shotputter, and a broad-jumper) show the new opportunities available for girls today.

1975; 17 min; 16 mm; color; JR, HS, A; Depression Era, World War II, Post World War II.

PHENIX; PENNST

GLOBAL VICTORY

Documentary of first participation by United States teams in a world tournament. Filmed in the United States and Mexico. Highlights four titles won by ABC-sponsored men's and three by WIBC-sponsored women's team.

NL; 27 min; 16 mm; NL; JR, HS, A; Post World War II.

ABC

GLORY OF THEIR TIMES, THE

At the turn of the century, when young men's dreams lingered on leisure things, there was a love affair between America and baseball. Rare footage and priceless tapes from Bud Greenspan (who gave us *Jesse Owens Returns to Berlin*), recall the era of John McGraw, Christy Mathewson, Babe Ruth, and other giants of baseball.

NL; 50 min; 16 mm; NL; JR, HS, A; Modern.

NBHF

GOALS, CHALLENGES, AND CHOICES

Shows how believing in oneself and refusing to accept the limitations and negative concepts set by others is basic to any great achievement. A 70-year-old ski instructor, a youthful motorcyclist, and a talented, untiring water skier are three individuals who set goals, reaffirm their belief in themselves, and then follow through. Through breathtaking action sequences, they reveal experiences, insights, and values necessary for self-fulfillment.

1975; 8 min; 16 mm; color; JR, HS, A; Post World War II.

AIMS; UILL

GO FOR BROKE

Features outstanding athletes, pushing their talents to the utmost. Narrated by Jack Whitaker.

NL; 8 min; VHS, U-Matic; color; JR, HS, A; Post World War II.
SFTI

GOING FOR THE GOLD . . . : THE STORY OF BLACK WOMEN IN SPORTS

Female sportscaster Jayne Kennedy hosts this profile of 17 black women who have excelled in sports. Individual stories of past and present champions that tell of the courage and determination needed to overcome difficult odds. A complete training and nutritional program for prospective athletes is also included.

NL; 20 min; 16 mm, VHS; color; JR, HS, A; Post World War II.
MTPS

GOING THE DISTANCE

Looks at the Eleventh Commonwealth Games held in Canada. Describes how eight athletes go the distance physically, emotionally, and psychologically. Shows how the athletes alternate training schedules with their daily activities.

1979; 89 min; 16 mm; color; JR, HS, A; Post World War II.
NFBC

GOING THE DISTANCE

Featuring Frank Shorter, American Olympic champion in the challenging marathon. No event in sport captures the drama and emotion of this grueling event where winners must go beyond all limits.

NL; 7 min; NL; NL; JR, HS, A; Post World War II.
TMA

GOLDEN ANNIVERSARY, THE

Records the important events of the 1966-1967 season, when the Women's International Bowling Congress celebrated its 50th anniversary.

NL; 19 min; 16 mm; NL; JR, HS, A; Post World War II.
WIBC

GOLDEN BREED, THE

This look at the world of the surfer features 26 of these top athletes doing their thing. The action ranges from shots of these golden people riding 35-foot waves to sky diving, with some motorcycle riding thrown in for good measure. Actor Richard Boone described *The Golden Breed* as " . . . one of the most exciting films I have ever seen." This is a film not only for surfing fans, but for all viewers who appreciate beautiful motion photography.

1968; 90 min; 16 mm; color; Jr, HS, A; Post World War II.
BUDGET

GOLDEN THREAD, THE

Traces the history of the Young Men's Christian Association (YMCA) from its founding in 1854 and presents a panorama of its programs in sports, academics, continuing educational and vocational training, and camping.

1980; 12 min.; 16 mm; color; JR, HS, A; Making of Modern Sport to Post World War II.
WSTGLC

GOLDEN TWENTIES

Recaptures the exuberant and extravagant tempo of the jazz age and the individuals who made it a high point in American history, emphasizing the fashions, fancies, and feelings of the era. Included is commentary by Elmer Davis, Frederick Lewis Allen, Robert Q. Lewis, and Red Barber, and newsreel footage.

1952; 68 min; 16 mm; NL; JR, HS, A; Golden Age of Sport.
MGHT; UCB

GOLD IN THEM THAR GILLS

Jos. Schlitz Brewing Company's $500,000 fishing derby.

NL; 15 min; 16 mm; NL; JR, HS, A; Post World War II.
CINES

GOLF AT FIRESTONE

A behind-the-scenes look at two great courses in Akron, Ohio. Sports fans and pros all over the world have become familiar with the Firestone Country Club's famous South and North courses. Intimate glimpses of such players as Arnold Palmer, Gary Player, Jack Nicklaus, and Lee Trevino reveal them in tough situations during competition, where total concentration and unique skills are needed to avoid the bogeys. The camera also leaves the golf battleground itself for a glimpse behind the scenes as television technology gives the armchair viewer closeups often missed by the spectator.

NL; 26 min; 16 mm; NL; JR, HS, A; Post World War II.
ASF

GOLF SPECIALIST, THE

W. C. Fields poses as a golf instructor at a fashionable hotel and gives some golf lessons to the wife of the jealous house detective. This very funny comedy presents Fields in his famous golf act he used often on the stage prior to this film. This was his first sound picture.

NL; 21 min; 16 mm; BW; JR, HS, A; Depression Era.

UILL

GONE FISHIN'

There is a new kind of fishing vehicle sweeping the country these days, one that combines utility and fun. It is called the water wagon, and this film shows what these unique one-man boats offer fishermen.

NL; 12 min; 16 mm; NL; JR, HS, A; Post World War II.

SOLANA

GONE WITH THE WAVE

An exciting, full-length feature that takes you into the surfing world. See Fred Hemmings, Dewey Weber, Paul Stroute, Jr., and Johnny Fain riding the waves of Mexico, California, and Hawaii.

1965; 80 min; 16 mm; color; JR, HS, A; Post World War II.

BUDGET

GOOD BADMINTON

Explains the game and discusses its history. Includes a championship badminton match.

NL; 10 min; 16 mm; NL; JR, HS, A; Premodern to Post World War II.

UGA (may not be available)

GOODNIGHT MISS ANN

Cinema-verite look at the lives of the professional boxers who train and fight at the historic Main Street Gym and the Olympic Auditorium in Los Angeles. Focuses on young Mexicans and Mexican-Americans in the lighter weight divisions, showing them training, before and after fights, and during the bouts themselves. Includes commentary by managers, trainers, and boxers, and captures the gritty reality—as well as the dreams and romanticism—of the boxing world.

1978; 28 min; 16 mm; VHS, U-Matic; color; JR, HS, A; Post World War II.

PYRAMID; UCB

GOOD OLD DAYS, THE

Fascinating, often humorous look at man's quest for excitement, thrills, and speed. Events such as chariot races, log-rolling contests, old-time slapstick comedy races, hand-car races, oddball events, and even a quick look at the development of the auto and racing vehicles help make this a nonstop piece of film entertainment, all with an upbeat music track.

1976; 22 min; 16 mm; color; JR, HS, A; Post World War II.

BUDGET

GOOD SPORT GAME, THE

A young girl learns the difference between good and bad sportsmanship from an old friend and discovers that being a good sport helps her feel good about herself.

1978; 11 min; 16 mm, VHS, U-Matic; color; JR, HS, A; Post World War II.

HIGGIN

GOOD SPORTS TOGETHER

Documents the Southern Alberta Summer Games, in which handicapped people participated with nonhandicapped people in a variety of sporting events.

NL; 17 min; 16 mm, VHS, U-Matic; color; JR, HS, A; Post World War II.

STNFLD

GRAMBLING-TEXAS SOUTHERN

The 1968 game between two of the top southern football college teams.

NL; 28 min; 16 mm; NL; JR, HS, A; Post World War II.

CINES

GRAVITY NEVER SLEEPS

From the drama of deep-powder tree skiing to the excitement of high volume kayaking and the incredible skill and grace of barefoot waterskiing, this exploration of gravity sports illustrates the powerful synergy that exists between athletes in search of the ultimate performance and gravity that never sleeps.

NL; 7 min; 16 mm; color; JR, HS, A; Post World War II.

PYRAMID

GREAT AMERICAN HARNESS HORSE, THE

One of ABC's "Discovery" series on TV. Film shows the raising and training of harness horses; visits to Castleton Farm in Trenton, Florida, and Pompano Park in Florida; features an interview with Delvin Miller on breaking of young horses; life of a standardbred from foaling to racing.

NL; 30 min; 16 mm; NL; JR, HS, A; Post World War II.

USTA

GREAT CHALLENGE, THE

This is the story, in two parts, of a mountaineering expedition. Twelve men left for Nepal in February, 1982, in order to tackle one of the most dangerous peaks in the Himalayas: Dhaulagira, over 26,500 feet. The climbers finally made it to the top on May 5.

1982; 55 min; 16 mm; color; JR, HS, A; Post World War II.

BELGIUM

GREAT ENGLISH GARDEN PARTY, THE

It's Wimbledon's 100th birthday, and this Emmy-award-winning-film, narrated by Peter Ustinov, celebrates this special occasion with a look at this great championship, beginning with the first matches held in 1877.

NL; 52 min; 16 mm; color; JR, HS, A; Making of Modern Sport to Post World War II.

USTEN

GREATEST GAME EVER PLAYED

Baltimore Colts 23-New York Giants 17 (sudden death overtime). Eleven Hall of Fame players were starters in this thriller, including Frank Gifford, Sam Huff, John Unitas, and Gino Marchetti.

1958; 16 mm, VHS, U-Matic; NL; JR, HS, A; Post World War II.

NFL; TMA

GREATEST PERFORMANCES OF 1984

A wrapup of the 1984 football season with a twist of humor to spotlight the achievements of unusual excellence in a year that had many highlights, lowlights, and bizarre sights, as well as record number of fans in attendance. Spotlights focus on Charlie Joiner, Dan Marino, Walter Payton, Eric Dickerson, Art Monk, Mark Clayton, James Lofton, and others.

1984; 8 min; VHS, U-Matic; color; JR, HS, A; Post World War II.

NFL; TMA

GREAT GAME (SOCCER)

Presents the division play leading to the F. A. Cup Final between Chelsea and Bolton at Stamford Bridge on June 2, 1945. While the importance of football to the youth and regions of Great Britain is shown, it is more interesting today for the picture it gives of the British people and their hopes immediately after World War II. (Historical Reserve Collection.)

1945; 23 min; 16 min; BW; JR, HS, A; Post World War II.

UWASH

GREAT GAME OF BASKETBALL, THE

With former Cincinnati Royals star Jack Twyman as your guide, this film takes viewers to Basketball's Hall of Fame for a look at how the sport began. Then we go onto the basketball court, where Twyman demonstrates the finer points of offensive and defensive play.

NL; 27 min; 16 mm; NL; JR, HS, A; Modern to Post World War II.

ASF

GREAT MOMENTS IN THE HISTORY OF TENNIS

Highlights from the history of tennis include scenes of Bill Tilden, Pancho Gonzales, Ken Rosewall, Rod Laver, Suzanne Lenglen, and Helen Wills.

1963; 40 min; 16 mm; BW; JR, HS, A; Golden Age to Post World War II.

CCCD

GREAT MOMENTS IN THE HISTORY OF TENNIS

Tracing the game of tennis from its inception to 1968 by a unique compilation of old movie clips, this film features all-time greats such as Tilden, Budge, Gonzales, and Kramer, as well as more contemporary stars such as Ashe, Okker, Gibson, and King.

NL; 40 min; 16 mm; BW; JR, HS, A; Renaissance to Post World War II.

USTEN

GREAT TRADITION, THE

How the country's tradition of marksmanship is given to the new generation. Shows children learning about guns, hunting, wildlife management, sportsmanship, and conservation.

NL; 30 min; VHS; JR, HS, A; Post World War II.

KAROL

GREEN BAY PACKERS FOOTBALL

Highlights (Various seasons)
1966 Championship
1967 Championship
1966 Super Bowl
1967 Super Bowl
1967 Rams vs. Packers
1967 Giants vs. Packers
1968 Bears vs. Packers
1968 Bears vs. Packers
NL; 30 min each; 16 mm; NL; JR, HS, A; Post World War II.

GBP

GREEN BAY PACKERS HIGHLIGHTS

14 films. Order by year. Films cover the years 1950 through 1962.

NL; NL; 16 mm; BW; JR, HS, A; Post World War II.

MILLER

GREEN BAY PACKERS HIGHLIGHTS

The great Lombardi years of 1964, 1965, 1966, and 1967 come through strongly in these four individual films on the powerful Packers under the late Vince Lombardi.

NL; 28 min; 16 mm; NL; JR, HS, A; Post World War II.

HAMMS

GREEN TABLES

Focuses on participants in a championship snooker match and on the history of the game. Invented by British Army officers in India in 1875, snooker counts only forty professional players in the world, but millions of amateurs and much enthusiasm. Includes also some of the history of billiards, invented by the Greeks and the favorite game of an unlikely royal amateur, Mary, Queen of Scots.

1978; 26 min; 16 mm; color; JR, HS, A; Making of Modern Sport to Post World War II.

UILL

GRENOBLE

The 1968 Winter Olympics at Grenoble, France. Captured on film by Academy-Award-winning director Claude Lelouch (*A Man and a Woman*), all the events of the Winter Olympics come to vivid life. Highlighting the film is the skiing mastery of Jean-Claude Killy and the graceful skating of Peggy Fleming.

1969; 95 min; 16 mm; color; JR, HS, A; Post World War II.

BUDGET

GROW HIGH ON LOVE

Presents highlights of Special Olympic state meets in Colorado, Connecticut, and California.

1978; 23 min; 16 mm; color; Post World War II.

NBC

GUNS OF AUTUMN

Overview of hunting in the United States, emphasizing its commercial and ritualistic aspects and the attitudes and motivations of America's 20 million hunters. Focuses on recent innovations that have taken most of the sport out of hunting, particularly the "hunting preserves" in which animal are "har-

vested" for a price. Also considers the role of game management in the United States. Allows hunters to state their point of view, but on balance suggests that hunting is basically a ritual that is becoming increasingly commercialized, inhumane, and cruel. Controversial and hard-hitting.

1975; 77 min; 16 mm; color; JR, HS, A; Post World War II.

CAROUF; UCB

GYMNAESTRADA, BASEL

The annual international gymnastic festival took place in Basel, Switzerland, in 1969. First the thousands of participants from all over the world appear in the colorful costumes, then you see a dazzling display of acrobatics, modern dancing, twirling, rhythmic exercises, somersaulting, and every other gymnastic activity imaginable. What is particularly appealing about the 1969 festival is that the participants ranged from the very young to the middle-aged of both sexes. No narration.

1969; 13 min; 16 mm; NL; JR, HS, A; Post World War II.

TRIBUNE; SNTO

GYMNASTICS WORLD CHAMPIONSHIPS 1966

Both educational and documentary in nature, this film, made at the 1966 world championships in Dortmund, compares the styles of individual gymnasts and features those exercises which were outstanding by virtue of their perfection, individuality, or originality.

NL; 29 min; 16 mm; BW; JR, HS, A; Post World War II.

MTPS

GYM PERIOD

A tense, taut story of a teen-age boy who lacks the skill and coordination to be successful in sport-related activities. Frustrated and alienated during his gym period, the last of the semester, he decides, after the other boys have left the gym, to make one more attempt to succeed in the activity that seems to symbolize his overall failure—the rope climb. He climbs slowly, painfully, until . . . the unexpected climax is profoundly effective and startling. A film that has many levels of meaning.

NL; 14 min; 16 mm; color; JR, HS, A; Post World War II.

FRAN

GYMNAST

Insight into the world of women's gymnastics and the effort required to compete at the international level highlights this feature. Top gymnasts from countries around the world are shown practicing and competing in Ft. Worth, Texas, at the first world championship ever held in the United States.

NL; 11 min; 16 mm; color; JR, HS, A; Post World War II.

CCCD

GYMNASTIC FLASHBACKS

Film clips from the Olympic Games and other gymnastic events are interwoven to show how gymnastics historically evolved from early group performances to current individual competition. Internationally renowned men and women gymnasts are seen performing their particular specialties: individual acrobatics, floor exercises, parallel and horizontal bars, vaulting, and balance-beam competition. Musical accompaniment.

1970; 10 min; 16 mm; color; JR, HS, A; Depression Era to Post World War II.

MICHMED; PYRAMID

GYMNASTICS USA

Shows the best men and women gymnasts in the United States performing in the qualifying competition for membership on the 1976 Olympic Team; also shows some younger athletes who may be champions in the future. Rather than being a record of a competition, the film is a visual poem on accomplishment, demonstrating how these gifted young athletes display the combination of talents that characterizes this sport and the skill, strength, and endurance required for all top-level athletic competition.

1977; 27 min; 16 mm; color; JR, HS, A; Post World War II.

UCB

HABIT OF WINNING, THE

An inspiring collection of interviews with some of the finest football players ever to dominate the game, this film shows how the habit of winning and the desire for excellence in one arena were successfully carried over into the world of business.

NL; 28 min; 16 mm, VHS, color, HS, A; Post World War II.

CCCD

HACKERS AND HEROES

A look behind the scenes at tennis as it is played today. Narrated by Bud Collins, it is also a study of tennis pros playing before an enthusiastic crowd in the U. S. Professional Singles Championship held at the Longwood Cricket Club, Boston. Arthur Ashe, the runner-up of the tournament, chats about the sport, as does young Jimmy Connors, the final winner.

NL; 28 min; 16 mm; NL; JR, HS, A; Post World War II.

ASF

HALF CENTURY 500

A "celebration" of 50 years of Indianapolis auto races, beginning with footage from the first race, in 1911, up to the race won in 1961 by A. J. Foyt. Lots of racing thrills . . . as well as a few crashes.

NL; 25 min; 16 mm; NL; JR, HS, A; Modern to Post World War II.

BUDGET

HALF-HALF-THREE QUARTERS FULL

Beautifully conveys, without narration, the drama and high suspense of a championship rowing meet. Captures the excitement and physical exertion of a demanding sport, the tense wait for the starting signal, and the overwhelming strain for victory as anxious coaches and spectators watch and cheer. Lyrically edited to a background of electronic music that accentuates each movement, and filmed with long lenses to capture the details of motion in striking close-ups.

1972; 8 min; 16 mm; color; JR, HS, A; Post World War II.

IFB; NFBC; UCB

HAMBLETONIAN AND LITTLE BROWN JUG

Films for recent years of the Hambletonian and Little Brown Jug. These films may be shown as separate 15-minute presentations.

NL; 30 min; 16 mm; NL; JR, HS, A; Post World War II.

USTA

HAP: AMERICA AT ITS BEST

Deals with physical and social therapy of mentally and physically handicapped children and young people through team-oriented athletics.

1971; 27 min; 16 mm; color; HS, A; Post World War II.

CFOP

HAPPINESS IS . . .

Shows some of the skiing attractions of western Canada.

1973; 13 min; 16 mm; color; JR, HS, A; Post World War II.

CTFL

HAPPY SUMMER EVENING, A

Tells the story of the organization of a local league, spring training, with a visit with Ted Williams and the Boston Red Sox, and the playing of a Little League game.

NL; NL; 16 mm; NL; JR, HS, A; Post World War II.

LLBI

HARDBALL

Major-league baseball is a hard-nosed business like any other, as the new owners of the Oakland A's quickly learn.

NL; 30 min; 16 mm; color; HS, A; Post World War II.

UCB

HARD CHARGERS, THE

Stock car racing has become more than a sport; it's a folkway. From the moments of excitement to the personalities of its heroes, it is shown to be a part of the fabric of American life. Includes interviews with Richard Petty, Cale Yarborough, and others.

1971; 53 min; 16 mm; color; JR, HS, A; Post World War II.

TIMLIF; UILL

"THE HARDER I WORK, THE LUCKIER I GET"

No one believed the Villanova Wildcats could win the 1985 NCAA Basketball Championships—no one except coach Rollie Massimino and his team. Set against the backdrop of America's college basketball playoffs, this color videotape recounts the hard work, perseverance, and determination that it took to become winners. Massimino and his players share their goals, objectives, and philosophies about the values of mutual respect and teamwork and the benefits of the American work ethic.

NL; 20 min; VHS, U-Matic; color; HS, A; Post World War II.

TMA

HARD RIDER

The rodeo circuit is a rough ride, but in his private life, Kenny McLean, champion bronco buster, is the steadiest of men. *Hard Rider* follows the long road of this man, his wife, and infant son, as they travel to rodeo towns in their camper. What Kenny doesn't say about his life, or about himself, the film fills in by watching him at work and at ease. Taking that jolting, bone-cracking ride through the dust or mud of the arena is what Kenny McLean does best. It is his job and has a lot to do with his (and others') idea of being a man.

1972; 58 min; 16 mm, VHS, U-Matic, Beta; color; JR, HS, A; Post World War II.

FI; NFBC

HARD ROAD TO GLORY, A

A compelling look into the early rise of black athletes, including Jesse Owens, Joe Louis, and Jackie Robinson.

NL; 45 min; VHS; NL; HS, A; Depression Era to Post World War II.

KAROL

HARLEM GLOBETROTTERS

Greatest moments of the early Globetrotters.

NL; 30 min; VHS; NL; E, JR, HS, A; Depression Era to Post World War II.

KAROL

HARLEM GLOBETROTTERS, THE

The Harlem Globetrotters bring their own brand of laughs and excitement to the screen. The story involves a college student who leaves his chemical research studies to join the team on tour. He soon learns the team's clowning, but it takes longer for him to catch on to the teamwork that makes the Globetrotters the great team that it still is. Thomas Gomez portrays the Globetrotters' manager, Abe Saperstein, in this excellent sports feature for all ages.

1951; 80 min; 16 mm; NL; JR, HS, A; Post World War II.

KAROL

HAUDENOSAUNEE : WAY OF THE LONGHOUSE

Intercuts scenes of traditional Iroquois Indian ceremonies with scenes of Native Americans in their roles as students, teachers, artisans, artists, athletes, and farmers in the modern world.

NL; 13 min; 16 mm, VHS, U-Matic; color; JR, HS, A; Post World War II.

ICARUS

HEALTH AND LIFESTYLE: POSITIVE APPROACHES TO WELL-BEING

Promotes the concept that the individual has a responsibility for the quality of his or her life. Emphasizes the connection between lifelong habits and health.

1980; 28 min; 16 mm; color; JR, HS, A; Post World War II.

OSU

HEART OF WINNING, THE

Presents the year-round training features of the Special Olympics program for mentally handicapped children. Tells of the importance of volunteers to the success of the program.

1974; 12 min; 16 mm; color; JR, HS, A; Post World War II.

KENJPF

HEAVENLY DAZE

This well-photographed film brings out new aspects in ski photography through slow-motion and freeze-frame acrobatics, amateur hot-dogging, and of course, the snow streakers. Some nudity.

NL; 12 min; 16 mm; color; JR, HS, A; Post World War II.

BUDGET

HEISMAN TROPHY: THE POSSIBLE DREAM

Since 1935, the 25-pound Heisman trophy has been the goal of every collegiate football player. This film recalls the very best players year-by-year and features 1970 Heisman winner Jim Plunkett of the New England Patriots, as he teaches youngsters the fundamentals of playing quarterback.

NL; 24 min; 16 mm; NL; JR, HS, A; Depression Era to Post World War II.

WSTGLC

HELIX

Explores man's relationship to the Canadian Rocky Mountains. Shows how he can enjoy the sport of skiing through the use of the helicopter as a "liberator" and confront what used to be unreachable slopes. Extensive aerial, time lapse, and wildlife photography throughout.

1977; 24 min; 16 mm; color; JR, HS, A; Post World War II.

UU

HELLEGAT

Hellegat is the name of a hamlet in the Rupel region, where the film takes place. The setting is one of ruined brickworks and old claypits which, in former days, brought work and prosperity to the area but which are now used as dumps for toxic industrial wastes. Sam is a young man who is mad about football and whose popularity as the goalkeeper of his local team is rising steadily. Mr. Lagasse, manager of the football team, is also the owner of the last remaining brickworks, which gives employment to practically the entire village. In order to win greater support for his business from his workforce, and also hoping that a football transfer will one day make him

rich, Lagasse offers Sam a good, safe job in his brickworks. Sam becomes friendly with another worker, Louis, an older man who is actually on the point of retirement. Sam and Louis become involved in a campaign to stop the clandestine dumping of toxic wastes in the old claypits—an operation in which Lagasse seems to be playing a shady part. As soon as it appears that Sam's goalkeeping is nothing out of the ordinary after all, and that his transfer value is falling rapidly, the interest and protection surrounding him are abruptly withdrawn. Sam begins to realize that his football manager and employer has been using him to further his own ends; the bitter farewell speech made by Louis as he leaves the brickworks on pension finally leads Sam to understand that he is merely a minor cog in the machine.

1980; 96 min; 16 mm, 35 mm; color; JR, HS, A; Post World War II.

BELGIUM

HELSINKI: CAPITAL OF SPORTS

Shows Helsinki, the capital of Finland, with its white, modern buildings. The Finns, who are great sport enthusiasts, also proudly take you to see several Olympic contests held during the Olympic Games in 1952 in their big stadium, built especially for that event.

NL; 14 min; 16 mm; NL; JR, HS, A; Post World War II.

SAL

HERE I AM: THE INTERNATIONAL GAMES FOR THE DISABLED

The 1984 International Games for the Disabled witnessed a coming together of more than 1,700 athletes from 45 countries on Long Island, New York, in June of 1984. Audiences will see an unforgettable chronicle of spirit and determination.

NL; 13 min; 16 mm, U-Matic; color; JR, HS, A; Post World War II.

MTPS

HEWITT'S JUST DIFFERENT

A film about friendship, peer-group pressures, and prejudice toward the retarded. Willie Arthur wants to be a pitcher on the baseball team, but fails to make it on his first tryout. Hewitt Calder, Willie's 16-year-old retarded neighbor, is somewhat of an authority on baseball, and he volunteers to coach Willie every day. When Willie tries out a second time, the coach is really impressed with his progress and puts him on the team. With his newfound status, Willie finds new friends and a dilemma. While the rest of the boys on the team readily accept Willie, they still go out of their way to jeer at Hewitt and call him a "re-tard." Finally, Willie is forced to take a stand,

and after an accident in which Hewitt comes to the rescue, the other boys also begin to accept Hewitt as a friend.

1977; 46 min; 16 mm; color; JR, HS, A; Post World War II.

TIMLIF; UILL

HEY! WHAT ABOUT US?

Fresh insight into sex role stereotyping in physical activities in schools, including physical education classes, playground games, and boisterous behavior in the classroom. Begins with four situations in which sex role stereotyping is relatively absent, then depicts a wide range of incidents in which stereotyping often occurs. Considers the exclusion of girls from sports, the reinforcement of the hero ethic in boys, differential teacher treatment of girls and boys on the playground, exclusion of boys from dance, and differential physical interaction of teachers with boys and girls. The first four situations challenge the usual conceptions of "masculinity" and "femininity" by showing children engaged in activities "typical" of the opposite sex: a girl displays competence in football; a boy excels in dance. Most events occur in elementary school settings.

1974; 15 min; 16 mm; color; E, JR, HS, A; Post World War II.

UCB; MICHMED

HIGH IN THE HIMALAYAS

A mountain-climbing expedition which terminated atop Mount Tawech, 21,000 feet above sea level, is highlighted. The expedition, led by Sir Edmund Hillary, conqueror of Mount Everest, inched its way into the Himalayan range on a dual mission of reaching the top and bringing running water to native village.

NL; 27 min; 16 mm; NL; JR, HS, A; Post World War II.

ASF

HIGHLAND PLAYGROUND

Year-round sporting activities in Scotland. The theme of this film is winter sports, and beginners and experts alike can indulge in the many sports available at the "Centre."

NL; 13 min; 16 mm; NL; E, JR, HS, A; Post World War II.

AUDPLAN

HIGHLANDS FLING

Groovy McDougal stars in this story of a love affair where hotdogger meets ski instructor, hotdogger wins $10,000, hotdogger wins ski instructor!

Footage of skiing and hotdogging and Aspen highlands terrain.

NL; 20 min; 16 mm; NL; JR, HS, A; Post World War II.

MTPS

HIGH LIFE RACING ROUND-UP

Cool drivers and hot cars team with talented pit crews to demonstrate the sport of auto racing at its best.

NL; NL; 16 mm; NL; JR, HS, A; Post World War II.

MILLER

HIGH LIFE SPORTS SPECIAL

The 91st Kentucky Derby; PGA golf tourney; bobsled championships; Gateway Marathon ocean powerboat race; Purdue pounds Notre Dame gridders; national rodeo finals.

NL; NL; 16 mm; NL; JR, HS, A; Post World War II.

MILLER

HIGH LIFE SPORTS THRILLS

World High Diving Championships; 89th Kentucky Derby; Sebring 12-hour Grand Tour; waterskiing at Cypress Gardens; NFL Pro football bowl action.

NL; NL; 16 mm; NL; JR, HS, A; Post World War II.

MILLER

HIGH LIFE WORLD OF SPORTS

The 1966 Notre Dame-Michigan State grid clash for national honors; soccer, starring Pele; surfing; bike racing; PGA golf championship; NBA basketball, Boston vs. Los Angeles.

NL; NL; 16 mm; NL; JR, HS, A; Post World War II.

MILLER

HIGHLIGHTS OF SPORTS

National Open Golf Tourney; 90th Kentucky Derby; Indianapolis 500; Davis Cup tennis; U.S.-Russian track meet; American Cup yachting; Army-Navy football classic.

NL; NL; 16 mm; NL; JR, HS, A; Post World War II.

MILLER

HIGHLIGHTS OF THE IRA

A documentary illustrating how well rodeo finals are produced, including pageantry and contract acts. Provides a description of each championship event and points out that IRA rodeo is big league, professional event.

NL; 26 min; 16 mm; NL; JR, HS, A; Post World War II.

IRA

HIGHLIGHTS OF THE WORLD CUP GYMNASTICS

In Long Beach, California, top gymnasts from all over the world meet for the first time since the 1968 Olympics. Exciting and graceful competition displays each contestant's abilities.

1969; 20 min; 16 mm; color; JR, HS, A; Post World War II.

BUDGET

HIGH WIRE

On September 29, 1982, tightrope artist Philippe Petit brought his death-defying wizardry once more above the streets of New York. World famous for his incredible feat of walking a tightrope between the twin towers of the World Trade Center, Petit assailed the heights outside Manhattan's Cathedral of St. John the Divine. *High Wire* is *cinema verite* at its best; it reveals a unique, individual moment of daring and triumph.

NL; 29 min; 16 mm, VHS; color; JR, HS, A; Post World War II.

WOMBAT

HIKING THE APPALACHIAN TRAIL

Story of the world's most famous and popular hiking path, running 2,000 miles up the spine of eastern America. Correct backpacking techniques shown by national experts. Hiking shown from the peak of Mount Katahdin in Maine to Springer Mountain in Georgia. Analysis of the pecking order among hikers.

NL; NL; 16 mm; NL; JR, HS, A; Post World War II.

KLEINW

HISTORY OF BASEBALL, THE

Spanning over a century of American baseball, this collector's video includes rare footage from the major league baseball archives. This program contains all the greatest players and plays from the early years to today's current franchises; from the World Series stars to the biggest blunders ever made.

NL; 120 min; VHS, color; JR, HS, A; Modern to Post World War II.

KAROL; FOTH

HISTORY OF THE AFL, THE

A look back at the colorful characters and eye-popping plays that highlight the history of the American Football League, founded in 1960 by Lamar Hunt (owner of the Kansas City Chiefs) and a group of men who came to be known as the "foolish club."

NL; 17 min; 16 mm; VHS, U-Matic; NL; JR, HS, A; Post World War II.

NFL; TMA

HOCKEY: THE LIGHTER SIDE

Bone-crunching checks, silly slips and falls, strange circumstances on the ice, and players' pranks and gags. Featured are John Davidson, Glenn Anderson, Larry Robinson, and Cam Neely.

NL; 30 min; VHS, JR, HS, A; Post World War II.

KAROL

HOOFBEATS

The story of mankind's most adaptable and useful animal, the horse, started 50 million years ago, when it was a nomadic wanderer. Today the horse is primarily a recreation creature, competing in such sporting events as rodeos, racing, and show jumping. Members of the United States gold medal Olympic equestrian team are shown in Grand Prix action.

NL; 28 min; 16 mm; color; JR, HS, A; Post World War II.

MTPS

HORSEHIDE HEROES

Through rare footage, you'll see such outstanding figures as Grover Cleveland Alexander, Roger Hornsby, Carl Hubbell, Mel Ott, Ted Williams, Ty Cobb, Bob Feller, Joe DiMaggio, Walter Johnson, Pepper Martin, and Honus Wagner. Managers Casey Stengel and John McGraw are also seen, as well as two of baseball's legends, Babe Ruth and "Iron Man" Lou Gehrig. (Includes Gehrig's farewell speech.)

NL; 10 min; 16 mm; BW; JR, HS, A; Golden Age to World War II.

FILMIC

HORSES

Summarizes the horse's evolution and use in work, war, and recreation from ancient times.

1977; 23 min; 16 mm; color; JR, HS, A; Ancient to Post World War II.

AVATLI; USC

HORSES — HORSEMEN — VICTORIES

The German riding center in Warendorf and its most successful riders (Thielemann, Winkler) with their horses. German and English sound versions.

NL; 12 min; 16 mm; BW; JR, HS, A; Post World
War II.
MTPS

HOT DOG SKIING

Highlights "hot dog" skiing events—the crazy
kind of skiing that has become the rage. All sorts of
unusual ski events combine thrilling jumps, skiing,
races where form and style don't count and skiers are
rated not only for time, but for how spectacularly they
perform.
NL; 27 min; 16 mm; NL; JR, HS, A; Post World
War II.
MTPS

HOW'S THAT CRICKET

Traces the history and rules of cricket.
1975; 14 min; 16 mm; color; JR, HS, A; Ancient to
Post World War II.
FIARTS

HUGH MacELHENNY

Traces Hugh MacElhenny's exploits on film from
the time he was a track and field star at George
Washington High School in Los Angeles through the
years with the Forty-Niners, Vikings, and finally
with the Giants and his former teammate, Y. A. Tittle.
Includes some spectacular football scenes from the
late 50s and early 60s.
NL; 20 min; 16 mm; color; JR, HS, A; Post World
War II.
COUNFI; USC

HUNT: ADAPTED FROM, THE MOST DANGEROUS GAME

Presents the story of two men on a hunting trip,
one of whom discovers he doesn't enjoy shooting animals. His companion, an avid huntsman, leaves him
in disgust. He meets an older hunter so jaded with
killing that the only prize he yearns to stalk is human
prey. Follows a chilling pursuit that is a cliff-hanger
until the very end.
1975; 30 min; 16 mm; color; HS, A; Post World
War II.
EBEC; UU

HUNTING AND FISHING IN SOUTH AMERICA

Bow and arrow is the weapon for an unusual
safari in uninhabited jungles.
NL; 25 min; 16 mm; NL; JR, HS, A; Post World
War II.
CINES

HUNTING IN EAST AFRICA

Fred T. Huntington and his wife, Barbara, par-
ticipate in a hunt in Kenya. Game taken includes
record-class gazelle, gerenuk, and black rhinoceros.
NL; 34 min; 16 mm; NL; JR, HS, A; Post World
War II.
RCBS

HUNTING IN MOZAMBIQUE

Big-game hunting with Jack O'Connor and Fred
T. Huntington. Includes scenes of kudo, waterbuck,
impala, sable, and many other African game animals
in their natural habitat.
NL; 25 min; 16 mm; NL; JR, HS, A; Post World
War II.
RCBS

HUNTING IN THE YUKON

Includes hunts for Dahl sheep, moose, caribou,
and grizzly bear. With Jack O'Connor and Fred T.
Huntington.
NL; 20 min; 16 mm; NL; JR, HS, A; Post World
War II.
RCBS

HUNTING IN ZAMBIA

Story of a successful hunt in Zambia, Africa.
Includes scenes of many African game animals: leopard, waterbuck, impala, lion, sable, puku, and elephant. The leopard, waterbuck, sable, and puku are
record-class trophies and have been included in Rol-
lin Ward's book, *Records of Big Game*.
NL; 25 min; 16 mm; NL; JR, HS, A; Post World
War II.
RCBS

HUNT IS ON, THE

Ireland's lush, rolling countryside makes it a
perfect place to raise horses. The Irish do breed
thoroughbreds which are sold and raced around the
world. Several fox hunts and a stag hunt are shown,
and the need for the horses' speed, jumping ability,
and stamina becomes evident. Several internationally famous horses are shown.
NL; 16 min; 16 mm; NL; JR, HS, A; Post World
War II.
TRIBUNE

HURRICANE HIGGINS

Traces the rise to popularity of snooker as a
working-class sport, attributing it to the surprising
skill of Alex Higgins of Belfast, who became World
Professional Snooker Champion at the unprecedented age of 23. Fanatic for perfection and excite-

ment, Higgins shook the suave, professional snooker world with his rise to fame, documented in this film.

1974; 28 min; 16 mm; color; JR, HS, A; Post World War II.

UILL

I ALWAYS COME BACK TO THE HIMALAYAS

The life of Sir Edmund Hillary, internationally known mountain climber and explorer, is told in this documentary film of his travels throughout much of the unexplored world.

NL; 28 min; 16 mm; NL; JR, HS, A; Modern to Post World War II.

ASF

I & E SPORTS REEL (IESR 200)

Sports events of 1955. Baseball World Series; tennis thrills; battling the bulls; AAU diving and swimming; women wrestlers, etc.

1955; NL; 16 mm; NL; JR, HS, A; Post World War II.

USARMY

I & E SPORTS REEL (IESR 201)

Football upset of the season; modern pentathlon; Irish upset in last game; iron curtain thriller; canine caddy; Army vs. Navy.

1956; NL; 16 mm; NL; JR, HS, A; Post World War II.

USARMY

I & E SPORTS REEL (IESR 202)

Golden Gloves; winter sports on snow and ice; basketball; slightly fishy; the big streaks; fishing in Panama; Winter Olympics 1956.

1956; NL; 16 mm; NL; JR, HS, A; Post World War II.

USARMY

I & E SPORTS REEL (IESR 203)

Ski jumping; speed bike classic; golf; children's boxing tournament; track meets; soccer; deep sea fishing; bowling; baseball.

1956; NL; 16 mm; BW; JR, HS, A; Post World War II.

USARMY

I & E SPORTS REEL (IESR 204)

Landy loses and wins; Indianapolis 500; modern Atlas sets records; Olympic acrobats; bike jockeys go all out; Little Leaguers, etc.

1956; 31 min; 16 mm; BW; JR, HS, A; Post World War II.

USARMY

I & E SPORTS REEL (IESR 205)

Olympic trials; the lighter side; U. S. Open; ride 'em cowboy; All-Star game.

1956; 21 min; 16 mm; BW; JR, HS, A; Post World War II.

USARMY

I & E SPORTS REEL (IESR 206)

Army runners smash records; boats fly; model planes; antique cars still roll; AAU swimming and diving; Hambletonian.

1956; 21 min; 16 mm; BW; JR, HS, A; Post World War II.

USARMY

I & E SPORTS REEL (IESR 207)

Includes national tennis; Olympic women; king football takes over; sport flashes; Gold Cup power-boats, etc.

1956; 21 min; 16 mm; BW; JR, HS, A; Post World War II.

USARMY

I & E SPORTS REEL (IESR 208)

Air Force grid debut; interservice boxing; World Series.

1956; 20 min; 16 mm; BW; JR, HS, A; Post World War II.

USARMY

I & E SPORTS REEL (IESR 211)

Football bowls; a dog's life; barrel jump; handball; Cowboys buffaloed; lady wrestlers.

1957; 20 min; 16 mm; BW; JR, HS, A; Post World War II.

USARMY

I & E SPORTS REEL (IESR 212)

Court kings; crack-up; hot heads on ice; Golden Gloves; 4 minute man; handball; winter sports.

1957; 20 min; 16 mm; BW; JR, HS, A; Post World War II.

USARMY

I & E SPORTS REEL (IESR 213)

Winter sports on snow and ice; service sluggers; soldiers on skis; winter perils; ladies of the courts.

1957; 20 min; 16 mm; BW; JR, HS, A; Post World War II.
USARMY

I & E SPORTS REEL (IESR 215)
Court kings; Masters' golf; moppet maulers; six-day bikes; college acrobats; Stanley Cup hockey.
1957; 21 min; 16 mm; BW; JR, HS, A; Post World War II.
USARMY

I & E SPORTS REEL (IESR 216)
Modern pentathlon; Kentucky Derby; Soccer Cup final; Boston marathon; diamond dust.
1957; 24 min; 16 mm; BW; JR, HS, A; Post World War II.
USARMY

I & E SPORTS REEL (IESR 217)
World record pole vault; a dog's life; Wimbledon tennis; heel and toe; U. S. Open; pennant fever; All-Star.
1957; 20 min; 16 mm; BW; JR, HS, A; Post World War II.
USARMY

I & E SPORTS REEL (IESR 218)
Mile record falls again; tennis thrills; Army star wins diving; trumping Theodore; baseball old-timers; modern pentathlon.
1957; 21 min; 16 mm; BW; JR, HS, A; Post World War II.
USARMY

I & E SPORTS REEL (IESR 219)
National tennis; boys' baseball; interservice golf; All-Navy softball; national shoot; Hambletonian; Manhattan marathon; AAU divers.
1957; 20 min; 16 mm; BW; JR, HS, A; Post World War II.
USARMY

I & E SPORTS REEL (IESR 220)
Army vs. Notre Dame; Navy vs. Boston College; Air Force Academy vs. George Washington; farewell to Giants; World Series, 1957.
1957; 21 min; 16 mm; BW; JR, HS, A; Post World War II.
USARMY

I & E SPORTS REEL (IESR 221)
Campbell sets speed record; Japan's big sport week; Japan's World Series; climax on the turf; football highlights.
1958; 20 min; 16 mm; BW; JR, HS, A; Post World War II.
USARMY

I & E SPORTS REEL (IESR 222)
Highlights of Army-Navy football game (1957) played in Philadelphia; preseason training and earlier games played by both teams.
1958; 22 min; 16 mm; BW; JR, HS, A; Post World War II.
USARMY

I & E SPORTS REEL (IESR 223)
Lions win pro title; Mat mugs; Tar Heels halted; Brown Ko's Lopes; football bowls—Rose, Sugar, Orange and Cotton Bowls.
1958; 20 min; 16 mm; BW; JR, HS, A; Post World War II.
USARMY

I & E SPORTS REEL (IESR 224)
Golden Gloves; All-American basketeers; wrong way king pins; bad break for Campy; winter sports; new pay raise bill.
1958; 20 min; 16 mm; BW; JR, HS, A; Post World War II.
USARMY

I & E SPORTS REEL (IESR 225)
Baseball in the air; major league ball clubs in spring training; the boys from Planet O; meet Silky Sullivan.
1958; 20 min; 16 mm; BW; JR, HS, A; Post World War II.
USARMY

I & E SPORTS REEL (IESR 226)
Last ski jump; bowling; moppet maulers; Masters' golf; the Boys from Planet O; indoor sports; baseball.
1958; 21 min; 16 mm; BW; JR, HS, A; Post World War II.
USARMY

I & E SPORTS REEL (IESR 227)
Includes Kentucky Derby; service sports; Russian strong men; Penn relays; buzz bikes run wild; Stan the Man.

1958; 20 min; 16 mm; BW; JR, HS, A; Post World War II.
USARMY

I & E SPORTS REEL (IESR 228)

Crack up in 500; meeting of Milers; heavy seas for yachts; the boys from Planet O; Tim Tam beaten; baseball; bike racing; Open golf.
1958; 21 min; 16 mm; BW; JR, HS, A; Post World War II.
USARMY

I & E SPORTS REEL (IESR 229)

All-Star game; AAU track; the Boys from Planet O; tennis thrills; racing, town and country; Cut'n' Shoot fighting man.
1958; 20 min; 16mm; BW; JR, HS, A; Post World War II.
USARMY

I & E SPORTS REEL (IESR 230)

Mile record falls again; PGA golf; battling the bulls; old-timers baseball; service sports; the Boys from Planet O.
1958; 22 min; 16 mm; BW; JR, HS, A; Sports General; Post World War II.
USARMY

I & E SPORTS REEL (IESR 231)

National tennis; Little League; tale of a trotter; Polo Grounds; what a change; service sports.
1958; 20 min; 16 mm; BW; JR, HS, A; Post World War II.
USARMY

I & E SPORTS REEL (IESR 232)

1958 World Series; tale of a horse; (re-enlistment spot announcement); Globetrotters; service football.
1958; 20 min; 16 mm; BW; JR, HS, A; Post World War II.
USARMY

I & E SPORTS REEL (IESR 233)

The International Horse Race in Maryland; college and pro football; Army vs. Texas; Navy vs. Notre Dame; Cleveland Browns vs. Chicago Cardinals.
1959; 19 min; 16 mm; BW; JR, HS, A; Post World War II.
USARMY

I & E SPORTS REEL (IESR 234)

Service football; Air Force Academy vs.Colorado; sport spectacular; Army-Navy football classic; in and out of Orbit; Spon on safe driving.
1959; 20 min; 16 mm; BW; JR, HS, A; Post World War II.
USARMY

I & E SPORTS REEL (IESR 235)

Football bowls: Rose, Sugar, Cotton, and Orange; pro title playoff; football. Davis Cup tennis; grid thrills of 1958.
1959; 19 min; 16 mm; BW; JR, HS, A; Post World War II.
USARMY

I & E SPORTS REEL (IESR 236)

Winter sports; bowling; Basketball All-Stars; indoor track; spot announcement on observance of safety rules to prevent accidents.
1959; 19 min; 16 mm; BW; JR, HS, A; Post World War II.
USARMY

I & E SPORTS REEL (IESR 237)

Goodbye winter; wind up of baseball teams in training.
1959; 20 min; 16 mm; BW; JR, HS, A; Post World War II.
USARMY

I & E SPORTS REEL (IESR 238)

Basketball finals (NCAA and professional); Stanley Cup hockey; Grand National; table tennis; boxing; spot on benefits of USAFI sources.
1959; 20 min; 16 mm; BW; JR, HS, A; Post World War II.
USARMY

I & E SPORTS REEL (IESR 239)

Horse racing; Wood Memorial, Kentucky Derby, and Preakness; Alex Olmedo; bike racing; marathon; track; Killibrew.
1959; 19 min; 16 mm; BW; JR, HS, A; Post World War II.
USARMY

I & E SPORTS REEL (IESR 240)

The "500"; surfing; boatnik; the Boys from Planet O; pentathlon; horse racing; Open golf.
1959; 20 min; 16 mm; BW; JR, HS, A; Post World War II.
USARMY

IBMXF WORLD CHAMPIONSHIP IV

Program 1: BMX Souvenir Tape
Program 2: BMX Training Tape

The BMX Souvenir Tape is an action-packed hour of BMX bicycle racing, taped by Canada's finest video-journalists on location in Whistler, B.C., during the 1985 world championship. The BMX Training Tape features BMX professionals in interviews and demonstrations, sharing their skills in a sport that is attracting an increasingly large following of people around the world.

NL; 60 min; VHS; color; JR, HS, A; Post World War II.

CANBC

ICARUS SYNDROME, THE

This film focuses on the joys of hang gliding. In sharing the beauty and wonder of the earth's majesty from the vantage point of the hang glider, we are moved to ask, "What can we do for the Earth to keep it thus?" The film also touches on man's insatiable appetite for flight and some interesting thoughts on the psychology behind this yearning. A film for people of all ages and interests.

1975; 9 min; 16 mm; color; JR, HS, A; Post World War II.

BUDGET

ICE ROCK AND SKY

There are six degrees of difficulty in rock climbing—from the very easy to the absolute in human ability. This film shows two courageous men who start with the fourth degree and end with the sixth.

NL; 18 min; 16 mm; NL; JR, HS, A; Post World War II.

TRIBUNE; SNTO

IF

Poetry is the language of man set to paper. Football is the language of man set to action. Joined together in Rudyard Kipling's famous poem "If"— which reinforces the need of keeping calm and collected when everyone else is going crazy, and the need to forge on when all others have failed—football action enhances the significance of both poem and sport.

NL; 2 min; 16 mm, VHS, U-Matic; color; JR, HS, A; Post World War II.

NFL; TMA

IF WISHES WERE HEROES

The owner-trainer of a thoroughbred brood mare faces a moral and financial dilemma when he is forced to choose between the mare and the life of her unborn foal. Contrasts the exciting world of the racetrack with the realities of raising horses. The personal conflict felt by the owner, his judgment, and its consequences are topics for continued discussion of values and an analysis of the decision-making process.

1976; 24 min; 16 mm; color; JR, HS, A; Post World War II.

PYRAMID; LSU

IKAROS

Slow-motion, multiple-image photography and a musical background depict the freedom and poetry inherent in skiing. Expert skiers race around and across boulders of snow and seem to fly as they somersault through the air in long, graceful arcs and sail off snowy cliffs. One lone skier poses dramatically at the brink of a precipice, slowly throws himself off, flips in mid-air, lands upright, and skis away.

1972; 10 min; 16 mm; color; JR, HS, A; Post World War II.

PYRAMID; UILL

I'LL GO AGAIN

I'll Go Again is a film about four athletes and a team who competed in the 1976 Olympics. They had trained courageously to be among those who would mount the podium to receive a medal. None did. Was it worth it? The film answers the question.

NL; 42 min; 16 mm; color; JR, HS, A; Post World War II.

CCS

I LOVED JOHN RINGLING

Describes the character and career of the great circus magnate from the humble beginning of his circus in Baraboo, Wisconsin, through his eventual retirement and death.

1964; 29 min; 16 mm; BW; JR, HS, A; Modern Sport.

MICHMED

IMAGES

A sensitive look at children as they try to emulate their heroes by posing and playing just as the pros do.

NL; 3 min; 16 mm; VHS, U-Matic; color; JR, HS, A; Post World War II.

NFL; TMA

IMPACT OF JERSEY JOE WALCOTT, SHERIFF

He was poor and black, and he says that's as tough as it can get in America. He had a dream of becoming the Heavyweight Champ of the World, and this is the story of how he accomplished it. The further story of how Walcott became the first black sheriff of Camden, N. J., far surpasses his struggles in the ring. As Sheriff Arnold Cream, he is at the same time tough, compassionate, firm, understanding and, most of all, respected and loved by those who come in contact with him.

1972; 26 min; 16 mm; color; JR, HS, A; Post World War II.

SYRA

IMPOSSIBLE HOUR, THE

The Impossible Hour follows Danish racing star Ole Ritter as he tries to regain his record for the hour ride. He had set the record in 1968, only to have it shattered by Eddy Merckx in 1972. Ritter tried three times in one week to better Merckx's record of 49.431 kilometers. In so doing, he learned about human limits and the quest for the heroic."

NL; 48 min; VHS; NL; JR, HS, A; Post World War II.

GRADY

INCREDIBLE SAN FRANCISCO ARTISTS' SOAPBOX DERBY, THE

Covers an unusual soapbox derby staged by 104 Bay Area artists who designed their gravity-operated cars in a wide variety of unconventional vehicular shapes: a pencil, a shoe, a butterfly, a dome paved with pennies. Intercutting of scenes from the highly organized and competitive national soapbox derby offers sharp contrast to the free-wheeling and imaginative San Francisco version. Interviews with the artists serve as narration and provide insights into the creative process.

1977; 24 min; 16 mm; color; JR, HS, A; Post World War II.

PENNST; PHENIX

INCREDIBLE SCHOONER

Reenacts the yacht race in which the schooner *America* won first place, becoming the first winner of the America's Cup. Includes an account of events leading up to the race and subsequent achievements of the ship.

1975; 19 min; 16 mm, VHS, U-Matic; color; JR, HS, A; Making of Modern Sport.

AIMS, UILL

INDIANAPOLIS

Documents the emotions, challenges, and goals of the men who make up the sport of automobile racing, using the Indianapolis 500 as the example.

1971; 28 min; 16 mm; color; JR, HS, A; Post World War II.

STP

INDY 500

NL; NL; 116 mm; NL; JR, HS, A; Post World War II.

COCA

INNSBRUCK '76

Vignettes of the historic village of Innsbruck, alive with competition, and spectacular photography of the world's finest amateur athletes in action. Includes Dorothy Hamill and Linda Fratianne, American figure skaters; Sheila Young and Peter Mueller, speed skating; Cindy Nelson and Phil Mahre, giant slalom; Bill Koch, cross-country skiing; and Tai Babilonia and Randy Gardner, ice skating.

NL; 27 min; 16 mm; color; JR, HS, A; Post World War II.

USOC

INSIDE SPORTS

Highlights seven sports spectaculars from the year 1974. Covers Miller High Life Hobie Cat National Championships; Marlboro Cup; basketball's All-American David Thompson; trampoline thrillers; the Indy 500; U.S.-Germany dual swim meet; Henry Aaron's historic home run.

1974; 26 min; 16 mm; NL; JR, HS, A; Post World War II.

MILLER

INSTANT REPLAY

Jerry Kramer, All-Pro tackle of the Green Bay Packers, tells the story of the Packers' 1967 season. Coach Vince Lombardi emerged as professional football's greatest mentor as his team beat the Dallas Cowboys for the NFL Championship and the Oakland Raiders, the American Football League champions, in the Super Bowl.

NL; 22 min; 16 mm; NL; HS, A; Post World War II.

ASF

INTRODUCTION TO ENDURANCE RIDING, AN

Brief history of endurance riding. Covers preparation, choosing the correct equipment and horse, grooming, conditioning, familiarization with the trail, proper gait, and postride care.

1973; 16 min; 16 mm; color; JR, HS, A; Post World War II.

PENNST

INVITATION TO ARCHERY, AN

Offers an introduction to the sport of archery, with a look at its history.

1978; 10 min; 16 mm, VHS, U-Matic; color; JR, HS, A; Ancient to Post World War II.
ATHI

I OWN THE EARTH: DIANA NYAD

This film documents Diana Nyad's powerful speech at the New Agenda Conference. It expresses the physical and emotional effects which sport has had on her life.
NL; 15 min; 16 mm; color; HS, A; Post World War II.
WSF

IRISH FOOTBALL FINAL: 1968

The Irish have an annual football contest between two championship teams, just as we do. It takes place in Croke Park in Dublin and everyone, including the President of Ireland, attends. In this case the teams were Kerry and Down.
NL; 10 min; 16 mm; NL; JR, HS, A; Post World War II.
TRIBUNE

IRISH HURLING FINAL: 1968

Hurling is a game played with a ball and a curved stick. It is not uncommon for the stick to hit a player's head instead of the ball. This contest also takes place in Croke Park, every seat filled with people cheering for their favorite team. In 1968, the two teams which competed were Tipperary and Wexford. Miraculously, no one was seriously injured in this exciting game.
NL; 10 min; 16 mm; NL; JR, HS, A; Post World War II.
TRIBUNE

IRONMAN

Documents the supreme endurance test, the Ironman Triathlon, in which the most durable men and women athletes in the world test themselves and gain self-knowledge and personal honor. Set on the big island of Hawaii and narrated by Bruce Dern.
1982; 22 min; 16 mm; color; JR, HS, A; Post World War II.
OSU

...IS IT LE/ZHER OR LEZH/ER?

Describes how the public in general and professionals in particular interpret the meaning of leisure and recreation. Many types of people are shown in a variety of leisure-time pursuits and explain why they engage in them, while experts discuss the need for such activity to combat loneliness, boredom, and aimlessness and to achieve a sense of purpose, self-fulfillment, and satisfaction. Includes leisure counseling, activities for the disabled, program funding, and "work ethic" conflicts.
1976; 31 min; 16 mm; color; HS, A; Post World War II.
PENNST

IT ALL BEGAN WITH FARRAGUT

NL; NL; 16 mm; NL; JR, HS, A; Golden Age to Post World War II.
ASA

IT HAPPENS EVERY SPRING

A film devoted to the excitement of bowling in the Women's International Bowling Congress Championship Tournament.
NL; 19 min; 16 mm; NL; JR, Hs, A; Post World War II.
WIBC

IT'S ALL IN THE GAME

Should schools continue or curtail interscholastic sports competition? The positive value of competitive sports, sportsmanship, and good physical health are presented in this film produced by the Athletic Institute.
1975; 27 min; 16 mm; color; HS, A; Post World War II.
ATHI; IOWA

IT'S A MILE FROM HERE TO GLORY

Focuses on Early McLaren, a 15-year-old who is small for his age, as he becomes a long-distance runner whose self-esteem is totally dependent on winning. Follows his comeback after a crippling auto accident as he is forced to realize the importance of friendship and team spirit. Based on the novel by Robert C. Lee.
1978; 46 min; 16 mm; color; JR, HS, A; Post World War II.
TIMLIF; IU

IT SURE WENT UP IN SMOKE

The two Dons of drag racing, Garlits and Prudhomme, explain how to get from point A, the starting line, to point B, the finish line, in the shortest possible time. This is the world of the AA/F dragsters and of the men who race these 1800-horsepower monsters down the 1320-foot strip.
NL; 21 min; 16 mm; NL; JR, HS, A; Post World War II.
GTARC

IT'S TOUGH TO MAKE IT IN THIS LEAGUE

Walt Garrison, former Dallas Cowboy, narrates this look at the career of pro football. Traces the path to the National Football League, showing the pressures of grading and rating, which begin early. Players, agents, scouts, coaches, and owners converse on the qualities which enable a player to break into a professional league. Football personalities Joe Namath, Stan Gardner, Roger Staubach, Larry Brown, Ray Mansfield, and Pete Rozelle contribute to this exploration of a demanding and short-lived career.

1976; 54 min; 16 mm; color; JR, HS, A; Post World War II.

UILL

IT'S TOUGH TO MAKE IT IN THIS LEAGUE

The physical, emotional and, in some cases, financial punishment that is part of trying to achieve a career in professional football is the subject of this short that covers every aspect of the sport, from Little League competition through the pressures in the professional ranks.

1977; 55 min; 16 mm; color; JR, HS, A; Post World War II.

BUDGET

JABS AND JOLTS

A rowdy, funny, and often thrilling film of small boy boxers, girl pugilists, a free-for-all wrestling riot, and a hair-pulling brawl between two lady wrestlers.

NL; 10 min; 16 mm; NL; JR, HS, A; Post World War II.

BUDGET

JACK JOHNSON

Employs old stills and news footage to depict the life of Jack Johnson, the first black heavyweight boxing champion, who fought against racial prejudice, white supremacy, and legal harassment in his private life. Includes newsreel clips from his fights with Jim Jeffries, Jess Willard, and others. Excellent portrait of the man and the times in which he lived.

1970; 90 min; 16 mm; JR, HS, A; Modern Sport to Golden Age.

UCB

JACK LAMBERT

A microphone in the pads of Jack Lambert captures the game day intensity of football's fiercest linebacker. Says his coach, Chuck Noll, "Jack's the most even-tempered man I've ever known—always mad."

1985; 8 min; VHS, U-Matic; color; JR, HS, A; Post World War II.

NFL; TMA

JACK RABBIT

Biographical portrait of a remarkable centenarian, Herman Smith Johannsen, who introduced the sport of cross-country skiing to North America and who was nicknamed "Jack Rabbit" by Canadian Indians because of the way he cut rings around them on skis while they plodded along on snowshoes. Born in Norway, Johannsen came to Canada in 1903. Still active and vital in his hundredth year, he is seen skiing at the Canadian Ski Marathon near Montreal, where he is the honored guest, and on a memorable trip to Norway, where he is reunited with his two sisters, both in their nineties. His life is traced with the aid of sports newsreels, Norwegian archives, and his family album.

1977; 29 min; 16 mm; color; JR, HS, A; Modern to Post World War II.

NFBC; UCB

JACKIE ROBINSON

Robinson relates his experience as an Afro-American in an all-white California neighborhood. After he became a football, basketball, baseball, and track star at UCLA, Branch Rickey, Brooklyn Dodger general manager, chose him as the player most likely to break the baseball color line. His talented play forced fans and players to accept him, welded the Dodgers into a pennant-winning team, and earned him the title of Rookie of the Year. Robinson became a representative of his race, speaking out forcefully on housing and employment discrimination, injustice, and brotherhood.

1965; 26 min; 16 mm; BW; JR, HS, A; Post World War II.

SF; SYRA

JACKIE SMITH

Jackie Smith played gallantly throughout his 15-year NFL career as one of the most prolific pass receivers in the game. Smith was the prototype of the modern tight end, mixing speed and skill with the love of combat.

1985; 9 min; VHS, U-Matic; NL; JR, HS, A; Post World War II.

NFL; TMA

JAI-ALAI: THE FASTEST GAME
Presents the history and development of jai-alai.
1978; 20 min; 16 mm; color; JR, HS, A; Post World War II.
NAJAF

JANET GUTHRIE STORY, THE: "THE ULTIMATE CHALLENGE"
A documentation of Indianapolis 500 racecar driver Janet Guthrie, with actual footage taken at the Indianapolis Motor Speedway.
1978; 24 min; 16 mm; color; JR, HS, A; Post World War II.
ISLA

JAZZ AGE, THE: 1919-1929
Depicts social life and customs in America during the 1920s, a prosperous era of excessive pleasure-seeking which has come to be known as the Jazz Age. Traces important historical events of the period. Part I covers the Versailles Conference, the Harding political campaign and scandal, the Ku Klux Klan, American town life, new manners and morals for women, and widespread use of the automobile. Other subjects covered include nightclubs of the prohibition era, wild stock-market speculations, bootlegging industry, racketeering, and popularity of foreign travel. Part II shows night life of Paris, Lindbergh's flight, American sports, Hoover campaign, starts of show business, and the stock market crash in 1929. Illustrated throughout with archive newsreel footage, and narrated by the late Fred Allen.
1965; 52 min; 16 mm; BW; JR, HS, A; Golden Age.
MGHT; MICHMED; NBC

J. D. GOES HUNTING
An American's hunting holiday in New Zealand's Southern Alps. Authentic fishing and hunting sequences are set amid mountains and forests teeming with bird life and abundant quarry for the sportsman.
NL; 15 min; 16 mm; NL; JR, HS, A; Post World War II.
NZGTO

JEFF KEITH'S RUN ACROSS AMERICA
This documentary follows young Jeff Keith in his historic run across the United States, in spite of a severe handicap: Jeff had lost a leg to cancer some years earlier. The film culminates in California, where he receives a personal call from the president, congratulating him on his courageous achievement.
NL; 13 min; 16 mm, VHS, U-Matic; color; JR, HS, A; Post World War II.
MTPS

JEFFRIES - JOHNSON 1910
Documents the historic Jeffries-Johnson boxing match, the racist campaign that preceded it, and the manner in which an excited world awaited the results
1971; 21 min; 16 mm; BW; JR, HS, A; Modern Sport.
MGHT; PENNST

JESSE OWENS
Highlights the year 1936, during the Summer Olympics in Berlin. Explains how the catalyst for a devastating blow to the twisted concept of a "master race" was the black athlete named Jesse Owens. Explains how he was one of the early greats in track and field and talks about his exciting years as an athlete and sports personality.
NL; 20 min; 16 mm; color; JR, HS, A; Depression Era to Post World War II.
COUNFI; USC

JESSE OWENS RETURNS TO BERLIN
The world-renowned athlete returns to Berlin's Olympic Stadium for a recreation of his emotion-charged sweep of four gold medals in 1936. Narrating his own experiences, he recalls the action on the field, the Nazi mania, the strong friendship between Olympians, the pomp and ceremony. Includes old film clips and captured footage.
1965; 51 min; 16 mm; BW; JR, HS, A; Depression Era, World War II.
MGHT; MICHMED

JIGGING FOR LAKE TROUT
A Native American family makes an excursion for fresh fish from a lake. They build a karmak and move in the furs, cooking troughs, etc. The woman sets up her lamp, spreads the furs, and attends to the children. The man moves out on the lake ice and chips a hole for fishing. He baits his hook and lowers it, jigging the line to attract the fish. Crouched by the hole, he takes some fish, as does his wife, who has joined him. Both remain at the hole throughout a severe blizzard.
1967; 32 min; 16 mm, VHS, U-Matic, Beta; color; JR, HS, A; Post World War II.
NFBC

JIM BROWN
An action-packed profile of the powerful ball carrier. Includes all of Brown's greatest runs as well as comments of those who tried to stop him. "Everytime I tackled Jim Brown, I heard a dice game going on inside his mouth," said the Eagles' Tom Brookshier.

1985; 7 min; VHS, U-Matic; color; Jr, HS, A; Post World War II.
NFL; TMA

JOCKEY

Portrait of Penny Ann Early, the first woman jockey. Shows her in several races and interviews trainers, fellow jockeys.
NL; 25 min; 16 mm; color; JR, HS, A; Post World War II.
TEXTURE

JOE NAMATH AND THE MAGIC BEAN

A fairy-tale version of the most incredible and unforgettable of all Super Bowls—Super Bowl III—the game Joe Namath "guaranteed" he would win, and did, with the help of the "Magic Bean."
NL; 5 min; 16 mm; VHS, U-Matic; color; JR, HS, A; Post World War II.
NFL; TMA

JOHN BAKER'S LAST RACE

Tells the story of John Baker, who at 24 was young, gifted, athletic, an Olympic-class miler, but dying of cancer. Shows John as he finally comes to grips with his condition and lives his final months with shining courage. Presents John as he works with youth of the community, turning this bitter tragedy into a legacy of hope.
1976; 33 min; 16 mm; color; JR, HS, A; Post World War II.
BYU; UU

JOSHUA

Depicts the personal conflicts of an African-American boy who has always lived in Harlem but wins an athletic scholarship to a Texas College. As he is about to enter college, Joshua sees his identity as a black American threatened, and he sets off on a running spree though a park where he encounters a white boy and realizes the possibilities of a black-white partnership on terms of equality.
1968; 15 min; 16 mm; VHS, U-Matic; BW; JR, HS, A; Post World War II.
AIMS

JOURNEY: THE QUEST FOR SELF-RELIANCE

Follows a 70-mile solo wilderness hike through the Sierra Nevada by a young man with no food, no matches, and no compass; he finds or makes everything he needs for survival. Highlights of his arduous trek include attempting to catch fish barehanded; starting a campfire with a fire bow; and making a fire bed to sleep on in subfreezing temperatures. In voice-over he comments on how the experience helped him grow and know himself better, the preparation and study needed for such a journey, and the traditional Indian methods he employed to survive.
1976; 21 min; 16 mm; color; JR, HS, A; Post World War II.
PHENIX; UCB

JOE DIMAGGIO (THE YANKEE CLIPPER)

Features Joe DiMaggio reviewing his career through some of baseball's most legendary film footage.
NL; 20 min; 16 mm; color; JR, HS, A; Depression Era to Post World War II.
COUNFI; USC

JUDOKA

The unusual story of a young Canadian athlete, Doug Rogers, who developed, in Japan, a talent for judo that led him into competition for the world championships at the Tokyo Olympics and subsequent competition at the Pan-American Games. The film, produced in 1965, shows intensive judo training Rogers took at a Tokyo college, as well as glimpses of life in Japan.
1965; 18.5 min; 16 mm; NL; HS, A; Post World War II.
NFBC

JUG McSPADEN: GOLF PRO

Gathering of golf greats and famous personalities including Sam Snead, Byron Nelson, Bobby Locke, Sammy Kay, the Duke of Windsor, and Bob Hope in action.
1953; 20 min; 16 mm; NL; JR, HS, A; Post World War II.
BUDGET

JUMP

In a candid and introspective manner, 19-year-old Ruthy shares her experience of learning to sky dive. Descriptive footage of her training for, and execution of, her first parachute jump is matched by Ruthy's musing consideration of the motivation for, and trepidation about, such a feat.
1977; 17 min; 16 mm, VHS, U-Matic; color; JR, HS, A; Post World War II.
STRPRO

JUNGFRAU: ASCENT ON SKIS

Good mountain climbing and skiing. Emphasizes the slow, sure pace of experienced climber. Shows winds and clouds near summit of the mountains and the treacherous descent.

NL; 21 min; 16 mm; NL; JR, HS, A; Post World War II.

TRIBUNE; SNTO

JUNGFRAU: FIRST ROTTAL ASCENT

The first ascent up the inner Rottal ridge of the Jungfrau was accomplished in 1885. It became the shorter and safer way to climb this most challenging mountain.

NL; 20 min; 16 mm; NL; JR, HS, A; Modern to Post World War II.

TRIBUNE; SNTO

JUNGFRAU: FIRST ASCENT

This is a reenactment of the first ascent of the Jungfrau, made on August 3, 1811.

NL; 21 min; 16 mm; NL; JR, HS, A; Premodern.

TRIBUNE; SNTO

JUNIOR BRONCBUSTERS

Vicious horses and wild-eyed steers hold no terrors for these amazing juniors, who'll thrill the audience with their reckless riding, roping, and stunts.

NL; 10 min; 16 mm; NL; JR, HS, A; Post World War II.

BUDGET

JUST FOR ME

This film documents three women's experiences with fitness and sport: that of a homemaker with children, an office worker who has just moved to the city, and a married schoolteacher. The film looks at the women before they participate in a sport, as well as during and after the experience. Support material available.

1982; 27 min; 16 mm; NL; HS, A; Post World War II.

NFBC

JUST HORSES

Demonstrates the versatility of horses. Beautiful photography shows jumping horses, polo ponies, race horses, bucking broncos, and show horses. Also shown is jumping competition at the American Royal, one of the largest and most prestigious horse shows in the United States.

NL; 15 min; 16 mm; color; JR, HS, A; Post World War II.

BUDGET

J. W. COOP

A rodeo cowboy, free after ten years in prison, sets out to rebuild his life and climb to the top in the rodeo circuit. Cliff Robertson starred, directed, produced, and co-authored this film. He's J. W. Coop, who has set out on a grueling campaign to win the national rodeo championship for himself in one season! His story makes up this excellent motion picture that tells of a man's obsession and the price he is willing to pay to achieve it.

1971; 112 min; 16 mm; color; JR, HS, A; Post World War II.

BUDGET

KALEIDO-SKI

A quick view of the Grenoble Olympic games, a mass descent of ski instructors, parachuting skiers, the French ski team in action, fantastic dream sequence, acrobatics on skis, kaleidoscopic images, humor, soul-pop music, brief narration . . . Chamonix, Val d'Isere, Courchevel, Avoriaz, La Clusaz, etc.

NL; 20 min; 16 mm; NL; JR, HS, A; Post World War II.

FGTO

KANSAS CITY CHIEFS FOOTBALL

1970 highlights
1971 highlights
1972 highlights
1973 highlights

NL; 30 min each; 16 mm; NL; JR, HS, A; Post World War II.

KCCFC

KARATE

The ancient Oriental art of karate, presented as a way to individual self-control and self-realization.

1972; 10 min; 16 mm; color; JR, HS, A; Post World War II.

PYRAMID; UILL

KARATE: ART OR SPORT?

What is thought of in the Western world as a method of self-defense is, in the East, one of the ways of uniting body and mind. Its aspects as art, its spirit of humility that accommodates the discipline which is the only way to self-improvement, the grace of its forms are demonstrated by a team of masters.

1974; 19 min; 16 mm; color; JR, HS, A; Post World War II.

PARMT; LSU

KARATE: PART I

Introduces karate as it was before it became a sport. Deals with self-defense as well as the disciplines associated with the martial arts.

NL; 60 min; VHS; color; JR, HS, A; Post World War II.

MOHOMV

KARATE SHOTOKAN

Made in cooperation with the Japanese and Belgian masters of this martial art, this film demonstrates the efficacity of karate. We learn that "karate" stems from "kara" meaning foot, and "tie," meaning fist. But the ultimate purpose of karate is the development of the personalities of those who practice it. A French and Dutch language film with English subtitles.

1970; 16 min; 16 mm; BW; JR, HS, A; Post World War II.

BELGIUM

KARTING

Karting consists of motor races using a rudimentary chassis, with no body work, fitted with two-stroke engines, the cylinder displacement of which may not exceed 100 cubic centimeters. On these little vehicles (with a maximum width of 127 cm. and a length of 182 cm.), the steering may not be assisted, and there must be no brakes on the front wheels. Karting takes place on special tracks with numerous bends. Top speeds may attain 120 km. per hour. The film shows several national and international races, proving that the sport can be a dangerous one. Belgium can boast of several champions in the karting world. A French language film with Dutch and English subtitles.

1970; 15 min; 35 mm; BW; JR, HS, A; Post World War II.

BELGIUM

KASHIA MEN'S DANCES: SOUTHWESTERN POMO INDIANS

Preserves four authentic Pomo dances as performed in elaborate costumes and headdresses, on the Kashia Reservation on the Northern California coast. The Pomo build a brush enclosure for the dance ceremony, as they did in former times, and walk to the enclosure singing a special song. The dances we see are a blend of their ancient religion together with the nearly 100-year-old Bole Maru and more modern beliefs. They were used to celebrate many occasions, such as the arrival of spring, the coming of the first salmon up the streams, the harvest, an initiation of new members into a secret society of adulthood, and the curing of a sick patient.

1963; 40 min; 16 mm; color; JR, HS, A; Ancient to Post World War II.

UCB

KAYAK

The story of a modern adventure down the wild Colorado River by kayak and raft. This film emphasizes the drama of challenging the difficult white water of the Grand Canyon. The film demonstrates many of the techniques of running the river. Share the magnificent beauty of the Grand Canyon and hear stories of the early voyageurs.

1976; 20 min; 16 min; color; JR, HS, A; Post World War II.

LSU

KEEP FIT, STUDY WELL, WORK HARD

Photographed at schools in Peking, Shanghai, and Sian, this film is a revealing look at the life of the young in China. Discipline pervades their lives, as illustrated by scenes of hundreds of children exercising in unison to the marching beat of broadcast music. Among other activities, students in an English class practice pronunciation of the saying by Mao Tse Tung, "Keep fit, study well, work hard." Many Chinese schools have an attached factory where part of the students' time is spent working on factory products. Younger children make and assemble chess sets, while older students do more difficult jobs such as wiring generators. Concludes with the staging of a pageant honoring Lei Feng, a revolutionary hero.

1973; 13 min; 16 mm; color; JR, HS, A; Post World War II.

CF; UILL

KENNE DUNCAN—TRICK SHOOTING

Kenne Duncan, one of the most familiar bad guys of "B" westerns and early TV shows, demonstrates his sharpshooting skill. Interspersed with some excellent trick shooting are stills from Duncan's film appearances, as well as footage of his visit to Japan. A rare piece of footage.

NL; 10 min; 16 mm; color; JR, HS, A; Post World War II.

BUDGET

KID WHO CAN'T MISS, THE

Produced to illustrate the fun and sense of accomplishment young people can find in the shooting sports. Whether it's gun collecting, Olympic competition, or hunting in the field, shooting is open to nearly all young people.

NL; 24 min; VHS, U-Matic; 16 mm; NL; JR, HS, A; Post World War II.

NRA; KAROL

KIDS AND OTHER PEOPLE

This film explains the importance of play for people of all ages. The soundtrack carries the candid voices of children who express their own ideas about the necessity of play for *Kids and Other People*. The activities shown are all informal, with the emphasis being on doing something for the sake of itself alone. Children roll in the snow and do cartwheels on the beach, a little girl watches sea-gulls and dreams of flying, a boy lies on his back studying the sky and plans trips to as-yet-undiscovered galaxies, adults preen and parade at an extravagant fancy dress ball, two elderly women sit in the sun chatting about the weather.

The film is a celebration of the spontaneity of play, with emphasis on informal activities that are inexpensive and accessible to most people.

1982; 21 min; 16 mm; NL; JR, HS, A; Post World War II.

NFU

KIDS AND SPORTS INJURIES

The need for safety and protective measures in children's sports: how injuries can affect vulnerable young bones and ligaments and lead to deformity, and the consequences of adult and peer pressure on young athletes to perform beyond their physical abilities.

NL; 19 min; VHS; color; A; Post World War II.

FOTH

KIDS AT PLAY

Shows the many games children play and the fun they have doing it. Discusses the origin and development of various games that children have played from ancient times. Indicates that "Ring Around the Rosie" may have had its origins during the bubonic plague, while "London Bridge Is Falling Down" is supposed to represent prisoners cemented into the foundation of the bridge.

1980; 29 min; 16 mm; color; JR, HS, A; Ancient to Post World War II.

CANBC; IU

KIEL OLYMPIAD (OLYMPIC YACHTING 1972)

Records the 1972 opening ceremonies and sailing competition at the Olympic Yachting Center in Kiel, Germany. Six classes were raced: Dragon, Soling, Star, Tempest, Flying Dutchmen, and Finn Dinghy. As the details of each race and background information on the various sailboat classes are provided by an accompanying narrative, the camera captures the special beauty and excitement of each event. United States entrants describe their love of the sport, its special skills and techniques. Concludes with scenes of the award presentation.

1973; 28 min; 16 mm; color; JR, HS, A; Post World War II.

OFFSHR; PYRAMID; UILL; USC

KING OF THE HILL

Two seasons (1972 and 1973) with the Chicago Cubs and their incredibly talented pitching ace, Ferguson "Fergy" Jenkins, unveil the inner workings of major league baseball: the eternal hope of spring training and the agony of defeat for a soft-spoken, vulnerable individual of great attractiveness. A broadly appealing documentary of baseball and one of its true superstars.

1974; 57 min; 16 mm, VHS, U-Matic; color; JR, HS, A; Post World War II.

NFBC

KING PIN OF SPORTS

Bowling history, with trick bowling display and instructions in basics.

NL; 28 min; 16 mm; NL; JR, HS, A; Post World War II.

CINES

KINGS OF SPORT

A vintage look at the early kings of sport, including Babe Ruth and Bobby Jones.

NL; 10 min; 16 mm; NL; JR; HS, A; Modern to Post World War II.

BUDGET

KITEMAN

Witness the National Delta Wing Kite Tournament at Cypress Gardens and share the disappointment of the losers and the triumph of the winners as they skillfully soar on their manmade wings.

NL; 15 min; 16 mm; NL; JR, HS, A; Post World War II.

FLADC

KITES: A COLLAGE OF KITES AND KITEFLYERS

Places the craft of kite making in different cultural and historical contexts. Shows that kite building and flying is a skilled craft and always a source of great pleasure.

1983; 28 min; 16 mm, VHS, U-Matic; color; JR, HS, A.

LUF

KNUTE ROCKNE

This account of the great coach who led Notre Dame's football team to the top shows the amazing competitive spirit of the man and his contributions to the game. The forward pass, increased speed, and a wider variety of plays were first employed by his teams. His famous halftime talks and practice sessions are well documented with contemporary footage.

NL; 27 min; 16 mm, VHS; NL; JR, HS, A; Golden Age to Depression Era.

SF

KNUTE ROCKNE

Uses rare footage to portray the personal life and history-making deeds of Knute Rockne.

1965; 26 min; 16 mm; color; JR, HS, A; Golden Age to Depression Era.

WOLPER; USC

KYUDO: JAPANESE CEREMONIAL ARCHERY

Presents a unique and picturesque aspect of Japanese culture, showing how their traditions and spiritual beliefs are involved in the old method of archery—a combination of body training and discipline of the mind. A master teacher is shown working with pupils, then demonstrating Kyudo with other masters. Climax of the film is the ceremony of Toshogu Shrine, where archers in traditional costumes shoot at a target from a galloping horse.

1970; 10 min; 16 mm; color; JR, HS, A; Post World War II.

AIMS; UILL

LA COURSE DE TAUREAUX

A survey of art relating to bullfighting (prehistoric rock paintings, Greek vases, Cretan frescoes, drawings by Goya), followed by a study of the part played by bulls in traditional Spanish fiestas: bullrings improvised in village marketplaces, chases through the streets, fights to celebrate St. Frimin's Day at Pamplona. Analysis of the different phases of the bullfight, whether on foot or on horseback (Conchita Cintron). The bulls are raised and broken-in chiefly in Castlile and Andalusia, where there are a number of schools for the training of future toreadors. The unsophisticated atmosphere of the Novilleros is contrasted with the magnificence of the big fights (Manolo Gonzales). Each fighter has his own individual style: passes executed by Dominguin; death thrusts by El Galb, Ricardo Bambita, Juan Belmonte, Manolo Gonzales, etc. But for their courage and agility, accidents may happen. A French language film.

1951; 80 min; 35 mm; BW; JR, HS, A; Ancient to Post World War II.

PANTHEON

LACROSSE

Played by North American Indians long ago, lacrosse has changed a little. The film demonstrates how the game is played, how lacrosse sticks are made by Mohawk Indians at a Cornwall factory, and how the Canadian Lacrosse Association helps instruct teams.

NL; 14 min; 16 mm; NL; JR, HS, A; Post World War II.

CANEMB

LACROSSE: LITTLE BROTHER OF WAR

Traces the history of lacrosse from its origins as an Indian game of skill and bloodshed to its growing popularity today as an amateur sport and a professional spectator sport.

1974; 14 min; 16 mm; color; JR, HS, A; Ancient to Post World War II.

CANFDC

LAKE ONTARIO STORY, THE

How good fish and water management was employed to convert Lake Ontario from a body of water with few fishing opportunities to a great place to catch lake trout and salmon.

NL; 28 min; VHS; NL; HS, A; Post World War II.

KAROL

LAST AMERICAN HERO

Jeff Bridges portrays a country boy who makes it the hard way as a dirt racetrack driver. Good depiction of the pop culture world of auto racing—small-town style.

1973; 97 min; 16 mm; color; JR, HS, A; Post World War II.

FI

LAST GREAT RACE, THE

The annual 1,200-mile dog-sled race across the frozen wilderness of Alaska—the Iditarod—is a grueling test of human endurance. A BBC camera crew followed 56 mushers and 800 dogs in the three-week trek across some of the world's most tortuous terrain. For many competitors, the Iditarod has become a way of life, as they spend much of the year breeding and training sled dogs and planning for the next great race.

1979; 50 min; 16 mm, VHS, U-Matic; Post World War II.

BBC; FLSU; PMI

LEADERS FOR LEISURE

Stresses the importance of, and need for, professionally trained leaders to insure the success of a community recreation program. Dispels the idea that one can make a recreation program work by merely providing facilities. Shows dramatically why leadership is the key to success and how to utilize leaders to build an effective program.

1948; 20 min; 16 mm; color; HS, A; Post World War II.

UILL

LEADING THE PARADE

Spectacular baton twirling performances by leading high school and college majorettes.

NL; 14 min; 16 mm; NL; JR, HS, A; Post World War II.

FLADC

LEARNING THROUGH MOVEMENT

Focuses on children as they explore and expand their physical capabilities through self-expressed and structured exercises. Shows children developing a sensitivity to body movements in relation to space, speed, and size. Follows students as they adjust and coordinate their actions with others.

1968; 36 min; 16m; BW; HS, A; Post World War II.

IU

LE CONQUERANT DE L'INUTILE

This film recalls the fate of great mountain climber Lionel Terray, who disappeared in 1965. Thanks to pictures of his climbs in the Alps, the Andes, and the Himalaya mountains, and to his books, this film accurately portrays the highlander, movie maker, and writer.

NL; 32 min; 16 mm; color; JR, HS, A; Post World War II.

FACSEA

LE CYCLISTE

A young mailman participates each year in the famous bicycle race called the Tour de France. What is unusual is that he does it in his backyard in Paris, on a bicycle fastened to the ground while he follows the race via radio and various other gadgets. Very amusing and entertaining film. The language used in the film is coarse at times.

1980; 15 min; 16 mm/subtitled; NL; JR, HS, A; Post World War II.

FACSEA

LEFT WALL OF CENOTAPH CORNER

An exciting rock-climbing film which traces the development of the "chock" or "nut" as an alternative to the hammered piton. This worldwide revolution in climbing technique has made possible clean climbs which do not damage the rock and preserve magnificent climbs for future generations. The film includes historical footage of two climbers ascending the left wall of Cenotaph Corner in North Wales in 1964. Nonclimbers will find the ascent spectacular. Beginners will learn how to use nuts in an environmentally sound way, while advanced climbers will enjoy seeing how the "nut game" began. Climbers are Roland Edwards and Eric Jones.

NL; 13 min; 16 mm, VHS, U-Matic, Beta; color; JR, HS, A; Post World War II.

CRYSP

LEGACY OF CURRIER AND IVES, THE

Surveys 19th-century American life with Currier and Ives lithographs and period memorabilia. Includes such categories as general history, farming life, city life, sports and pastimes, river life, war scenes, life in the West, trains, and patriotism.

NL; 23 min; 16 mm; color; JR, HS, A; Premodern Sport, Making of Modern Sport, Modern Sport.

CREATW; ESMARK

LEGEND OF THE LIGHTING BOLT: THE HISTORY OF THE SAN DIEGO CHARGERS

Of the eight original AFL franchises, none has as vivid a history, as rich a collection of stars, as much impact on the shaping of pro football, as the San Diego Chargers. Chargers' stars from the Gillman era (Keith Lincoln, Ernie Ladd, Paul Lowe, Ron Mix, and Lance Alworth) through the Coryell teams (Dan Fouts, Kellen Winslow, Charlie Joiner, and Wes Chandler) are profiled. Includes over 10 minutes of footage never seen on television.

NL; 30 min; 16 mm, VHS, U-Matic; JR, HS, A; Post World War II.

NFL; TMA

LEISURE

A witty animated "history" of leisure from the caveman's first moment of play through the Industrial Revolution to today's novel situation in which we are beginning to care most about having a good environment for our leisure activities.

1976; 14 min; 16 mm; color; JR, HS, A; Ancient to Post World War II.

PENNST; PYRAMID; UCB; UWISC

LEISURE AND VACATIONS

At the end of the workday, on the weekend, or during his vacation, the average Frenchman has within his reach a variety of pastimes ranging from the typically French la petanque and the Tour de France to rugby and soccer. He may relax for a week in the country or at the beach, energetically climb mountains at Chamonix, or sail off the coast of Brittany.

NL; 11 min; 16 mm; color; JR, HS, A; Post World War II.

EBEC

LEISURE: LIVING WITH THE 20-HOUR WEEK

Predicts that the near future will bring an increase in most people's leisure time, and discusses the consumer products, both new and old, that will help fill it. Covers recreational activities, among them skiing, snowmobiling, and sailing; transportation improvements that will turn areas such as Tibet and Antarctica into vacation spots; and problems (for example, obesity) that will accompany a more abundant way of life.

1971; 22 min; 16 mm; color; JR, HS, A; Post World War II.

DOCA; UCB

LEISURE SPORTS

In the Woods at Rambouillet, a paradise for hunters of mushrooms, horseback riding, and cyclists, there is also a great zoo for children. *In the Mountains,* with France's thousands of mountaineers, the forest of Fontainebleau teaches youngsters how to climb. In Chamonix, in the French Alps, the mountain climbing capital, new mountain guides receive their training. *On the Water.* Sailing is very popular in France. Beginners get a chance at it on a pond at St. Quentin near Paris. More intrepid yachtsmen go to the Glenans school on the Brittany coast.

1978; 26 min; color; JR, HS, A; Post World War II.

FACSEA

LEISURE TIME: USSR

Examines how the Russian worker spends his increasing leisure time and how this affects the nature of Soviet society. Pictures common diversions such as concerts, the circus, amusement parks, and sports.

1968; 12 min; 16 mm; color; JR, HS, A; Post World War II.

IFF

LEISURE 2000

Dr. Robert Lee discusses the probable emergence of more leisure time in our future and the demands it will make upon us. Examines the growing trend toward sabbaticals and continuing education, and leisure's impact upon husband-wife relationships.

1972; 28 min; 16 mm; BW; HS, A; Post World War II.

PENNST

LE MANS : THE GRAND PRIZE

For the first time in modern racing history, street legal tires took on specially compounded racing tires. B. F. Goodrich radials were pitted against "The Big One"—the grueling 24 hours 1973 Grand Prix at Le Mans. The challenge was accepted by John Greenwood and his Corvette racing team. This film is a record of that event, its thrills, disappointments, and rewards.

NL; 17 min; 16 mm; NL; JR, HS, A; Post World War II.

MTPS

LENNY MOORE

Shows how Lenny Moore's speed and pass-receiving ability made him a football great. Follows his career from his days at Penn State University through the years with the Baltimore Colts and Johnny Unitas. Features Lenny talking about film footage of some of his games.

NL; 20 min; 16 mm; color; JR, HS, A; Post World War II.

COUNFI; USC

LENNY MOORE

His spectacular style and movement was like a symphony on a football field, but his instant fame in 1962 tarnished his desire and concentration. This is a story of tragedy and failure, and finally triumphant comeback of such magnitude that Moore was awarded Comeback Player of the Year and voted MVP in the NFL for 1964.

1985; 8 min; VHS, U-Matic; color; JR, HS, A; Post World War II.

NFL; TMA

LE PILIER DE LA SOLITUDE

A man scales a vertical, overhanging rock face 2600 feet high, in the aiguille de Chamonix. He spent six days and six nights clinging to that rock face, short of both food and drink. Nevertheless, he triumphs, thanks to his willpower and courage. Not new, but fine entertainment. A French language film.

NL; 21 min; 16 mm; NL; JR, HS, A; Post World War II.
FACSEA

LES NEIGHES DE GRENOBLE

This film is a panorama of the Winter Olympics at Grenoble in February, 1968, with an appearance by Jean-Claude Killy.
NL; 20 min; 16 mm; color; JR, HS, A; Post World War II.
FACSEA

LES NEIGHES DU CANTAL

Skiing in the Cantal region of France, which has remained very much as it was years ago. Beautiful photography of the environment and the people who live there year round. Skiing is second nature to these people, and a ski resort was built there which is in perfect harmony with the environment.
1974; 15 min; 16 mm; color; JR, HS, A; Post World War II.
FACSEA

LET ME LIVE IN YOUR WORLD

Strong family love and indomitable spirit not only help Ted Vollrath overcome the handicap of amputated legs, but carry him through a black belt in martial arts and the development of martial arts for the handicapped to pass on his unique training to others. His home life and his combat skills are both inspirational and fascinating.
1976; 25 min; 16 mm; color; JR, HS, A; Post World War II.
BUDGET

LIFECLIMB

Inspiring portrait of 65-year-old Stan Zundell. Confronted at age 58 with personal, medical, and career crises, he renewed himself physically, emotionally, and spiritually by taking up mountain climbing.
1977; 23 min; 16 mm; color; HS, A; Post World War II.
PYRAMID; UCB

LIFE IN THE QUICK LANE

An action-packed, colorful presentation about drag racing — once just a hobby, now a multimillion dollar business in which races are won and lost in the blink of an eye.
NL; 23 min; 16 mm, VHS, U-Matic; color; JR, HS, A; Post World War II.
MTPS; SEARS

LION HUNTERS

Ethnographic classic shows men of Niger who hunt lion with bow and arrow. Explains why hunters are a group apart from their kinsmen, and captures elaborate ceremonial preparations and intricacies of brewing poison for arrows. Follows action through to the kill.
1970; 68 min; 16 mm; color; JR, HS, A; Post World War II.
UCB

LIPIZZANER

The history of the Spanish Riding School in Vienna, and the training of the famous Lipizzan horses. German sound.
NL; 50 min; 16 mm; NL; JR, HS, A; Post World War II.
AUSINS

LISTEN TO THE MOUNTAINS

On a winter ski-mountaineering expedition in the high Sierras, five men and women seek a new awareness of their place within the rhythms of nature. In this vast world of snow and sky they gain a serenity which, once absorbed, "returns with us as energy, ready to apply to our daily lives."
NL; 22 min; 16 mm; color; JR, HS, A.
PYRAMID

LIVING WITH LEISURE

What leisure is, and what should be done with it, is a subject about which not everyone is in agreement. For one person it is the chance to travel; for another, leisure may come as a nuisance. The age of leisure has arrived, and it is time, according to a sociology professor in the film, to recognize the fact and make leisure a more significant part of life.
1972; 13 min; 16 mm; NL; HS, A; Post World War II.
NFBC

LOMBARDI

This is an indepth profile of Lombardi's career from his early days at Fordham to his retirement at Green Bay. Friends, members of his family, and several of his Packers provide a rare insight into Lombardi—the man who symbolized excellence throughout his life.
NL; 51 min; 16 mm, VHS, U-Matic; color; JR, HS, A; Depression Era to Post World War II.
NFL; TMA

LOMBARDI: COMMITMENT TO EXCELLENCE

A biographical documentary on Vince Lombardi, coach of the Green Bay Packers, and his dedication to football. Interspersed with scenes of football teams in action are Lombardi's comments about his life, his profession as a coach, his beliefs, and his philosophies.

1972; 26 min; 16 mm; color; JR, HS, A; Post World War II.

BBP; UILL

LONELINESS OF THE LONG-DISTANCE RUNNER, THE

The story of a young delinquent whose rehabilitation at a borstal (reformatory) consists of training to win a cross-country race. The film is a highly unconventional interpretation of the "sports builds men" cliché, since the youth halts before the finish line, well ahead of his opponents, and deliberately refuses to win. The film exposes many of the psychological ramifications of sports, particularly the vicarious experiences of the spectators.

1962; 103 min; 16 mm; BW; JR, HS, A; Post World War II.

TWYMAN

LOU GEHRIG'S GREATEST DAY

July 4, 1939, Yankee Stadium, a day of appreciation for one of America's great baseball champions who faces an incurable illness.

1955; 27 min; 16 mm; BW; JR, HS, A; Depression Era.

CBS; KENTSU; MGHT; UTEX

LOUIS vs. SCHMELING (1936)

On June 19, 1936, the great international heavyweight boxing contest was held in Yankee Stadium, New York.

1936; 32 min; VHS; BW; JR, HS, A; Depression Era.

BHAWK

LOVE TO KILL

Presents cultural attitudes toward killing, hunting, the value of life, killing as an instinctual heritage, and survival of the fittest in nature. Follows six boys at summer camp, who, after visiting a commercial buffalo preserve, are shocked at what they have seen and decide to take action into their own hands. Shows the boys as they themselves become the victims of society's violence in attempting to save the buffalo. Excerpted from the feature film *Bless the Beasts and the Children.*

NL; 12 min; 16 mm; color; JR, HS, A; Post World War II.

LCOA; UU

LUNKER LORE

How to catch more fish with an outboard motor. A new method of fishing that gets results when others fail is explained by expert angler Buck Perry. Patterned motor trolling locates the lunkers. Casting with bottom-bumping lures puts fish on the stringer.

NL; 22 min; 16 mm; NL; JR, HS, A; Post World War II.

SOLANA

LURE OF LABRADOR

Fishing for the "square tail" or brook trout in the unexplored land that is Labrador. Experts say that the world record brook trout will some day be caught in these waters. Other species shown in this film are the splake, quananiche, lake trout, and the great northern pike.

NL; 28 min; 16 mm; NL; JR, HS, A; Post World War II.

PICAD

LURE OF MONT BLANC, THE

Impressive documentary about the climbing of Mont Blanc (the highest peak in the Alps) by a French and German roped party aiding each other in difficulties.

1964; 2 min; 16 mm; NL; JR, HS, A; Post World War II.

MTPS

MAGIC OF THE BICYCLE, THE

Tracing the development of the bicycle from the time of the high wheelers to the present, the film uses animated sequences to show the old-time bicycle and the great popularity of the sport in the Gay Nineties. The modern rebirth of cycling is dramatically shown with scenes of present-day groups bicycling over recently built cycle paths and demonstrating the various kinds of modern bicycle equipment available today.

NL; 27 min; 16 mm; NL; JR, HS, A; Modern to Post World War II.

ASF

MAGIC ROLLING BOARD, THE

The mystique, joys, and skills of skateboarding come under scrutiny in this study of America's fastest-growing sport. How to fly at ground level is demonstrated by a mix of champions and "kids around the block." Featured are those who are serious racers out to beat a record, those who simply skate for fun and recreation, and those whose free-styling lifts it to an art form.

1976; 14 min; 16 mm; color; E, JR, HS, A; Post World War II.

PYRAMID; UILL

MAGIC WAY OF GOING: THE THOROUGHBRED

The horse has been associated with humans since before recorded history; a partner, a worker, a challenge. One spectacular branch of the horse family is the thoroughbred. Here is a film which examines the thoroughbred in every aspect: biological, historic, social, its breeding and nurturing, and the central role it performs in today's ever-growing world of horse racing. Crammed with fascinating scientific information, the film also contains footage of great visual beauty and excitement, as well as the breathtaking drama of such events as a multiple racetrack collision, the auctioning of one of the highest paid yearlings ever, and the birth and first moments of a thoroughbred foal. In breeding, the search is stamina, speed, the will to win. Today breeders rely on a complex system of genetics and scientific evaluation as well as traditional good luck. The goal is to produce a great new champion.

1981; 50 min; 16 mm; color; JR, HS, A; Post World War II.

UNL; WOMBAT

MAGNIFICENT MATADOR, THE

The color and pageantry of the bullring is interwoven with the story of a famous matador who suddenly deserts the arena. His reason: he is convinced that his 18-year-old son will be killed if he enters the bullring. Mexican villages, cities, and ranches provide colorful backgrounds.

1955; 94 min; 16 mm; color; JR, HS, A; Post World War II.

BUDGET

MAKING IT HAPPEN

Focuses on whether or not winning is a "feminine" attribute. Explores the lives of three sportswomen. Highlights women's major contributions to sports history.

NL; 17 min; U-Matic; color; JR, HS, A; Post World War II.

NFBC

MAN AND HIS SPORT, A: SPORTS MEDICINE

Shows how training methods of sports medicine specialists are used to improve performances of ath-

letes. Examines weight and interval training, strength and stamina testing, lung capacity, heart rate, psychological factors, and diagnosis and treatment of serious injuries. Describes the sport clinics of Australia that are being opened to aid athletes in assessing and developing their potentialities.

1970; 29 min; 16 mm; color; HS, A; Post World War II.

AUIS; UILL

MAN BEHIND THE WHEEL

Are racing machines going too fast? Does the man stay in control of the machine, or does the machine control the man? The contest between man and his machine is followed in stock car racing at Charlotte, N. C., at the drag racing scene in the Spring Nationals, and in championship racing at Indianapolis.

NL; 30 min; 16 mm; color; JR, HS, A; Post World War II.

BUDGET

MAN NAMED LOMBARDI

Narrated by George C. Scott and featuring clips from Lombardi's most memorable games with the Packers, this program presents a touching look at a true spiritual leader. Candid interviews with Hornung, Starr, Thurston, Jurgenson, and others give the insider's view of the man and his methods.

NL; 55 min; VHS; color; JR, HS, A; Post World War II.

FOTH

MAN OF KINTAIL

Tells how Robert Tate McKenzie improved the field of physical education through his interest in physical education and sculpturing. Depicts his constant struggle to place athletics on par with academic subject matter.

1968; 28 min; 16 mm; BW; JR, HS, A; Post World War II.

IFB; UWISC

MAN WHO SKIED ANTARCTICA

Follows Yulchiro Miura (the man who skied down Mt. Everest) as he seeks challenge and self-discovery on an icy Antarctic peak, where he encounters a storm, crevasses, and even an avalanche.

1979; 18 min; 16 mm; color; JR, HS, A; Post World War II.

CF; UCB

MARATHON, THE

Presents a television special from the CTV program "Olympiad," which highlights dramatic moments in the history of the Olympic marathon competitions. Includes newsreel footage from 1908 to 1976.

1976; 50 min; 16 mm; color; JR, HS, A; Modern to Post World War II.

CTV

MARATHON WOMEN

A documentary portrait that captures the spirit of an unusual athlete and her experience at a record-breaking 26.2 mile New York marathon.

NL; 28 min; 16 mm; color; JR, HS, A; Post World War II.

FLMLIB

MASSACHUSETTS, SALT WATER STATE

The Massachusetts coastline stretches over two thousand miles. It provides a variety of salt-water fishing that is an old salt's dream and novice's delight. This film captures the beauty of the Massachusetts waters and the spirit of her water worshipers. Curt Gowdy provides the narration for this film.

NL; 14 min; 16 mm; NL; JR, HS, A; Post World War II.

ASF

MASTER OF THE WIND

Three gliding champions (George Moffet, Wally Scott, and Gled Deujinsky) compete in the 36th National Speed Triangle in Texas in their special sailplanes. This is the longest speed test in history, and the three experts glide from Moffet to Macabee to Van horn and back to Moffet. Sailplaning at its very best.

1973; 11 min; 16 mm; color; JR, HS, A; Post World War II.

BUDGET

MASTERS GOLF SERIES, THE

1974 Masters. Gary Player repeats his 1961 triumph.

1973 Masters. Tommy Aaron is the surprise winner.

1972 Masters. Jack Nickaus, "The Golden Bear," conquers the Augusta course.

1971 Masters. Charles Coody wins the Masters Crown.

1970 Masters. Billy Casper beats Gene Littler in a playoff.

1969 Masters. George Archer takes the title.

1968 Masters. Bob Goalby triumphs over Roberto de Vicenzo.

1967 Masters. Gay Brewer edges out Bobby Nichols.

1966 Masters. Jack Nicklaus takes third Masters crown in four years.

1966-1974; 45 min each; 16 mm; NL; JR, HS, A; Post World War II.

MTPS

MASTERS GOLF TOURNAMENT

This film takes the viewer through the live action highlights of the Masters Golf Tournament held each year at the Augusta National Golf Club, Augusta, Georgia.

NL; 42 min; 16 mm; NL; JR, HS, A; Post World War II.

TEXACO

MATADOR

A poetic and authentic look at the bullfighter and his bull, the importance of bullfighting in Spanish society, and the human side of the matador. The program culminates at a bullfight at the Feria de Abril in Seville.

NL; 50 min; VHS, U-Matic, Beta; color; JR, HS, A; Post World War II.

FOTH

MATTERHORN

This is a centennial celebration of the first successful ascent of the Matterhorn, which took place on July 14, 1865.

NL; 38 min; 16 mm; NL; JR, HS, A; Making of Modern Sport to Post World War II.

SNTO; TRIBUNE

MEDIEVAL MANOR

Presents the concept of community life during the era of feudalism, emphasizing the dependence of the serfs and freemen upon the lord of the manor. Shows the people working the land and producing tools of war. Explains the place of the church in the life of the people, depicts preparation for the wedding of the lord's son, and describes sporting events, foods served, and some of the customs of the day.

1956; 21 min; 16 mm; color; JR, HS, A; Medieval.

EBEC; UMOC

MEDITATIONS OF HUNTING

The film is based on a book of the same name written by Spain's foremost twentieth-century philosopher, Jose Ortega Gasset. It is an analysis of the hunter who has inherited the urge to hunt from his ancestors. The sports hunter is synonymous with fair play, and the dedicated hunter always lives by a code of ethics.

NL; 28 min; 16 mm; color; JR, HS, A; Post World War II.

USD

MENDOZA DRESSES IN WHITE

About skiing and the winter activities in the beautiful province of Mendoza. Mendoza has as its west border the Andes, which provide great skiing.

NL; 14 min; 16 mm; NL; JR, HS, A; Post World War II.

EMBARGO

MEN OF THE TALL SHIPS

Made during the 1976 United States Bicentennial, this documentary celebrates the adventure and cooperative competition on board the world's big square-rigged sailing vessels—the tall ships.

1980; 56 min; 16 mm, VHS; color; JR, HS, A; Post World War II.

DIRECT

MICKEY MANTLE

Presents Mickey Mantle talking about his boyhood in Oklahoma and how he signed a contract with the Yankees right out of high school, and reviews film footage of many of the great moments in his playing days.

NL; 20 min; 16 mm; color; JR, HS, A; Post World War II.

COUNFI; USC

MICKEY WRIGHT: LONG GAME

NL; NL; 16 mm; NL; JR, HS, A; Post World War II.

LPGA

MIDGET MUSCLEMEN

The meanest maulers on the mat! Otto Bollman and Cowboy Bradley really draw crowds. As the narration puts it, "They don't have far to fall."

NL; 10 min; 16 mm; NL; JR, HS, A; Post World War II.

BUDGET

MIGHTY MOOSE AND THE QUARTERBACK KID

Benny Singleton, 12-year-old quarterback of the Jets, a Little League football team, plays the game only to placate his father, who is a football enthusiast and sponsor of the Jets. Benny would prefer to pursue his hobby of photography. "Mighty Moose" Novak, an injured professional football player (played by Alex Karas, former star with the Detroit Lions) agrees to be substitute coach for the Jets, and since his emphasis is on playing the game for fun rather than to win at any cost, the team begins to enjoy the sport more. "Mighty Moose" quickly discovers that Benny has no real aptitude for football, and through a series of humorous ploys, the coach brings father and son closer together. Benny begins to understand his father's dreams, and Mr. Singleton understands his son's aspirations.

1972; 32 min; 16 mm; color; JR, HS, A; Post World War II.

UILL

MILLER HIGH LIFE OPEN

Three films cover 1957, 1958, and 1959.

1957-59; NL; 16 mm; NL; JR, HS, A; Post World War II.

MILLER

MIND AND BODY: JUDO WORLDWIDE

Depicts the development of the international sport of judo from a cultural point of view. The film offers an introduction to the history and cultural tradition behind judo, explains the fundamental techniques employed in the sport, and presents judo as a medium for the spread of Japanese culture.

1978; 20 min; 16 mm; color; JR, HS, A; Ancient Sport to Post World War II.

FLSU

MINI-MARATHON

Women are running their way to a new sense of purpose and potency—and they are starting at all ages. This rousing account of some enthusiastic participants in New York's Mini-Marathon is not just for women and runners.

NL; 24 min; 16 mm, VHS; color; JR, HS, A; Post World War II.

WOMBAT

MINNESOTA VIKING HIGHLIGHTS

Pick your year, 1962 through 1971; ten individual films capsulizing each Viking season. (1962 and 1963 highlight films are in black and white.)

NL; 28 min; 16 mm; color, BW; JR, HS, A; Post World War II.

HAMMS

MINT 400, THE

CBs announce the arrival of the racers who have come to Las Vegas, Nevada, to take on the challenge of the desert in the richest off-road race in America: the Mint 400. Shown is all the excitement of the event from start to finish—the planning and preparation, support crews, the exotic racing machines, and finally the race itself.

NL; 19 min; 16 mm; NL; JR, HS, A; Post World War II.

MTPS

MIRACLES IN SPORT

A treasury of athletic moments—games, plays, events, and heroes.

NL; 30 min; VHS; NL; JR, HS, A; Depression Era to Post World War II.

KAROL

MISTROVSTVI SVETA V KRASOBRUSLENI

World championship in figure skating.

1962; NL; 16 mm; NL; JR, HS, A; Post World War II.

CZECHEM

MITSUBISHI BEATS THE BAJA 1000

Baja, California, has long been known for its torturous terrain, grueling heat, and terrible toll on man and machine. This is the story of how John Baker, Team Mitsubishi, and his Class 7 2WD mini-pickup conquered Baja in 1983 to bring home off-road racing's most coveted win.

1983; 12 min; 16 mm, VHS; JR, HS, A; Post World War II.

MTPS

MODERN AFRICA: SPORTS AND ENTERTAINMENT

Explains important cultural aspects of Africa's history and society in terms of organized sports and professional entertainment. Shows how colonists introduced soccer, the Peace Corps introduced basketball, and indigenous sports of boxing and wrestling have become Westernized. Like sports, African entertainment is seen as a blend of tradition and innovation. Musical pieces by Miriam Makeba and the City Five Singers clearly show how much American music has been affected by African music and vice versa. We see that wandering minstrel shows still exist alongside more sophisticated dramatic productions (ABC Documentary On Africa Series).

1967; 14 min; 16 mm; color; JR, HS, A; Post World War II.

ABCS; MGHT; UCONN

MOEBIUS FLIP, THE

Presents a science-fiction fantasy based on the riddle of the Moebius strip, using some of America's finest skiers as its actors. While the group is skiing in the mountains, the world's polarity is suddenly reversed, causing the skiers to find themselves on the opposite side of "normal" perception. Only by performing a Moebius flip can they return to the world they know. Graceful acrobatic figures twist and somersault in slow-motion efforts to "flip" back to reality.

Multiple images and vibrant color solarizations are used, along with an original musical score.

1969; 29 min; 16 mm; color; JR, HS, A; Post World War II.

PYRAMID; UILL

MOMENTS OF THE RUNNER

Examines the popularity of running in the United States and traces the roots of long-distance running from ancient Greece. Shows America's most popular road races.

1979; 28 min; 16 mm; color; JR, HS, A; Ancient to Post World War II.

DARRAH.

MONICA GOERMANN, GYMNAST

Monica Goermann is a young Winnipeg gymnast on her way to becoming an international celebrity. Under the watchful supervision of her mother, who is her coach, Monica trains daily, executing difficult moves. In this film she is shown preparing for the 1978 Commonwealth Games at Edmonton, where she tied for the Silver Medal.

1980; 28 min; 16 mm, VHS; NL; JR, HS, A; Post World War II.

NFBC

MONTREAL OLYMPIAD

In 80 minutes of compelling action selected from over 200 hours of ABC television coverage, *Montreal Olympiad* captures the drama and excitement of the twenty-first Olympic Games, focusing on the physical virtuosity of its individual performers. Part I of *Montreal Olympiad* emphasizes boxing, track and field, and women's swimming (with a comparison of East Germany's Kornelia Enders and America's Shirley Babashoff) and contains an engaging portrait of Rumania's young gymnast Nadia Comaneci. Part II covers basketball, men's swimming, Bruce Jenner's winning decathlon performances, an examination of the competition between Nadia Comaneci and Olga Korbut, and a glimpse into the life of Vasily Alexiev, the Russian weightlifting gold medalist. Each of the two segments contains highlights of many other Olympic contests, interwoven with the in-depth coverage and profiles of some of the better-known competitors.

1977; 80 min; 16 mm; color; JR, HS, A; Post World War II.

BUDGET

MONTREAL 1976, PART I: BEST OF THE BEST

With flags of 100 nations waving in salute, some 7,000 Olympians enter the field for the opening ceremony. Features track and field, including coverage of Lasse Viren, Dwight Stones, Dave Roberts, and the race between Frank Shorter and Waldemar Cierpinksi for the marathon's gold. Also features the stunning display of accuracy and consistency as the United States archery and shooting teams set Olympic and world records.

NL; 28 min; 16 mm; color; JR, HS, A; Post World War II.

USOC

MONTREAL 1976, PART II: THE SWIFT, THE STRONG, THE BEAUTIFUL

Features highlights of the combat sports with Leo Randolph, John-John Davis, Sugar Ray Leonard, and the Spinks brothers winning gold medals in boxing events; the United States swim team, led by Shirley Babashoff, John Naber, Bruce Furniss, and Jim Montgomery, shattering records and setting a gold-winning pace; and coverage of gymnastic events, including Nadia Comaneci, Nelli Kim, Olga Korbut, Shun Fujimoto, and America's Peter Kormann.

NL; 28 min; 16 mm; color; JR, HS, A; Post World War II.

USOC

MONTREAL 1976, PART III: HIGHER, FASTER, STRONGER

With the Olympic motto as its title, this fast-paced film features boating, weightlifting, cycling, basketball, equestrian competition, and Bruce Jenner's record-breaking decathlon win. Also highlighted are the closing ceremonies.

NL; 28 min; 16 mm; color; JR, HS, A; Post World War II.

USOC

MONTEREY HISTORIC, THE

A most unusual auto race, the Monterey Historic features some of the classic racing cars of yesteryear in competition once again. These rare machines are driven by racing luminaries including some of their original drivers. A gathering of priceless vintage autos competing for new honors in a delightful viewing experience.

NL; 28 min; 16 mm; color; JR, HS, A; Post World War II.

MTPS

MOODS ON SURFING, THE (SURFERS LIVE THE LIFE THEY LOVE)

Filmed at several beaches in California and Hawaii, this film is an impressionistic description of ocean surfing. The camera records different surfing situations, waves of every size and intensity, a comedy sequence revolving around the freeway-like jams at a crowded shoreline, and concludes with a performance by well-known surfer David Nuuhiwa. Musical background takes the place of narration.

1968; 16 min; 16 mm; color; JR, HS, A; Post World War II.

PYRAMID; UILL

MOST UNDERRATED PLAYERS

A collection of unsung heroes who play in the shadow of others, yet consistently demonstrate the kind of effort that has earned them respect of their teammates and opponents. Appreciate the skills of Green Bay tight end Paul Coffman, St. Louis receiver Pat Tilly, New England running back Mosi Tatupu, and San Francisco defensive end Dwaine Board.

1985; 7 min; VHS, U-Matic; color; JR, HS, A; Post World War II.

NFL; TMA

MOTO BRAVE

Filmed simultaneously with four cameras, this film shows the first motorcycle Tour de France in 1973 and the audiovisual impressions derived from this race. A French language film.

1973; 11 min; 16 mm; color; JR, HS, A; Post World War II.

FACSEA

MOUNT MCKINLEY HANG GLIDE

This film illustrates dramatically the significance of setting high goals, the importance of planning and training to achieve goals, and the personal characteristics that contribute to success in any undertaking. It tells the true story of four Americans who set out to fly hang gliders from the top of Alaska's Mount McKinley. At 20,320 feet, Mount McKinley is the tallest peak in North America and presents one of the sheerest vertical faces of any mountain in the world.

1978; 19 min; 16 mm; color; JR, HS, A; Post World War II.

BUDGET

MOUNTAIN DOES IT FOR ME, THE

Telling the story of teaching youngsters with cerebral palsy to ski, the film looks at both the skiing and the special training and educational approach in the hospital. One of the skiers in the movie describes how he feels about skiing: "It's kind of like a dream because movement, like walking, doesn't come easily for me. But in skiing, I don't have to fight it, the mountain does it for me."

NL; 12 min; 16 mm; VHS, U-Matic, Beta; color; HS, A: Post World War II.
CRYSP

MOUNTAIN SILENCE

Shows hearing-impaired young people participating in many outdoor summer and winter activities at Mountain Silence, a camp school for the deaf in the Rocky Mountains. Here, the children gain the confidence they need to become successful adults and find that the mountains themselves are great teachers of self-reliance. Skiing, rafting, horseback riding, dance, mime, crafts, backpacking, and mountain climbing are among the many activities available at the camp school, where reinforcement of sign language is also emphasized.
NL; 18 min; 16 mm, VHS, U-Matic, Beta; color; HS, A; Post World War II.
CRYSP

MOVEMENT: TO LIVE IS TO MOVE

This film explores the possibility of movement as a way of developing a total, unified feeling of self. Edith Shrank, an early childhood teacher, explains how children experience "total movement," completely involving themselves in any one physical activity. Footage of various physical activities shows how unity of the physical and mental aspects of ourselves can again be achieved. Scenes of children at play, modern dancers, physical education classes, and aikido fighters show young people developing an awareness of their own and others' bodies moving through space.
NL; 26 min; 16 mm; color; HS, A; Post World War II.
CNEMAG

MOVEMENT EXPLORATION: WHAT AM I?

Records the movements of birds, animals, machines, and water and shows children as they imitate some of these movements. Includes sea gulls, pigeons, penguins, porpoises, monkeys, a merry-go-round, an oil pump and derrick, a tractor, trees, and waves. Suggests that birds, animals, and the elements have restricted movements, while man has the capacity to imitate them all.
1968; 11 min; 16 mm; color; JR, HS, A; Post World War II.
IU; PHENIX

MR. MOTO vs HENRY HANK

Mr. Moto, judo and karate expert, matches brawn with Las Vegas favorite Henry Hank in a knockdown brawl of a wrestling match and defeats not only Henry Hank, but manages to become involved in a physical bout with the announcer and referee Joe Wood. The crowd boos as the overbloated Mr. Moto takes his ceremonial bows.
NL; 10 min; 16 mm; NL; JR, HS, A; Post World War II.
BUDGET

MR. ROSSI GOES CAMPING

Searching for a peaceful campsite leads Mr. Rossi into a series of wildly improbable adventures with cows, dirt bikes, and bulldozers. A comedy posing deeper questions about the damage we do to our environment, *Mr. Rossi Goes Camping* is a mischievous romp in the great outdoors.
NL; 11 min; 16 mm, VHS; color; JR, HS, A; Post World War II.
DIST16

MUCH ADO ABOUT GOLF

When W. C. Fields is selected to drive the first ball dedicating the new golf course, he asks his caddy for the special driver he got in Toronto—his Canadian Club! His caddy hands him a bottle. From then on it's a 4-way conflict between Fields, caddy, ball, and club.
NL; 9 min; 16 mm; BW; JR, HS, A; Depression, Post World War II.
OSU

MUHAMMAD ALI: SKILL, BRAINS, AND GUTS!

In this sometimes funny, consistently entertaining, and slick biography of Ali, we see that Ali's brassiness, verbal prowess, and talent were evident from his first big win—the Olympic gold medal at age 18. Through the fight sequence, the taunting of his opponents before a match, and his loss and recapture of his boxing license, he shows himself to be quick and strong in the ring and full of chutzpa outside the ring.
1975; 90 min; 16 mm; color; JR, HS, A; Post World War II.
MACMIL

MUNICH '72: PART I

Features the opening ceremony, equestrian events, modern pentathlon, shooting, fencing, wrestling, and track and field.
NL; 15 min; 16 mm; color; JR, HS, A; Post World War II.
USOC

MUNICH '72: PART II

Scenes of opening ceremony, plus the cycling road race, team handball, women's gymnastics, judo, soccer, boxing, and the final minutes of the controversial USA-USSR men's basketball game.

NL; 15 min; 16 mm; color; JR, HS, A; Post World War II.

USOC

MUNICH '72: PART III

Features aquatic sports, including scenes of Mark Spitz, Melissa Belote, Sandra Neilson, Mike Burton, and others.

NL; 15 min; 16 mm; color; JR, HS, A; Post World War II.

USOC

MUSCLE

A social worker by profession, Pat Ferris spends much of her free time in a gym. She is a dedicated body builder. The film shows her fine-tuning her body for, and competing at, the Manitoba Women's Provincial Body Building Championship.

1983; 11 min; 16 mm; NL; HS, A; Post World War II.

NFBC

MVP, 1981: KENNY ANDERSON AND JOE MONTANA

In 1981, two distinguished themselves to become co-MVPs, Cincinnati's Kenny Anderson and San Francisco's Joe Montana, quarterbacks who led their respective teams to their greatest seasons ever and who ultimately met to decide the world championship. This program depicts the two superstars in their finest moments.

1981; 24 min; 16 mm, VHS, U-Matic; color; JR, HS, A; Post World War II.

NFL; TMA

MVP, 1982: JOHN RIGGINS

The unstoppable Riggins propelled Washington to the championship. His exceptional achievements during the 1982 season are highlighted.

1982; 24 min; 16 mm, VHS, U-Matic; color; JR, HS, A; Post World War II.

NFL; TMA

MVP, 1983: MARCUS ALLEN

Allen capped an outstanding year with a 74-yard cut-back run in the Super Bowl that has become legend. Relive his outstanding year in this exciting highlight show.

1983; 24 min; 16 mm, VHS, U-Matic; color; JR, HS, A; Post World War II.

NFL; TMA

MVP, 1984: DAN MARINO

Marino spent the season picking apart the defenses of other teams, then rewrote NFL history to become the youngest player to ever lead the Dolphins to the Super Bowl.

1984; 24 min; 16 mm, VHS, U-Matic; color; JR, HS, A; Post World War II.

NFL; TMA

MY KINGDOM FOR A HORSE

Traces, through drawings and dramatizations, the history of horse racing in Britain, from its humble beginnings in the fields to the pomp and circumstance of Royal Ascot and the big business of today's offtrack betting. Anecdotes, complete with colorful language, illustrated how seriously this nation of horse lovers has always taken the Sport of Kings.

1977; 28 min; 16 mm; color; JR, HS, A; Renaissance to Post World War II.

UILL

MY LAST CHANCE IN LIFE

In this CBS News segment, Maury Wills tells interviewer Robert Lipsyte about his rehabilitation from cocaine addiction. A record-setting base-stealer for the Los Angeles Dodgers (104 in 1962), Wills tells of his long struggle to become a manager of a major league baseball club.

1985; 11 min; VHS, U-Matic, Beta; color; HS, A; Post World War II.

LAWREN

MY NAME IS TED WILLIAMS

Outstanding athlete, sportsman, and Marine veteran, Ted Williams tells the story of his life and his philosophy in this documentary narrated by Tom Harmon.

NL; 28 min; 16 mm; NL; JR, HS, A; Depression Era to Post World War II.

ASF

MY OWN YARD TO PLAY IN

Photographed on the streets of New York, this film shows the very special world children create at play. The sound track is actual sounds of children talking, singing, and playing.

1959; 6 min; 16 mm; BW; A; Post World War II.

COLU

MYSTERIOUS WHITE LAND

Skiing on the Tasman Glacier at Mt. Cook and Coronet Peak, Queenstown, with Japanese professional skiers.

NL; 24 min; 16 mm; NL; JR, HS, A; Post World War II.

NZGTO

MY TOWN

A baseball game between two rival teams from Matsumoto, on the island of Honshu, is the vehicle for introducing us to the neighborhoods and various members of the community as the children prepare for the big game.

NL; 25 min; VHS; color; JR, HS, A; Post World War II.

AS

NAME OF THE GAME IS . . . BASEBALL, THE

Little Leaguers and big leaguers—all winning players—base their achievements on physical fitness. Young players learn the fundamentals of baseball from big league stars. Narrated by Curt Gowdy.

NL; 29 min; 16 mm; NL; E, JR, HS, A; Post World War II.

MTPS

NAME OF THE GAME IS . . . BASKETBALL, THE

In slow-motion, Oscar Robertson, John Havlicek, Wes Unseld, Elvin Hayes—and 11 more great stars of the NBA—demonstrate the techniques that brought them stardom. Includes fitness tips.

NL; 28 min; 16 mm; NL; JR, HS, A; Post World War II.

MTPS

NATIONAL FOOTBALL LEAGUE CHAMPIONSHIP GAMES

Detroit vs. Cleveland - 1957
New York vs. Chicago Bears - 1956
Los Angeles vs. Cleveland - 1955
Detroit vs. Cleveland - 1954
Detroit vs. Cleveland - 1953
Detroit vs. Cleveland - 1952

NL; NL; 16 mm; NL; JR, HS, A; Post World War II.

MILLER

NATIONAL PARKS: PLAYGROUND OR PARADISE, PARTS 1 AND 2

Poses the question: Can we both use and preserve our national parks? Visits to Yellowstone, Yosemite, and the Grand Canyon point out the dilemma. Shows how Alaska has set aside land as a wilderness reserve, while urban parks are emerging as a new park frontier.

1980; 58 min; 16 mm; color; JR, HS, A; Post World War II.

PENNST

NCAA BASKETBALL HIGHLIGHTS: 1979

Exciting highlights are shown of the 1979 NCAA basketball tournament. Included are the semifinals with Michigan State (led by Magic Johnson and Greg Kelser) defeating Pennsylvania and Indiana State (with Player of the Year Larry Bird) edging by DePaul 76-74. The finals set Michigan State Spartans against Indiana State with the Spartans winning their first NCAA title.

1980; 20 min; 16 mm; color; JR, HS, A; Post World War II.

NCAA; OSU

NEGRO IN SPORTS, THE

Jesse Owens, winner of five Olympic titles in track, takes the viewer on a brief look at many black athletes in the world of sports. Jackie Robinson and Joe Louis are seen, and for the grand finale, the amazing Harlem Globetrotters go into action!

NL; 10 min; 16 mm; NL; JR, HS, A; Depression to Post World War II.

BUDGET

NELLIE KIM

The story of the Korean gymnast and her participation in the 1976 Montreal Olympics, where she won two gold medals for the USSR team.

NL; 29 min; 16 mm; color; JR, HS, A; Post World War II.

NFBC

NEW AGENDA SUMMARY, THE

This film highlights the activities of the historic three-day national conference on the status of women in sports in America. The film contains important moments from speeches delivered by Billie Jean King, Donna de Varona, Carol Mann, Diana Nyad, and Sally Ride. It discusses many of the resolutions passed by the conference delegates. The six primary issues of discussion and those resolutions which were adopted from the issues include physiological concerns of women in sport, promotion and public acceptance of women in sport, resources for women in sport and fitness, athleticism and sex role, socialization of women in sport, and organization and regulation of sport for women.

NL; 28 min; VHS; color; HS, A; Post World War II.

WSF

NEW ENGLAND PATRIOTS '73

Narrated by sports announcer Don Gillis. Highlights of the 1973 Patriots season. The team being revamped by first-year coach Chuck Fairbanks to fight the toughest 1974 schedule in the NFL. See Jim Plunkett match sage passer Roman Gabriel play-for-play, in the thriller with the Eagles; a heartbreaker decided by one point and the clock. See newly arrived running backs Sam Bam Cunningham and mini Mack Herron. On kick-off returns alone, Herron gained 1,092 yards, and the film portrays Cunningham as a player with skills to become the new prototype for power backs. And see new receiver Darryl Stingley as he takes an active role in the receiving corps along with Reggie Rucker, Randy Vataha, and tight end Bob Windsor.

NL; 28 min; 16 mm; NL; JR, HS, A; Post World War II.

ASF

NEW YORK GIANTS HIGHLIGHTS

Six films, covering the years 1950 through 1955. Order by year.

NL; NL; 16 mm; BW; JR, HS, A; Post World War II.

MILLER

NEW YORK YANKEE BROADCAST

Deals with the 1980 New York Yankee American League championship. Analyzes the history of the baseball broadcast.

NL; 34 min; VHS, U-Matic; color; JR, HS, A; Post World War II.

KITCHN

NFL AND YOU, THE

A fascinating inside look into the glamorous and exciting world of the NFL family, from the league office, NFL Proprieties (the promotional arm of the NFL), NFL Films (the production company of the NFL), to the 28 teams and hundreds of players that make it all happen. A must for anyone interested in all aspects of the NFL.

NL; 30 min; VHS, U-Matic; color; JR, HS, A; Post World War II.

NFL; TMA

NFL CRUNCH COURSE

Interviews with top defenders, their teammates, their coaches, and offensive players who tell what qualities an outstanding defensive player possesses.

NL; 43 min; VHS; NL; JR, HS, A; Post World War II.

KAROL

NFL '83; NFL '82; NFL '81

Separate stories of the 1983, 1982, 1981 seasons, featuring the surprise successes enjoyed by some teams and the hard times experienced by others. The playoffs and All-Pro teams are featured.

1981, 1982, 1983; 24/47 min; 16 mm, VHS, U-Matic; color; JR, HS, A; Post World War II.

NFL; TMA

NFL FILMS 1984 ALL-PRO TEAM

A look at the magical moments of the 1984-1985 season's most memorable players, covering offense, defense, and some special positions as well. An education in excellence for the avid football fan as well as the younger player. Thirty-five players representing seventeen teams.

1984; 50 min; VHS, U-Matic; color; JR, HS, A; Post World War II.

NFL; TMA

NFL FOLLIES GO HOLLYWOOD, THE

Funny and unusual footage of NFL films in the context of the silver screen.

NL; 23 min; VHS; NL; JR, HS, A; Post World War II.

KAROL

NFL HEAD COACH: A SELF-PORTRAIT

The story of NFL head coaches is told through interviews with each of the 28 then-current head coaches, including Landry, Shula, and Noll. Their intimate conversations cover a wide range of topics, from motivation to strategy to pressure and burnout. This program presents a never-before-seen glimpse of this elite fraternity.

NL; 43 min; VHS; color; HS, A; Post World War II.

FOTH

NFL HEAD COACH: A SELF-PORTRAIT

This unique production, which has no narration, allows fans to eavesdrop on head coaches as they go through trials and tribulations of coaching in the NFL. Utilizing more than 45 different live sound wirings, *Head Coach* provides informative insights —often hilarious—of the strategic geniuses of the NFL. A good opportunity to learn some of their secrets of success.

1985; 53 min; VHS, U-Matic; color; JR, HS, A; Post World War II.

NFL; TMA

NFL HIGHLIGHTS

1957-1963 (BW); 1964, 1965, 1967 (Color)

NL; 30 min each; 16 mm; both; JR, HS, A; Post World War II.
MILLER

NFL's BEST EVER COACHES, THE

There have been over 300 head coaches in NFL history, but only a select few have been worthy enough to be called "The Best Ever." This program not only examines the records of distinction set by these sideline generals, but also takes an introspective look at their contrasting personalities. Vince Lombardi's ability to motivate, Sid Gillman's offensive innovations, and Paul Brown's trend-setting techniques are featured. Also analyzed are George Halas, Don Shula, Tom Landry, and Chuck Noll. A unique wired-for-sound montage.
NL; 46 min; 16 mm, VHS, U-Matic; NL; JR, HS, A; Post World War II.
FOTH; NFL; TMA

NFL's BEST EVER QUARTERBACKS

This program is a history of the pro passing game as seen through the careers of some of the NFL's greatest quarterbacks. It is also a story about the personalities of some of the unique individuals in the annals of sport. Updated in 1985 to include Dan Marino and Joe Montana. The careers of outstanding pass masters John Unitas, Fran Tarkenton, and Roger Staubach are profiled, among others.
1985; 46 min; VHS, U-Matic; color; JR, HS, A; Post World War II.
NFL; TMA

NFL's BEST EVER RUNNERS

Who was the greatest running back of all time, and why? Find out in this program about the finest runners in football history. Updated in 1985. Viewers can analyze and compare the running styles of Walter Payton, Eric Dickerson, Jim Brown, Gale Sayers, Hugh McElhenny, O. J. Simpson, and Earl Campbell.
1985; 46 min; VHS, U-Matic; color; JR, HS, A; Post World War II.
NFL; TMA

NFL's BEST EVER TEAMS, THE

This program explores the personalities and accomplishments of seven teams spanning 30 years. Which team was the NFL's best? Was it the Packers during the sixties or the Dolphins of the seventies? Or was it the flashy Cowboys, the tough Raiders, or the balanced Steeler's squad in the 1970s? All seven teams left an indelible imprint on the history of professional football.

NL; 46 min; 16 mm; VHS, U-Matic; color; JR, HS, A; Post World War II.
NFL; TMA

NFL's GREATEST GAMES, THE

Clips and interviews from five great games.
NL; 30 min; VHS; NL; HS, A; Post World War II.
KAROL

NFL T. V. FOLLIES WITH JOHATHAN WINTERS

A station schedules 24-hour football coverage. Winters hosts football game shows and home shopping programs. Features bizarre and hilarious games.
NL; 70 min; VHS; NL; JR, HS, A; Post World War II.
KAROL

NIAMBI: SWEET MELODY

Tells the story of Niambi Robinson, a little Afro-American girl who, at the age of five, broke the world's record for her age in the 100-meter dash. Explores the values and constant nurturing of her loving family and shows Niambi at school, at ballet class, on the track, and at home.
1979; 25 min; 16 mm, VHS, U-Matic; JR, HS, A; color; Post World War II.
FI

NICHOLS AND DIMES

An insider's view of Arabian horse breeding. Film and stage producer/director Mike Nichols describes his personal and business involvement with these beautiful, spirited animals.
1981; 25 min; 16 mm, VHS; color; JR, HS, A; Post World War II.
COLU; DIRECT

NINE IN A ROW

Presents a documentary record of a college rowing team in action, showing the experiences the team encounters during the race through psychedelic visual images.
10 min; 16 mm; color; JR, HS, A; Post World War II.
CFS

1911 INDIANAPOLIS 500-MILE RACE

The first Indianapolis 500. The winner was Ray Harroun, and he drove a Marmon Wasp. His speed was 74.59 mph. No sound, but has subtitles.

NL; 10 min; 16 mm; BW; JR, HS, A; Modern Sport.
  PES

1960 BASEBALL HIGHLIGHTS
Major league and All-Star action.
  NL; 28 min; 16 mm; NL; JR, HS, A; Post World War II.
  CINES

1960 GOLF HIGHLIGHTS
Arnold Palmer and other golf greats swing into action.
  NL; 28 min; 16 mm; NL; JR, Hs, A; Post World War II.
  CINES

1960 SUMMER OLYMPICS
Covers the eighteen days of the Seventeenth Modern Olympiad, with competitors matching speed, strength, skill, and endurance in eighteen forms of athletic competition.
  1960; 7 min; 16 mm; BW; JR, HS, A; Post World War II.
  UCOLO

1962 SPORTS THRILLS
Penn Relays; 88th Kentucky Derby; pro basketball, Boston vs. Philadelphia; Milwaukee Jaycee Women's Open golf tourney; NFL championship, Green Bay vs. New York.
  NL; NL; 16 mm; NL; JR, HS, A; Post World War II.
  MILLER

1962 PRO FOOTBALL HIGHLIGHTS
Top pros in the year's great games.
  NL; 28 min; 16 mm; NL; JR, HS, A; Post World War II.
  CINES

1964 PRO FOOTBALL HIGHLIGHTS
Year's most exciting plays and players.
  NL; 28 min; 16 mm; NL; JR, HS, A; Post World War II.
  CINES

1964 WOMEN'S NATIONAL ALL-STAR GAME HIGHLIGHTS (FAST PITCH)

1965 WOMEN'S NATIONAL ALL-STAR GAME HIGHLIGHTS (FAST PITCH)

1970 WOMEN'S NATIONAL ALL-STAR GAME HIGHLIGHTS (FAST PITCH)

1974 WOMEN'S NATIONAL ALL-STAR GAME HIGHLIGHTS (FAST PITCH)
NL; NL; 16 mm; NL; JR, HS, A; Post World War II.
  ASA

1965 AAWU FOOTBALL HIGHLIGHTS
An exciting compilation of great moments on the gridiron. Sports fans will thrill to footage from such college games as USC vs. Washington and Stanford, Washington State vs. Oregon State, and many others. Besides footage of such football greats as John Reed, Mike Garret, Dale Lewis, and Glenn Meyers, the film also features scenes of the 1966 Rose Bowl and the Tournament of Roses Parade with Walt Disney as the Grand Marshall.
  NL; 32 min; 16 mm; color; JR, HS, A; Post World War II.
  BUDGET

1965 NFL HIGHLIGHTS
Exciting football action is highlighted with scenes of the Dallas Cowboys, Minnesota Vikings, and the San Francisco 49ers.
  NL; 20-30 min; 16 mm; color; JR, HS, A; Post World War II.
  BUDGET

1966 AND 1967 NFL CHAMPIONSHIP GAMES, THE
"One Big Play:" Green Bay Packers 34 - Dallas Cowboys 27—January 1, 1967. "The Chilling Championship:" Green Bay 21 - Dallas 17—December 31, 1967. These two cliff-hanger contests featured rosters which were loaded with superstars from that era, including Bart Starr, Forrest Gregg, Ray Nitschke, Don Meredith, Bob Hayes, and Bob Lilly. The 1967 game was played in 13-degree temperatures and is referred to as the "Ice Bowl." (Also championship games from 1962-66.)
  1962-67; 25 min each; 16 mm, VHS, U-Matic; Post World War II.
  NFL; TMA

1967 MEN'S NATIONAL CHAMPIONSHIP HIGHLIGHTS (FAST PITCH)

1968 MEN'S NATIONAL CHAMPIONSHIP HIGHLIGHTS (FAST PITCH)

1969 MEN'S NATIONAL CHAMPIONSHIP HIGHLIGHTS (SLOW PITCH)

1972 MEN'S NATIONAL CHAMPIONSHIP HIGHLIGHTS (SLOW PITCH)

NL; NL; 16 mm; NL; JR, HS, A; Post World War II.

ASA

1968 COLLEGE FOOTBALL REVIEW

All-Americans in action.

NL; 28 min; 16 mm; NL; JR, HS, A; Post World War II.

CINES

1969-70 COACHES ALL-AMERICAN BASKETBALL TEAM

This is a five-part film with each segment featuring a member of the 1969-70 Coaches All-American basketball team. Pete Maravich of LSU, Charlie Scott of North Carolina, Bob Lanier of St. Bonaventure, Dam Issel of Kentucky, and Rick Mount of Purdue are included.

NL; 12 min; 16 mm; NL; JR, HS, A; Post World War II.

NINEFC

1970 KODAK ALL-AMERICAN TEAM

1971 KODAK ALL-AMERICAN TEAM

1972 KODAK ALL-AMERICAN TEAM

NL; 28 min; 16 mm; NL; JR, HS, A; Post World War II.

KODAK

1971 MASTERS GOLF TOURNAMENT FILM, THE

Charles Coody, who lost the 1969 Masters when he bogied the last three holes of the tournament, begins the final day of play with a 7 under par. Jack Nicklaus, with three Masters championships behind him, is tied with Coody. Johnnie Miller begins the last round 3 under. In one of the most brilliant performances in the history of the Masters, Miller finished the 14th hole 9 under with a lead of 2 strokes over Nicklaus and Coody. But Coody refused to yield under pressure and goes on to win the 1971 Masters by 2 strokes.

NL; 40 min; 16 mm; NL; JR, HS, A; Post World War II.

WSTGLC

1972 MASTERS GOLF TOURNAMENT FILM, THE

On the first day, defending Masters champion Charles Coody electrifies the huge gallery with a hole-in-one on the 190-yard 6th, then triple-bogies the 7th. Fifty-nine-year-old Sam Snead, Arnold Palmer, and Paul Harney all have good first rounds. But it is Jack Nicklaus all the way as he becomes the only golfer to break par for the 72 holes. Despite a brilliant challenge from Jim Jamieson, Nicklaus joins Arnold Palmer as a 4-time winner of the Masters.

NL; 40 min; 16 mm; NL; JR, HS, A; Post World War II.

WSTGLC

1972 SPECIAL OLYMPICS: "WE'VE ONLY JUST BEGUN"

The spirit of courage, determination, and enthusiasm through athletic competition is captured by this film, which covers the National Summer Olympics for the mentally retarded. Vividly depicts the grace, agility, skill, and confidence of the contestants. Each event (basketball, track and field, gymnastics, swimming) produces victories and defeats. But the end result is victorious, because the Special Olympics have opened the door for thousands of mentally retarded young people to take their rightful place in society with dignity and pride. Pat Lawford, Eunice Shriver, Ethel Kennedy, and Rosey Greer are on hand to present the awards. Without narration, the film is augmented by a popular musical theme, "We've Only Just Begun," sung by the Carpenters.

1976; 16 min; 16 mm; color; JR, HS, A; Post World War II.

MEDIAG; UCLA; UILL

1973 KODAK ALL-AMERICAN FOOTBALL TEAM

Meet the official 1973 team selected by the American Football Coaches Association. Shown in exciting footage from many games are 23 outstanding players, including Heisman Trophy winner John Cappelletti of Penn State and "Lineman of the Year" John Hicks of Ohio State. Others are Notre Dame's Dave Casper; Ohio State's Randy Gradishar (the lone repeater from the 1972 team); Oklahoma's Lucius Selmon and Rod Shoate; Southern California's Booker Brown, Lynn Swann, and Richard Wood; Roosevelt (Rosey) Leaks and Bill Wyman, both of Texas; Dave Jaynes of Kansas; Nebraska's Daryl White and John Dutton; and Michigan's Dave Brown and Dave Gallagher.

NL; 28 min; 16 mm; NL; JR, HS, A; Post World War II.

KODAK

1973 MASTERS, THE

Englishman Peter Oosterhuis leads going into the fourth and final day of play, but it is Tommy Aaron—the perennial runner-up of golfdom—who cards a four-under-par 68 to win by a stroke. In one of the most exciting Masters finishes in years, Aaron beats off a brilliant but belated rally by defending champion Jack Nicklaus, who ties for third with Oosterhuis and young Jim Jamieson. J. C. Sneed finishes second in the tourney marked by unusual penalty strokes and another mismarked score card.

NL; 40 min; 16 mm; NL; JR, HS, A; Post World War II.

WSTGLC

1981 AIAW DIVISION III TRACK AND FIELD CHAMPIONSHIPS

Covers all 17 events of this meet; helpful for recruiting and financial support.

NL; 30 min; VHS; NL; HS, A; Post World War II.

GSVP

1984 COTTON BOWL (A BOUNCE OF THE BALL)

Highlights of Georgia's come-from-behind 10-9 victory over the University of Texas. It was a sweet victory for the underdog Bulldogs led by a senior class that had the best record in college football the past four years. For Texas, appearing in the Cotton Bowl for an unprecedented 18th time, the defeat perhaps cost the great Longhorn squad a shot at the national title.

1984; 16 mm; JR, HS, A; Post World War II.

MTPS

1984 LIBERTY MUTUAL LEGENDS OF GOLF

Fifty-two of the biggest names in golf pair up to compete for top honors in the Liberty Mutual Legends of Golf. The winning team of Gay Brewer and Billy Casper capture the title at the Onion Creek Country Club in Austin, Texas. Highlights of the play feature such crowd-pleasers as Sam Snead, Arnold Palmer, Julius Boros, Gene Sarazen, and Don January.

Color; JR, HS, A; Post World War II.

MTPS

1986 LIBERTY MUTUAL LEGENDS OF GOLF

Audiences join the gallery of spectators at the Onion Creek Club in Austin, Texas, for a gathering of golf's greatest champions. The sport comes alive as viewers see teammates Don January and Gene Littler win the tournament for the second consecutive year. Greats, including Palmer, Player, Snead, and Boros, compete in highlights from the NBC-TV network telecast.

1986; 27 min; 16 mm, VHS, U-Matic; NL; JR, HS, A; Post World War II.

MTPS

1987 KEEBLER INTERNATIONAL PREP TRACK AND FIELD INVITATIONAL

Each summer nearly 200 of the world's best high school athletes travel to Elmhurst, Illinois, to compete in the Keebler International Prep Track and Field Invitational. Watch the 1987 winners as they strive to break records set by previous champions Greg Foster, Carl Lewis, and Renaldo Nehemia.

1987; 50 min; VHS; NL; JR, HS, A; Post World War II.

MTPS

99 DAYS TO SURVIVAL

Astronaut Walter Schirra narrates, as his family and a group of CBS newsmen retell and redo the journey of John Wesley Powell, first to run the rapids of the Colorado and to map the region. The vivid film takes away nothing from the courage of those first men and their life-and-death struggle in scientific exploration.

1971; 50 min; 16 mm; color; JR, HS, A.

CBS; PYRAMID; UILL

NO ADULTS ALLOWED

The world of children is the subject of this short, beginning with infants crawling furiously in a baby derby or turning a cop to putty in their tiny hands. Some junior golfers prove good enough to make adult duffers grind their teeth in envy. There are also young swimmers and divers, and juvenile boxing involves some very spirited competitors, even if they aren't too steady on their feet.

NL; 10 min; 16 mm; NL; JR, HS, A; Post World War II.

FILMIC

NO MAN'S LAND

A look at what it takes to battle in the trenches— offensive line vs. defensive line. Several coaches tell about line play changes and developments. Meet players such as Dennis Harrah, guard, L.A. Rams, and Bruce Matthews, offensive tackle, Houston Oilers. Good advice from the pros.

1985; 9 min; VHS, U-Matic; color; JR, HS, A; Post World War II.

NFL; TMA

NOBLE ART, THE

Depicts the history of boxing from a largely British perspective, beginning with early bare-knuckled encounters. The entire boxing scenario, including the development of promoters and of the fight audience, is examined. To illustrate boxing's transformation from local brawling and carnival contests to an Olympic sport and professional athletic event, uses archival and live footage of bouts involving international championship matches. Explores effects of racism, poverty, morality, and crime on boxing. Contrasts professional with amateur boxing, showing how amateur boxing, particularly in combination with boys' clubs, has furnished a healthy outlet for aggressive and potentially destructive impulses.

1977; 28 min; 16 mm; color; JR, HS, A; Ancient to Post World War II.

UILL

NO LAWS TODAY

Tells the story of the chaos that ensues when a day without laws is declared. Shows the importance of laws and rules for traffic, consumer affairs, and even sports.

1982; 12 min; 16 mm, VHS, U-Matic; color; JR, HS, A; Post World War II.

GFILM; JOU

NO SIMPLE ROAD

The excitement and joy of handicapped children participating in outdoor sports and activities is reflected sensitively in this award-winning film produced by Children's Hospital. Children with muscular dystrophy, polio, cerebral palsy, spina bifida, and other physical handicaps learn to play tennis, golf, ski, and experience the pleasures of rafting, fishing, hayrides, and mountain excursions. These experiences allow youngsters to better accept their disabilities, gain self-confidence, and react positively to their able-bodied peers.

NL; 18 min; 16 mm, VHS, U-Matic, Beta; Post World War II.

CRYSP

NO TIME TO SPARE

Rip Van Winkle theme stresses the fun of bowling; includes Andy Varipapa's trick shots and pro stars Dick Hoover, Dick Weber, Bill Lillard, Joe Wilman, and Lee Jouglard.

NL; 18 min; 16 mm; NL; JR, HS, A; Post World War II.

ABC

NO WAY THEY WANT TO SLOW DOWN

This documentary takes an informal look at how the best Canadian skiers work and live. The Canadian Ski team is on a tight schedule down in Chile and Argentina. Two-and-a-half tons of equipment,

speeds of up to 140 km/h, grueling workouts, and a dramatic theft are all par for the course.

1975; 28.5 min; 16 mm; NL; JR, HS, A; Post World War II.

NFBC

NORTH COUNTRY LADY

Whether they ski or not, audiences will enjoy this fast-moving impression of skiing at one of the country's leading ski resorts. An original musical score sets the mood for New England winter at its finest. Beautiful skiing, Vermont scenery, laughs, spills, night life, and people enjoying themselves.

NL; 30 min; 16 mm; color; JR, HS, A; Post World War II.

MTPS

NORTH AMERICAN CHAMPIONSHIPS

1960 - "Winning Winds," Tawas, Michigan
1961 - "Spinakers West," Mission Bay, San Diego
1962 - "Sails, Ales and Tales," Buffalo
1963 - "Sails and Seagulls," Tawas, Michigan
1964 - "Seas and Sails," San Diego
1966 - "The Year of the Lightning 10,000"

NL; NL; 16 mm; NL; JR, HS, A; Post World War II.

ILCA

NORTHERN GAMES

A film about the traditional games of the Inuit as they are practiced 800 kilometers north of the Arctic Circle by youth in competition from communities across the North. The film describes the skills required to play them; the traditions behind the games; and the spirit of cooperation, as opposed to hard competition, that inspires the participants.

1981; 26 mm; 16mm; NL; JR, HS, A; Ancient to Post World War II.

NFBC

NOTHIN' BUT A WINNER

Presents former University of Alabama football coach Bear Bryant illustrating and explaining his techniques for motivating his players toward athletic excellence. Interviewed by behavioral scientist Dr. John Geier.

NL; 30 min; VHS, U-Matic; color; JR, HS, A; Post World War II.

SFTI

NOTHING'S STOPPING YOU

Presents an adventure guide, who is also a diabetic, teaching teenage diabetics mountain climbing skills. Diabetics used to be limited in the activities they could do. Now, thanks to a new method of monitoring their blood sugar levels—chemstrip—diabetics do not have to let the disease interfere with what they like to do best: nothing can stop them.

NL; 7 min; 16 mm, VHS, U-matic; color; JR, HS, A; Post World War II.

MTPS

NOT JUST A SPECTATOR

Depicts sports and recreational activities open to the handicapped person if proper facilities are provided.

1974; 35 min; 16 mm; color; JR, HS, A; Post World War II.

IREFL

NOT THE TRIUMPH BUT THE STRUGGLE (THE STORY OF THE AAU-SEARS NATIONAL JUNIOR OLYMPICS)

Victory is only a small part of competition, as seen in this film from the AAU-Sears National Junior Olympics at the University of Nebraska-Lincoln. Interviews with coaches, parents, and the participating athletes reveal the many other facets—from developing one's skills to teamwork, to the ultimate goal of competition, when the victory of the feat is realized. A central theme is found in the attitudes of all who are involved: it is not to win, but to take part . . . not the triumph, but the struggle.

1977; 28 min; 16 mm; color; JR, HS, A; Post World War II.

UEVA; UNL

NOW AND FUTURE CHAMPIONS

An intensive look at the running of the major harness races for 1975: the Hambletonian, the Little Brown Jug, the Kentucky Futurity, and the U.S. Pacing Championship, featuring the great horses Flirth, Melvin's Woe, Arnie Almahurst, and Sir Dalrae.

NL; 26 min; 16 mm; JR, HS, A; Post World War II.

USTA

NUTRITION AND EATING DISORDERS SERIES

This three-part video series focuses on nutrition and eating disorders in athletics. The material covers the problems created by the drive to lower weight without regard for proper diet, the devastating consequences of eating disorders, and what coaches, teachers, and others can do to help the student athlete with an eating disorder. A comprehensive set of printed material includes handout masters on eating disorders, nutrition, weight loss, amenorrhea, and a resource referral list.

Afraid to Eat: Eating Disorders and the Student-Athlete. This program uses interviews with student athletes, coaches, and medical personnel to define anorexia and bulimia and provides information about incidence rates. The videotape also covers the characteristics and warning signs and dramatically shows the consequences of eating disorders.

Out of Balance: Nutrition and Weight. This videotape addresses the effects of nutrition and weight on athletic performance as well as their difficulty of achieving a weight goal without sacrificing proper nutrition.

Eating Disorders: What Can You Do? Being well informed about eating disorders is especially important for those who influence student athletes during their college careers. This program will assist coaches, medical personnel, and administration in understanding the underlying causes of eating disorders, recognizing the warning signs, and planning appropriate action.

1990; 15 to 17 min; VHS; color; JR, HS, A; Post World War II.

KAROL

OAKMONT AND THE OPEN

A semidocumentary of the Oakmont Country Club near Pittsburgh. Scenes in the U.S. Open Championship won by Tommy Armour, Sam Parks, Jr., and Ben Hogan (in black and white); round-by-round action in the 1962 Open, including the playoff between Jack Nicklaus and Arnold Palmer.

1962; 33 min; 16 mm; BW; JR, HS, A; Golden Age to Post World War II.

USGA

ODE TO O. J.

A poem dedicated to O. J. Simpson at a time when injury threatened to end his career.

NL; 3 min; 16 mm, VHS, U-Matic; color; JR, HS, A; Post World War II.

NFL; TMA

OFFICIALS, THE

Tells the story of football officials. Highlights of major NCAA games are also featured.

NL; 28 min; 16 mm; NL; JR, HS, A; Post World War II.

ASF

OFF THE WALL

This lighthearted, action-packed look at racquet-ball shows players of all ages, from all walks of life, competing with drive and enthusiasm. Entertaining viewing for anyone motivated to try this popular sport.

1979; 15 min; 16 mm; color; JR, HS, A; Post World War II.

PENNST; PYRAMID

OFF YOUR DUFF

This ode to the benefits of exercise opens with the testimony of a 40-year-old who was 26 pounds over-weight and, although she felt foolish doing it, began to run. She admits it did not turn her into an 18-year-old beauty, but it did help her shed tensions and feel on top of things. Kim Prince, the narrator, notes that exercise doesn't have to hurt to do good. Dr. Kenneth Cooper explains how the heart can benefit from exer-cise. Bonnie Prudden discusses keeping fit in later life. A fitness program stressing noncompetitive par-ticipation is looked into at Trailwood Elementary School in Shawnee Mission, Kansas. Exercise for treatment of depression is explored by Dr. Robert Brown. Maggie Letvin, fitness instructor and author, proposes that even vanity is a good reason to exercise.

1979; 30 min; 16 mm; color; JR, HS, A; Post World War II.

LCOA; UILL; WGBH

OF HORSES AND MEN

Animation is used to illustrate men's role in the spread of horses across the American continents. Man's dependence upon the horse has existed since before modern time.

1968; 10 min; 16 mm; color; JR, HS, A; Premodern Sport to Post World War II.

DISNEY; OKSU

OF TIME, WORK AND LEISURE

A documentary presentation of the concepts set forth in Sebastion de Grazia's provocative study by the same name. Points out that in our work-oriented, clock-dominated society, we have won "time off," but we have lost the ability to appreciate true leisure.

1963; 30 min; 16 min; BW; HS, A; Post World War II.

NET; UTEX

OHIO STATE UNIVERSITY FOOTBALL HIGHLIGHTS: 1974

Compilation of highlights from Ohio State's 1974 football season, in which the Buckeyes were Rose Bowl victors. Features Archie Griffin.

1975; 45 min; 16 mm; color; JR, HS, A; Post World War II.

OSU

O HOKEJI JINAK

Hockey as you don't know it.

NL; NL; 16 mm; NL; JR, HS, A; Post World War II.

CZECHEM

OLE THE BULL

A 19-year-old matador is pitted against a menac-ing bull. Here the matador demonstrates his coolness under pressure by braving death at each turn of the cape.

NL; 10 min; 16 mm; color; JR, HS, A; Post World War II.

BUDGET

OLGA

Portrays the efforts and frustrations that go into the making of an "overnight sensation," and shows the results of many years of grueling practice. Olga Korbut, a member of the Russian gymnastics team, won three gold medals in the 1972 Olympics. Only seventeen when the film was made, Olga has been a gymnast since she was eleven. Gives an insight into the special athletic schools that choose and train young Russian athletes, and where Olga began her training.

1975; 47 min; 16 mm; color; JR, HS, A; Post World War II.

CAROUF; GRATV; MICHMED

OLYMPIA

Olympic games from 776 B.C. to A.D. 393. Viewers can feel the spirit of the games and see the breath-taking sculpture and artifacts.

NL; 16 min; 16 mm; NL; JR, HS, A; Ancient Sport.

RSTF

OLYMPIA (THE DIVING SEQUENCE)

The tension built throughout *Olympia* between men as men and men as gods is resolved in "The Diving Sequence." A breathtaking film. (From the film directed by Leni Riefenstahl in Nazi Germany.)

1938; 4 min; 16 mm; BW; JR, HS, A; Depression Era.

UWASH

OLYMPIA MARATHON SEQUENCE

Celebrated sequence from *Olympia, Part 1*, that follows Japan's Kitel Son to his triumph in the 26-mile marathon. Renowned for its brilliant camera work and editing, this montage celebrates the athlete's triumph over the natural human inclination to be complacent and comfortable and to accept less than can be achieved.

1938; 13 min; 16 mm; BW; JR, HS, A; Depression Era.

PHENIX; UCB

OLYMPIA, PART I: THE FESTIVAL OF THE PEOPLE

Epic documentary on the Berlin Olympiad of 1936, directed and edited by Leni Riefenstahl. An artistic masterpiece of the cinema that, despite its underlying Nazi ideology, contains some of the finest blending of image, sound, and music ever achieved. From the opening sequence of mist-shrouded Grecian ruins, the viewer is caught up in an idealized world of strength, grace, and beauty, in which competitive sports are celebrated as heroic ritual. Part I consists of the introduction, the carrying of the torch by more than 3,000 runners from Olympia to Berlin, and track and field events, including Jesse Owens' achievements, the famous *Olympia Marathon Sequence,* and the beautiful slow-motion sequence of the high jump.

1938; 115 min; 16 mm; BW; JR, HS, A; Depression Era.

PHENIX; UCB

OLYMPIA, PART 2: THE FESTIVAL OF BEAUTY

Part I of *Olympia* centers on the games held within the stadium; Part 2 mostly records the games held outside. With a freer, more visual style, it begins with a long prologue, then builds gradually, moving through scenes in nature to the human form and finally to the ravishing diving sequence (see *Olympia Diving Sequence*). The tension of competition in sailing and rowing builds from repose to strain to exhaustion. Soccer, equestrian events, bicycle races, mass calisthenics, and the decathlon.

1938; 97 min; 16 mm; BW; JR, HS, A; Depression Era.

PHENIX; UCB

OLYMPIC CAVALCADE

Highlights the history of the Olympic games from their beginnings in 776 B.C.

NL; 15 min; VHS, U-Matic; color; E, JR, HS, A; Ancient to Post World War II.

HEARST

OLYMPIC FRAGMENTS

Comments on the normal media appraisal of sport. Emphasizes the skill, beauty, and joy of kineticism.

NL; 12 min; VHS, U-Matic; color; JR, HS, A; Post World War II.

KITCHN

OLYMPIC HARMONY

Highlights the 1976 Winter and Summer Olympic Games.

1976; 30 min; 16 mm; color; E, JR, HS, A; Post World War II.

COCA; USOC

OLYMPIC HIGHLIGHTS

The drama of the 1936 Olympic Games, held in Berlin, Germany, lives again in this selection of various moments and events. As the athletes of many countries (including track star Jesse Owens) compete in the many events, the viewer not only views their efforts, but also gets a glimpse of Hitler's Reich, Hitler himself, and gains a feeling of what it was like during this particular edition of the Olympic Games.

1936; 10 min; 16 mm; BW; JR, HS, A; Depression Era.

BUDGET

OLYMPIC GAMES

A special issue of the monthly newsreel devoted to the XX Olympic Games in Munich in 1972. German and English sound versions available.

NL; 16 min; 16 mm; NL; JR, HS, A; Post World War II.

MTPS

OLYMPIC GAMES OF GRENOBLE

Next best thing to having been at the world Olympics held in Grenoble in 1968. Hockey, men's downhill with Killy, cross-country, bobsled, figure skating, women's slalom, ski jumping, women's downhill, giant slalom with Killy, speed skating, women's special slalom, men's special slalom with Killy. Split-screen montages and modern zoom effects.

NL; 30 min; 16 mm; NL; JR, HS, A; Post World War II.

FGTO

OLYMPIC PREVIEW

A look at the 1975 Pan Am Games in Mexico City, emphasizing their value as a proving ground for athletes, and showing the effort and preparations of athletes for the 1976 Summer Olympic Games. Features Bruce Jenner training.

NL; 14 min; 16 mm; color; JR, HS, A; Post World War II.

USOC

OLYMPICS IN MEXICO, THE

All the drama, excitement, tragedy, humor, laughter, and spirit of the XIX Olympic Games held in Mexico, with 119 countries participating, has been captured in this classic motion picture documentary. A crew of 81 cameramen shot every possible angle, exposing 1.5 million feet of film to capture not only the most exciting events, but to create an unforgettable portrait of a sports event.

1969; 112 min; NL; color; JR, HS, A; Post World War II.

BUDGET

OLYMPIC SKATES AND SKIS

A review of the 1968 Winter Games in Grenoble, France.

NL; 13 min; 16 mm; color; JR, HS, A; Post World War II.

USOC

OLYMPICS OF RACING

The cream of the crop in thoroughbred race horses and jockeys challenge the legacy of Gulfstream Park.

NL; 14 min; 16 mm; NL; JR, HS, A; Post World War II.

FLADC

OLYMPICS: THE ETERNAL TORCH

Presents actual footage from highlights of Olympic games, from their modern revival in 1896 in Athens through the tragic 1972 games at Munich. Includes commentary by United States decathlon winner Rafer Johnson regarding the high ideals of Olympic competition.

1974; 28 min; 16 mm; color; JR, HS, A; Modern to Post World War II.

LSU; PENNST

OLYMPIC WINTER THRILLS

Depicts the 1948 Olympics held in Switzerland. Includes scenes of hockey, figure skating, skate racing, bobsled racing, and skiing.

1948; 9 min; 16 mm; BW; JR, HS, A; Post World War II.

UILL

OLYMPICS, THE

Tells the story of the quadrennial Olympic Games from their beginnings and shows highlights from several.

1965; 26 min; 16 mm; BW; JR, HS, A; Ancient to Post World War II.

CBS; USC

ON ANY SUNDAY

Bruce Brown explores the world of motorcycling, one of the most rugged and exhilarating of popular sports. In two years of filming the world's greatest racers, Brown captured the breathtaking speed and excitement of many kinds of motorcycle racing.

Whether he is filming a thousand motorcycles ready to take off across the desert at the sound of a gun or Steve McQueen and friends out on a pleasure ride, Brown succeeds in creating rare film that is as informative as it is entertaining.

1971; 89 min; 16 mm; color; JR, HS, A; Post World War II.

BROWN; ALMI

ONCE BEFORE I DIE

Intrepid mountain climbers pit their skills against the dangers of the Himalayas in this documentary. Eleven people, led by the Dozier brothers, journey 20,000 feet to the summit, while the camera captures all the drama, excitement, danger, and final exhilaration of conquest that comes with reaching their goals. Several members of the Dozier party add their words to Ross Martin's narration in this tribute to the determination of those who climb such peaks.

Note: Please specify short or long version. Feature version also available.

1970; 25 or 52 min; 16 mm; color; JR, HS, A; Post World War II.

BUDGET

100 JAHRE FUSSBALL

This film reviews and highlights one hundred years of soccer in Germany. Only parts I and III are available; part II withdrawn from collection.

NL; 90 min; 16 mm; color; JR, HS, A; Modern to Post World War II.

CGFRG

ONE MORE SEASON: THE CHARLIE WEDEMEYER STORY

This award-winning documentary tells the story of a former All-Star athlete who waged a 10-year battle against Lou Gehrig's disease (ALS). With the support of his family and the high school football team, Wedemeyer all but ignored the obstacles of nearly total disability and defied the odds of his terminal illness. Coaching from a wheelchair, with his players reading his lips, Wedemeyer guided his team to a state championship. Called "more affecting and astounding than *Brian's Song*" by the Los Angeles *Times*.

NL; 52 min; VHS; color; JR, HS, A; Post World War II.

FOTH

ONE OF A KIND

What makes the American Bowling Congress national championship tournament the most popular sporting event of its kind surfaces in the beautiful setting of the Indianapolis Convention Center. The march down center aisle in 1974, Hall of Fame night, the collegians and juniors going through their paces in the grand setting, and the prestigious Masters championship are all included. A special look at the Classic division, with its star-studded field.

NL; 25 min; 16 mm; JR, HS, A; Post World War II.

ABC

ONE TOUGH TEXAN

A. J. Foyt does not win every race he runs, but every race driver knows the Texan is the man to beat when the green flag flies. From Daytona to Riverside, from Indianapolis to LeMans, Foyt has won them all. Five times USAC National Driving Champion, three times winner of the Indianapolis 500, now the talented Texan adds one more USAC Championship win to his total with a victory at Phoenix International Raceway. Foyt shows where it all begins, at his shop in Houston, Texas, and where it all ends, with a checkered flag in Phoenix. In between, his crew tells a little of what it is like to work for one tough Texan.

NL; 21 min; 16 mm; NL; JR, HS, A; Post World War II.

GTARC; IVCH

ONLY THE BALL WAS WHITE

Vintage photographs, historic film clips, and colorful interviews document a bygone era in baseball and the men who were denied stardom by the color line. Among those sharing recollections are Satchel Paige, Don Newcombe, Roy Campanella, and Jimmie Crutchfield. The story they tell leaves little doubt that the isolation of black baseball talent was more our loss than theirs. Narrated by Paul Winfield.

1980; 30 min; 16 mm, VHS, U-Matic; color; JR, HS, A; Golden Age, Depression Era, World War II, Post World War II.

PMI

ON THE FIFTH DAY: STORY OF THE AMERICAN QUARTER HORSE

This film, narrated by Lorne Green, shows the evolution of the American quarter horse from prehistoric times to the present. Shows how its predecessors were used in battle during the Middle Ages and during the fall of Rome, and how the Quarter Horse is such an important factor in the cattle business in Southwest America.

1970; 30 min; 16 mm; color; JR, HS, A; Ancient to Post World War II.

AQHA; IOWA

ON THE GO

The world of high-speed thrill-seekers is the basis of this short subject. Men who revel in excitement compete with each other in such events as the grueling Indianapolis 500 (with such famed drivers as Graham Hill and Bobby Unser behind the wheel). Off-road racing in the rugged desert terrain in Las Vegas. Air racing in Reno, and hydroplane racing with boats skimming across the water at breakneck speeds.

NL; 25 min; 16 mm; color; JR, HS, A; Post World War II.

BUDGET

ON THE ROCKS

On the Rocks offers a unique, lighthearted perspective on rock gymnastics, the exciting sport which applies the natural grace and rhythm of gymnastics to the art of rock climbing. Filmed during spectacular climbs in California, Colorado, and Wyoming and featuring interviews with some of the world's best climbers, it reveals the motivation and the methods of these daring men and women.

NL; 29 min; 16 mm; color; JR, HS, A; Post World War II.

PYRAMID

ON THE RUN

Dazzling cinematography shows the world's best distance runners in action, capturing their motivations and their drive to win. Particularly spectacular footage of runs through the primeval New Zealand landscape.

1980; 22 min; 16 mm; color; JR, HS, A; Post World War II.

PYRAMID; UCB

ON THE TRAIL: AN INTRODUCTION TO TRAIL WALKING

Hiking groups of different types and ages are seen on trails in the city and country, state parks, and on trails laid by permission through private land. Demonstrates map and compass reading, trail maintenance, and finding the way by blazes and markers. Emphasis is on day hikes, which require no expensive equipment, training, or great physical strength.

1975; 9 min; 16 mm; color; JR, HS, A; Post World War II.

UILL

ON YOUR OWN

The importance of self-motivation is the subject of this very unusual and popular film. Breathtaking cinematography and thought-provoking narration combine to drive home the point that no matter what training and education you receive, or the number of motivational programs you attend, in the end, it's really up to you.

The film opens with the birth of a foal. As we watch him grow, we see him undergo extensive training at the hands of top professionals to prepare him to be the best racehorse he can be. As the foal's first real test nears, the narrator contrasts the training a racehorse receives with the educational opportunities we're provided with throughout our lives. As the race begins and the horses thunder toward the finish line, slow-motion photography and the narrator's comments combine to make the film's final point: in running the races of your life, what you do with the educational opportunities provided you is really up to you.

NL; 7 min; 16 mm, VHS; color; HS, A; Post World War II.
CCCD

ORANGE BOWL 1972-73

One year's planning culminates in 18 days of exciting festivals and sporting events. The King Orange Jamboree Parade highlights New Year's Eve in downtown Miami. Focal point of the celebration is the annual gridiron classic on New Year's night, this year, between Nebraska and Notre Dame.

28 min; 16 mm; NL; JR, HS, A; Post World War II.
FLADC

ORIENTEERING

Explains the rules of the sport, which originated in Sweden in 1918 and is now gaining popularity in the United States and Canada. Orienteering combines vigorous exercise with the of compass and map-reading skills. Each participant is equipped with a topographical map of the course and a compass, must check in at all the intermediary control points in the proper order, and the first to reach the finish line is the winner.

NL; 10 min; 16 mm, VHS; color; JR, HS, A; Modern, Golden Age to Post World War II.
IFB

OUR WONDERFUL BODY: HOW WE KEEP FIT

Shows how exercise, a proper diet, rest, proper clothing, and annual doctor's examinations are all necessary to maintain a healthy body.

1973; 10 min; 16 mm; color; JR, HS, A; Post World War II.
IU

OUT OF THE DUST

Off-road racing's Frontier 500 comes to life as audiences experience one of the most grueling courses for man and machine. Sportscaster Bill Flemming narrates this racing classic as viewers watch competitors battle soaring temperatures, zero visibility, harsh elements, and nightime hazards through a jarring course where just finishing is an achievement.

NL; 23 min; 16 mm, VHS; NL; JR, HS, A; Post World War II.
MTPS

OVER THE MIDDLE

You'll get an inside view of the "guts" it takes for a pass receiver to go *Over the Middle* . . . ferocious contact . . . not for the faint-hearted!

1985; 6 min; VHS, U-Matic; color; JR, HS, A; Post World War II.
NFL; TMA

PARADE OF THE TALL SHIPS

Presents sailboat crews and captains as they prepare for a transatlantic race. Follows the ships as they parade into New York Harbor on July 4, 1976.

1977; 20 min; 16 mm; color; JR, HS, A; Post World War II.
IBM; MTPS

PARALYMPICS

A very different kind of sports film, *Paralympics* was produced by the United States Wheelchair Sports Fund. It was made during the twelfth international meet for the physically handicapped, held in England. Four hundred entrants from twenty nations are shown competing. Cheerful, and done with a light touch, this film would be of particular inspiration to young people who are interested in working with the handicapped.

NL; NL; 16 mm; color; JR, HS, A; Post World War II.
CONTEMP

PARENTS CAN MAKE A DIFFERENCE

A 15-minute film focusing on the importance of parents in the development of their children's sports habits.

NL; 15 min; 16 mm; color; A; Post World War II.
WSF

PASSION OF SPAIN, THE
Examines the sport of bullfighting in Spain, pointing out that the viewing audience participates in the sport.
NL; NL; NL; NL; NL; Post World War II.
RCPDF; VIACOM

PASSPORT TO PLEASURE
The excitement of trout fishing in the beauty of New Zealand scenery.
NL; 16 min; 15 mm; NL; JR, HS, A; Post World War II.
NZGTO

PASSPORT TO PLEASURE
Get "inside" the ABC, find out what makes the world's largest participation organization really tick. Learn the benefits of ABC membership, the "passport to pleasure" on the lanes.
NL; 25 min; 16 mm; NL; JR, HS, A; Post World War II.
ABC

PAT FISCHER
In 17 years with the NFL, Fischer played more games at cornerback than anyone in the NFL. He proved that size and speed are not always prerequisites for playing football. Fischer was a smart player whose fearless and tenacious talent were the cornerstones of his success.
1985; 7 min; VHS, U-Matic; color; JR, HS, A; Post World War II.
NFL; TMA

PATTERNS OF PLAY
Describes the history of tennis, squash, table tennis, and badminton.
NL; 14 min; 16 mm; color; JR, HS, A; Making of Modern Sport to Post World War II.
MTPS

PAUL HORNUNG
Interviews Paul Hornung. Presents some action-filled segments of Paul's career at Notre Dame and with the championship Green Bay Packers. Discusses the difficulties and pleasures of being a recognizable athlete and sports commentator.
NL; 20 min; 16 mm; color; JR, HS, A; Post World War II.
COUNFI; USC

PAUL HORNUNG
A portrayal of the bittersweet career of the "Golden Boy" of the Packers. He was known for his colorful personality, which went far beyond the boundaries of the football field. After being suspended from play for a year, he made a comeback and returned to the limelight. This is a story of the character and courage it takes to learn from the school of hard knocks.
1985; 10 min; VHS, U-Matic; JR, HS, A; Post World War II.
NFL; TMA

PEACH BOWL FILMS
1970 - Arizona State vs. North Carolina
1971 - Georgia Tech vs. Ole Miss
1972 - North Carolina vs. West Virginia
1973 - Georgia vs. Maryland
1974 - Vanderbilt vs. Texas Tech
NL; NL; 16 mm; NL; JR, HS, A; Post World War II.
PEACH

PEOPLE'S GAME, THE
Shows the history, development, and nature of one of the chief national sports of Britain: soccer. Spread throughout the British empire, and characterized as "its most enduring sport," the game's importance caused England to withdraw from the Olympics for more than 20 years because of concern over the amateur status of its own players while other countries employ professional athletes. The pervasiveness, appeal, and general popularity of the sport is demonstrated through newsreels, interviews, and coverage of stadium events.
NL; 28 min; 16 mm; color; JR, HS, A; Modern to Post World War II.
UILL

PERFECT BALANCE, THE
Featuring Ann Meyers, four time UCLA women's basketball All-American and star of the USA's 1976 Olympic silver medal team in Montreal.
NL; 7 min; NL; NL; JR, HS, A; Post World War II.
SFTI; TMA

PERFECT MOMENT, THE
A poetic visualization of those "perfect moments" when natural skill and preparation are ready for the external "ideal conditions" of chance, weather, or natural forces which carry men beyond themselves and their mundane perceptions of life, to the full realization of doing something exactly right. Features Chris Price, champion hang glider pilot, Corky Fowler, professional skier, and Orson Welles as narrator.

1979; 12 min; 16 mm; color; JR, HS, A; Post World War II.
PYRAMID; UILL

PERSISTENT ONES, THE

Presents a television special from the CTV program "Olympiad,"which focuses on athletes who have overcome physical or emotional handicaps to become Olympic gold medal winners.
1976; 50 min; 16 mm; color; JR, HS, A; Post World War II.
CTV

PHILADELPHIA EAGLES FOOTBALL

A film dealing with the club and its games.
NL; NL; 16 mm; NL; JR, HS, A; Post World War II.
PEFC

PHILADELPHIA EAGLES HIGHLIGHTS, 1952

NL; NL; 16 mm; BW; JR, HS, A; Post World War II.
MILLER

PHYSICAL FITNESS

Tells how research has helped extend the life span of the average individual. Includes interviews with the Reverend Bob Richards, Olympic pole vaulter, and Roger Banister, runner of the four-minute mile. Demonstrates physical fitness measurements, exercises, and training developed through research at the University of Illinois.
1955; 27 min; 16 mm; BW; JR, HS, A; Post World War II.
CBS; UILL

PHYSICAL FITNESS AND GOOD HEALTH

Entertaining animation conveys the message that true physical well-being depends upon equal parts of exercise, rest, and good nutrition. Shows how food intake, energy expended, and rest are interrelated, and illustrates the effects of modern man's inactivity upon his muscles, heart, and capillary system.
1969; 11 min; 16 mm; color; JR, HS, A; Post World War II.
UILL

PHYSICAL FITNESS: IT CAN SAVE YOUR LIFE

Provides an overview of past and present exercise and eating habits, indicating that current levels of physical inactivity and overeating contribute to poor physical health. Examines the eating and exercise habits of Gene Washington, then with the San Francisco 49ers, and relates his activities to the activities of people in general. Suggests that a well-balanced diet and a daily exercise program can lead to improved physical fitness, health, and well-being.
1977; 23 min; 16 mm; color; JR, HS, A; Post World War II.
AVATLI; EBEC; IU

PHYSICAL FITNESS: THE BIG PICTURE

Describes the Army's emphasis on physical training to develop physically fit men and women to protect the interests of the United States.
1968; 28 min; 16 mm; NL; JR, HS, A; Post World War II.
USARMY

PIGS VS. THE FREAKS

Fast-moving, humorous, and irreverent document on the annual football game between the long-haired students of Michigan State University (the Freaks) and the local police force (the Pigs). Shows pregame activities and postgame reactions, as well as the game itself. Excellent portrayal of understanding between people with conflicting life-styles.
1974; 15 min; 16 mm; color; JR, HS, A; Post World War II.
PYRAMID; UCB

PIERRE DE COUBERTIN

Thanks to the Baron de Coubertin, Olympic games, invented by the Greeks, have been restored.
1964; 26 min; 16 mm; NL; JR, HS, A; Modern to Post World War II.
FACSEA

PIKES PARADISE

Shows fisherman Ed Ebbinger fishing for northern pike in the wilderness of northern Ontario. Includes information on the feeding and breeding habits of pike and information about local wildlife and history.
NL; 25 min; 16 mm; color; JR, HS, A; Post World War II.
BRNSWK; KAROL

PILOT FOR GLACIER SKIERS

Presents Mike Buckland, chief pilot of the Mount Cook Air Service, and describes his job, carrying tourists and skiers to the glaciers by ski-plane. Portrays difficult landings on the glaciers and very beautiful scenery from the air. Tells the history of the ski-plane.

1967; 25 min; 16 mm; color; JR, HS, A; Post World War II.

UNIJAP

PING-PONG

NFB's filming of the table tennis competitions between teams of young Canadians and Chinese that took place in the People's Republic of China in the summer of 1973, the first time in twenty-five years that such filming was made possible. Shown are highlights of the play at the China-Canadian Friendship Meet, as well as some of the sightseeing taken in by the young Canadians—a visit, for example, to the Great Wall of China. A film without commentary.

1974; 13.5 min.; 16 mm; cikir; JR, HS, A; Post World War II.

NFBC

PIONEER LIVING: EDUCATION AND RECREATION

Shows how pioneer communities in the early 1800s planned for their educational and cultural needs. We see school being conducted in a combination church and school building and the enjoyment of recreational activities, including quilting bees, box socials, square dancing, hay rides, and a pioneer wedding followed by the traditional shivaree.

1970; 11 min; 16 min; color; JR, HS, A; Premodern.

UILL

PITTSBURGH STEELERS HIGHLIGHTS

Four films covering the years 1951 through 1954. Order by year.

1951-54; NL; 16 mm; BW; 16 mm; JR, HS, A; Post World War II.

MILLER

PIZZA PIZZA DADDY-O

An anthropological and folkloric record of eight singing games played by fourth-grade Afro-American girls on the playground of a school in a Los Angeles ghetto: My Boy Friend Gave Me A Box, This a-way Valerie, When I was a Baby, Imbileenie, This a-way Batman, Mighty Mighty Devil, My Mother Died, and Pizza Pizza Daddy-O. All action is undirected; the organization of the games is entirely the work of the children themselves, based on the essential structure and characteristics handed down from one generation of schoolchildren to the next. The primary game form, the ring, is demonstrated. The other principal play form, parallel lines of players facing each other, is also shown. The major stylistic feature is call and

response; almost every phrase is echoed both in singing and movement patterns. Study guide including text of the songs is available.

1969; 18 min; 16 mm; NL; JR, HS, A; Post World War II.

UCB

PLAY AND CULTURAL CONTINUITY, PART 1: APPALACHIAN CHILDREN

Captures spontaneous play of children in a rural coal-mining community in the Appalachian mountains. Children from infancy to school age are seen in a variety of situations, including family life, kindergarten, rambling in the mountains, and fishing. Regional environmental influence on the content of their play is discernible.

1975; 23 min; 16 mm; color; HS, A; Post World War II.

CFDC; PENNST

PLAY AND CULTURAL CONTINUITY, PART 2: SOUTHERN BLACK CHILDREN

Presents children's vivid, dramatic play in Houston and surrounding countryside. Cultural entities such as music, dancing, intricate hand-clapping improvisations, and traditional folk games show the easy interaction between generations.

1975; 27 min; 16 mm; color; HS, A; Post World War II.

CFDC; PENNST

PLAY AND CULTURAL CONTINUITY, PART 3: MEXICAN-AMERICAN CHILDREN

Setting is the Rio Grande Valley near Edinburg, Texas, an area where traditional values are maintained and passed on to children. Episodes show domestic play and enactment of experiences at clinics and livestock auctions. Illustrates the culturally defined, prescribed modes of interaction between boys and girls, and the emphasis on mutual respect between generations.

1975; 28 min; 16 mm; color; HS, A; Post World War II.

CFDC; PENNST

PLAY AND CULTURAL CONTINUITY, PART 4: MONTANA INDIAN CHILDREN

On the Flathead Indian Reservation and surrounding countryside, the play of Indian children ranges from the universal domestic activities and "monster" play themes to those mirroring individualistic cultural elements, such as wrapping up babies, drumming, singing, and hunting.

1975; 29 min; 16 mm; color; HS, A; Post World War II.
CFDC; PENNST

PLAY CHAMPIONSHIP BASKETBALL

Basketball fundamentals are demonstrated by the two-time national championship Oklahoma A & M team with All-American Bob Kurland and Coach Henry Iba. Includes shooting, passing, dribbling, tapping, screening, blocking, use of arms and hands, defense on jump, guarding the shooter, infractions, drills, types of plays, and all major phases of court play. Specifically designed as a coach's training aid.
1947; 60 min; 16 mm; BW; JR, HS, A; Post World War II.
ASF; UILL

PLAY HANDBALL

Reviews the history of the game of handball, exhibits basic equipment, demonstrates basic shots, and presents tips on play strategy for both singles and doubles. Basic demonstrations by Jim Jacobs and Stuffy Singer. Film endorsed by the U.S. Handball Association.
1968; 16 min; 16 mm; color; JR, HS, A; Post World War II.
GN; MICHMED

PLAYING TO WIN: FRAN TARKENTON'S BUSINESS STRATEGIES FOR SUCCESS

The famed quarterback, who completed more passes for more touchdowns than any other quarterback in the history of the NFL, has parlayed his impressive statistics and leadership principles into successful business strategies. This film (based on Fran's book by the same title) emphasizes that success in sports or business can come only from a team effort and smart playmaking. As head of his own firm, Tarkenton Productivity Group in Atlanta, Fran has consulted with more than 300 businesses on "human engineering" problems. His leadership theories—referred to as "Tark's Truths"—and game plans for success are straightforward and provide a good primer or refresher course for managers and leaders of all types. An excellent motivational program with interesting information and exciting NFL action.
1984; 12 min; 16 mm, VHS, U-Matic; color; JR, HS, A; Post World War II.
NFL; TMA

PLAYTOWN, U.S.A.

Shows a typical instance of the hazards faced by youth when they have no play facilities other than the city streets. Discusses reasons for the inability of schools to cope with the problem alone and the mu-

tual stake that adults, with increasing leisure hours, have with youngsters in a municipal, tax-supported, year-round program of recreation for all ages and both sexes. Describes in detail the organization of Decatur, Illinois, as proof that just such a program can be operated efficiently and economically.
1946; 25 min; 16 mm; color; A; Post World War II.
UILL

POINT OF NO RETURN, THE

The average kick-off return in 1983 was only 19.5 yards, the lowest in the history of the league. This is the story of the Kamikaze teams and the awesome collisions of the men who sacrifice their bodies covering kicks. Bill Bates, the wild wedge buster of the Dallas Cowboys, is miked for sound as he makes the dangerous journey to the point of no return.
1985; 5 min; VHS, U-Matic; color; JR, HS, A; Post World War II.
NFL; TMA

POISED FOR ACTION

Major football stars demonstrate, on and off the field, the need for physical fitness. Grid superstars such as Frank Ryan, Gayle Sayers, Merlin Olsen, and Sonny Randall tour various military camps as well as demonstrate the close proximity between football and regular exercise for a long and healthy life.
NL; 25 min; 16 mm; color; JR, HS, A; Post World War II.
BUDGET

PORTALET

Shows the difficult ascent of the "Petit Cloucher du Portalet," using modern equipment.
NL; 14 min; 16 mm; NL; JR, HS, A; Post World War II.
SNTO; TRIBUNE

PORTRAIT OF A CHAMPION: DIVING ALYSA GOULD

Value and hard work in becoming a champion for junior and senior high school.
NL; 12 min; 16 mm; color; JR, HS, A; Post World War II.
GEMILL

PORTUGUESE HORSE

The film shows several aspects of horse training—for bullfighting, riding, shows, etc.—at the breeding stations of Fonte Boa and Alter de Chao.
NL; 9 min; 16 mm; NL; JR, HS, A; Post World War II.
PNTIO

POUR UN MAILLOT JAUNE

This film on the Tour de France of 1965 gives an objective image of that annual race: hard sportive trial and popular entertainment.

1965; 27 min; VHS, U-Matic; NL; JR, HS, A; Post World War II.

FACSEA

POWER AND WHEELS : THE AUTOMOBILE IN MODERN LIFE

Surveys the social and cultural impact of the automobile on American life in the past fifty years, emphasizing the influence it has had on geographical mobility, recreation sports, and the nation's economy. Points out that the automobile has created serious problems—accidents, air pollution, and increasing traffic.

1972; 17 min; 16 mm; color; JR, HS, A; Depression Era, World War II, Post World War II.

EBEC; UILL

PREFERRED STOCK

Recounts the growth of NASCAR, the world's leading stock-car race-sanctioning organization, and the creation of its premiere arena of speed, the Daytona International Speedway. The program surveys the beginnings and development of big-league stock-car racing, and features Daytona Speedway's 25th Anniversary "500" and nostalgic footage of races on Daytona Beach.

NL; 26 min; 16 mm, VHS, U-Matic; color; JR, HS, A; Depression Era, World War II, Post World War II.

CCCD; SEARS

PRESERVING THE CHALLENGE

Modern technology and imagination, while providing all sorts of ways of impelling and controlling the flight of golf balls, also poses a serious threat to the basic character of the game of golf. The film illustrates how the U.S. Golf Association is dealing with the problem of preserving the element of skill in this game. Featuring Tom Watson and narrated by Jim McKay.

NL; 28 min; 16 mm; color; JR, HS, A; Post World War II.

MTPS; USGA

PRO BOWL CLASSIC

1959, 1960, 1961, 1962. Order by year.

1959-62; NL; 16 mm; NL; JR, HS, A; Post World War II.

MILLER

PROFESSIONALS, THE: THE NFL'S "BEST EVER"

The Professionals is a program as much about men as it is about football. Jim Plunkett, Dick Butkus, Larry Brown, Jim Marshall, Billy Kilmer, and Dick Vermeil are featured in portraits of men in crisis who have overcome obstacles to achieve success in the NFL. Whether it was illness, ridicule, or the specter of mediocrity, each subject in *The Professionals* is an example of perseverance through difficult times. Ultimately their triumphs are celebrations of the human spirit.

NL; 46 min; 16 mm, VHS, U-Matic; NL; JR, HS, A; Post World War II.

NFL; TMA

PRO FOOTBALL FUNNIES

Eavesdrop on huddles and pep talks, then watch as football's finest stumble, fumble, trip, stagger, drop, and bungle their way through pro-football lowlights.

NL; 30 min; VHS; NL; JR, HS, A; Post World War II.

KAROL

PRO FOOTBALL LEGENDS

The history of football's legends and great plays.

NL; 30 min; VHS; NL; JR, HS, A; Post World War II.

KAROL

PRO FOOTBALL: THE LIGHTER SIDE

More funny moments from America's favorite spectator sport.

NL; 30 min; VHS; color; JR, HS, A; Post World War II.

KAROL

PROS, THE

This excellent documentary depicts both the tragic and triumphant moments of tennis stars at the 1972 U.S. Open—the sadness of Ashe in defeat; the glory of Nastase in victory. Slow-motion clips are set to a rock music background.

1972; 25 min; 16 mm; color; JR, HS, A; Post World War II.

USTEN

PRZEZYJMY TO JESZCE RAZ (LET'S SEE ONCE AGAIN)

The greatest sports achievements and meetings of Polish sportsmen in recent years are present here. A Polish language film.

NL; 45 min; 16 mm; BW; JR, HS, A; Post World War II.
POLEMB

PSYCHLING

Chronicles John Marino's third (and last) attempt to break his own cross-country world record in 1980. Follows Marino and his crew through all stages of the trip from Los Angeles to New York City in twelve days, three hours, and forty-one minutes. Shows that setting and achieving goals leads to satisfaction, while fear of failure often inhibits people from attempting realistic goals. Through the example of Marino, one learns that willingness to set goals, the right attitude, and hard work will enable one to accomplish realistic expectations.
1981; 25 min; 16 mm; color; HS, A; Post World War II.
MGHT; MICHMED

PSYCHOLOGY OF SPORT

Introduces applications of sports psychology.
1974; 19 min; 16 mm; color; HS, A; Post World War II.
SARBO

PSYCHOLOGY OF SPORTS

Discusses the importance of psychological factors in motivating athletes to perform at their best, how to communicate through positive reinforcement, how to be a good listener, and the importance of skill improvement.
1982; 25 min; VHS, U-Matic; color; JR, HS, A; Post World War II.
EBEC

PSYCHOLOGY OF WINNING, THE

Explores the characteristics of successful people in all walks of life, including astronauts, returning POWs, and sports figures.
1981; 20 min; 16 mm; color; HS, A; Post World War II.
SOLIL

PUMPING IRON

Focusing on the competition for the World Bodybuilding Championship, *Pumping Iron* examines the lives of men who undergo grueling training with the hope of transforming their bodies into copies of Greek sculptures. *Pumping Iron* features Arnold Schwarzenegger, the six-time winner of the Mr. Olympia title.

1977; 90 min; 16 mm; color; JR, HS, A; Post World War II.
ALMI

PURINA RODEO EDUCATIONAL FILM

Film about rodeo's seven major competitive events.
NL; 26 min; 16 mm; NL; JR, HS, A; Post World War II.
IRA

PURITAN FAMILY OF EARLY NEW ENGLAND

A Puritan family, living in a small New England coastal village, participates in many activities and chores. The children learn from a hornbook, dig clams, spin wool; the mother cooks cornbread, makes soap and candles; the father hunts and dresses skins.
1950; 11 min; 16 mm; BW; JR, HS, A; Premodern Sport.
CORF; OKSU

QB OR NOT QB?

The question is, should the coach or the quarterback call the plays? The answer is supplied by Tom Landry, John Elway, Tom Flores, Dan Henning, Joe Theisman, and Paul Brown (the first coach to call plays from the sideline). Wireless microphones on Falcon coach Dan Henning and on his spotters in the press box give a rare insight into the intricate decision-making process of calling plays in the NFL.
1985; 7 min; VHS, U-Matic; color; JR, HS, A; Post World War II.
NFL; TMA

QUARTER HORSE: THE HORSE AMERICA MADE

Documents the versatility of the American quarter horse. Shows the many ways it provides pleasure for its owners and enthusiasts. Demonstrates its quickness of action and its natural tendency to get along well with man. Includes many action shots of the horses' work at rodeos.
1970; 39 min; 16 mm; color; JR, HS, A; Post World War II.
AMQH; UWISC

QUEEN BEA

Portrait of the premiere woman harness racing driver, Bea Faber.
NL; 14 min; 16 mm; color; JR, HS, A; Post World War II.
USTA

QUEST FOR FLIGHT

Includes historic footage of man's efforts to fly. Covers ballooning, sky-flying, and space travel.

1976; 23 min; 16 mm; color; JR, HS, A; Modern to Post World War II.

UWISC

QUESTION OF HUNTING, A

This film points out the ecological, financial, and emotional benefits for both hunters and society. It presents with candor the confrontation between pro-hunting and antihunting viewpoints. Spokespersons on both sides offer opinions, facts, and evidence. Shows the work of conservation and wildlife preservation groups. One of the film's most beautiful sequences shows a waterfowl refuge that was bought with hunters' money.

NL; 28 min; 16 mm; VHS, color; JR, HS, A; Post World War II.

CCCD; KAROL

RACE FOR GOLD, THE

What was it that gave East German athletes the edge in the 1976 Olympics? Was it rigorous, highly structured, government-sponsored training? Or was it drugs that gave their women swimmers masculine bodies, along with record-breaking speed? Can new training programs help our amateur athletes win? And who should be responsible for the cost involved?

1980; 57 min; 16 mm; color; HS, A; Post World War II.

IOWA; TIMLIF

RACE FOR PROFESSIONALS, A

Shows the 59th running of the Indianapolis 500, in which Bobby Unser took the checkered flag. Includes the spectacular crash survived by Tom Sneva and memories of earlier races that are now part of Indy lore.

NL; 25 min; 16 mm; color; JR, HS, A; Post World War II.

GTARC

RACE OF HORSES, A

The story of a horse race, with its glitter, flash, and excitement, is intercut with the parallel story of the breeding and training of the thoroughbred horse. Displays the roles of the many people involved in the horse-racing industry: strappers, handlers, trainers, jockeys, veterinarians, and breeders. Contains a sequence on the foaling, breaking in, and handling of the race horse.

1974; 10 min; 16 mm; color; JR, HS, A; Post World War II.

UILL

RACE TO LIVE

Stock-car racing, from workshops to crashes.

NL; 28 min; 16 mm; NL; JR, HS, A; Post World War II.

CINES

RACETRACK

Racetrack is about Belmont Racetrack, one of the world's leading racetracks for thoroughbred racing. The film highlights the training, maintaining, and racing of thoroughbred horses. Everyday occurrences are shown: the grooming, feeding, shoeing, and caring for horses, and the preparation for races, the various aspects of training, exercising, and timing the horses, the prerace presentation of the horses, and betting and watching the races. The film also has sequences showing the variety of work done by trainers, jockeys, jockey agents, grooms, hot walkers, stable hands, and veterinarians.

NL; 114 min; 16 mm; JR, HS, A; Post World War II.

ZIPPORAH

RACING ON THIN AIR

Relates the external challenge of Pikes Peak through its history and the excitement of the Pikes Peak Auto Hill Climb. Interviews the winners of the 1966 race.

NL; 30 min; 2" videotape; BW; JR, HS, A; Post World War II.

KRMATV; PUBTEL

RACING RIVERS

Six rivers with spectacular rapids, a lake, and the open sea combine to make this the longest, toughest jet boat race ever staged.

1976; 22 min; 16 mm; NL; JR, HS, A; Post World War II.

NFU

RACING RIVERS, THE

Old-car lovers and drivers came from across the world for the international rally at Rotorua, New Zealand. This film report of the event concentrates on the men and their machines. Music, the sights, the activities, complete this picture of old-car buffs at their most important international event.

1981; 25 min; 16 mm; NL; JR, HS, A; Post World War II.

NFU

RACING: THE WILL TO WIN

Shows competitors of all ages in several different kinds of races, learning about the preparation, discipline, knowledge, and endurance necessary to compete successfully.

1978; 17 min; 16 mm; color; JR, HS, A; Post World War II.

UWISC

RACING TRADITION

Hialeah Park Racetrack features the best in horse racing history.

NL; 14 min; 16 mm; NL; JR, HS, A; Post World War II.

FLADC

RACQUETBALL: MOVING FAST

Mark Morrow, professional player and teacher of this fast-moving sport discusses the rules and skills for racquetball. Played outdoors or indoors the game requires more safety consciousness than many involving larger spaces. Positions for the skip ball, Z-ball, pinch shot, kill, and fly kill are illustrated in discussion and in play.

1978; 15 min; 16 mm; color; JR, HS, A; Post World War II.

CBS; UILL

RAFER JOHNSON STORY, THE

The story of Rafer Johnson, world decathlon champion, captain of the 1960 United States Olympic Team, honor student, president of his grade school, high school, and college classes, and first member of the Peace Corps.

1963; 55 min; 16 mm; BW; JR, HS, A; Post World War II.

SF

RAG TAG CHAMPS

Presents the story of a young black growing up against a background of sports, school, and family dilemmas. Jake lives with his Uncle Lenny, a former baseball player who works as a musician. Jake's baseball team needs a coach, his attendance record at school needs improving, and Uncle Lenny needs a place to rehearse. The ideal place is a warehouse that belongs to the sponsor of the rival baseball team. How these elements are worked together by Jake is an inspiring story. From the ABC Weekend Special Series, based on the novel *Jake,* by Alfred Slate.

1978; 48 min; 16 mm; color; E, JR, HS, A; Post World War II.

ABCS; UILL

RAINBOW (ALASKAN TROPHY TROUT)

Alaska is famed for its gamefish, and one of the most prized of all is the giant rainbow trout. You will join Fishing Hall of Famer Bill Cullerton as he successfully stalks the mighty rainbow among the scenic lakes and rivers of Alaska.

NL; 27 min; 16 mm; NL; JR, HS, A; Post World War II.

SOLANA

RALLYE DES NEIGHES

An account of the winter rally sponsored annually by the Montreal Motorcar Club.

NL; 26 min; 16 mm; NL; JR, HS, A; Post World War II.

CCG

RALLY: A RACE AGAINST TIME

Here's rallying at its finest — and toughest. Drivers, navigators, and their equipment are pitted against unrelenting terrain under the most demanding and varied conditions imaginable. Racing against the clock from San Francisco to Sacramento, California, and on to Reno, Nevada.

NL; 19 min; 16 mm; color; JR, HS, A; Post World War II.

MTPS

RASSLIN' REDSKINS

Chief Yaukie vs. Carol Kawalski (The Terrible Pole) in a knockdown free-for-all of bone-crushing (added to the sound track) brutality.

NL; 10 min; 16 mm; NL; JR, HS, A; Post World War II.

BUDGET

RASSLIN' ROCKETS

It's Convention Hall in Wildwood, New Jersey, and two of the biggest bruisers in the world of wrestling, Lou Klein and Gene DeBuch, go to it.

NL; 10 min; 16 mm; NL; JR, HS, A; Post World War II.

BUDGET

RAYMOND BERRY

The Fred Astaire of the football field. Berry's dedication, hard work, and obsession for detail carried him to the Hall of Fame in 1973. His motto was, "luck is what happens when preparation meets opportunity." Inspiring and thoughtful story.

1985; 6 min; VHS, U-Matic; color; JR, HS, A; Post World War II.

NFL; TMA

READINESS: THE FOURTH R

Interprets, for lay groups, the values and outcomes of physical education, including athletics in schools and colleges. Shows astronaut John Glenn, athletics at Michigan State University, elementary school classwork, and various physical education classes. Defines "readiness" as the quality of being ready physically, emotionally, and mentally for anything.

1962; 20 min; 16 mm; color; HS, A; Post World War II.

UILL

READING POETRY: CASEY AT THE BAT

With vigor and appropriate drama, George Maharis narrates the poem, "Casey at the Bat," by Ernest Lawrence Thayer. The visual treatment of the film is twofold. The first reading is done against the background of a Little League baseball game; the poem is recited again with words superimposed over a slow-motion sequence from a major league game.

1972; 12 min; 16 mm; color; E, JR, HS, A; Post World War II.

OXFORD; UILL

REAL DEPARTURE, THE

Ever since he was a small boy, Cyrille Deborchere dreamed of being bicycle racer. But there was a big gap between boyhood dreams and reality, a gap that took a great deal of effort to bridge. It took ten years for the boy to become a man and to reach his peak as a racer. Ten years, during which his illusions received many hard knocks, but it was a period which taught him courage, endurance, and what life is all about.

1978; 52 min; 16 mm; color; JR, HS, A; Post World War II.

BELGIUM

REBOUND

This film, dealing with basketball, shows the best Belgian teams in action and the training beginners undergo. Basketball is, above all, a sport in which team spirit must predominate. Clubs tend to select very tall players, but this sport is open to all, and it is played for amusement by amateurs of all origins and physiques. A French language film with English subtitles.

1972; 13 min; 35 mm; color; JR, HS, A; Post World War II.

BELGIUM

RECORD BREAKERS

The establishment of a new world speed record for outboard-powered boats involves several men and their boat. Filmed against a background of Lake Havasu, the film shows behind-the-scenes activity as the crew prepares for the assault on the record. In the action sequences, Gerry Walin drives *Starflite IV* twice through the measured kilometer course at an average 131.05 miles per hour. Boat owner W. Jones tells what is involved in setting world speed records.

NL; 14 min; 16 mm; NL; JR, HS, A; Post World War II.

SOLANA

RECREATION: THE JAPANESE WAY

Colorful woodblock prints and scenes from everyday life depict the Japanese enjoying their recreational activities . . . from Sumo wrestling to Kabuki Theatre and cherry blossom viewing. In rural Japan, festivals celebrating the harvest are still held today, affording a tie to the past as well as a recreational outlet. Employees are shown joining in company subsidized activities.

NL; 30 min; 16 mm; NL; JR, HS, A; Post World War II.

MTPS

RED AUERBACH

Features Red Auerbach, of the Boston Celtics, speaking candidly about his philosophy, some of the great players he has coached, and other issues in professional basketball.

NL; 20 min; 16 mm; color; JR, HS, A; Post World War II.

COUNFI; USC

RED DEVILS

As the *Red Devils,* the stunt pilots of the Belgian air force have earned a measure of fame which is amply justified by the daring aerobatics they perform. The Red Devils Patrol is composed of volunteers whose average age is about 26 years. During a session on the ground, the *Red Devils* discuss the aerobatics to be performed at the next air show, and the language they use is for the most part English.

1976; 20 min; 16 mm; color; JR, HS, A; Post World War II.

BELGIUM

REFEREE

Deals with the work of Jess Kersey, who has been blowing a whistle and calling the shots for basketball games across the country as a National Basketball Association referee.

NL; 30 min; VHS; color; JR, HS, A; Post World War II.

RMIBHF; WTBS

REMEMBERING JACKIE ROBINSON

Examines the historical implications and social significance of Jackie Robinson's breaking the color barrier to become the first black man to play in the major leagues.

1983; 14 min; VHS, U-Matic; color; JR, HS, A; Post World War II.

KINGFT

REST AND LEISURE IN THE USSR

Narration in Russian describes how Russian families spend their leisure time. Shows them visiting the Park of Culture and Rest in Moscow, swimming, skiing, skating, boating, and fishing in the mountains. Closes with scenes of a young workers' resort, where a visiting American couple joins in songs and dances.

1963; 14 min; 16 mm; color; JR, HS, A; Post World War II.

UU

REQUIEM FOR A RACE TRACK

Sebring is no more. After 21 years, the last endurance race has been run around the twisting 5.2-mile airport road course. Sebring, Florida, will always be remembered for bringing international automobile racing to the United States. In 1950, the Allards, Jags, and MGs were averaging 52 miles per hour around the flat Sebring layout. In 1972, the Ferraris and Alfas were running 120 miles per hour on the same course. Endurance racing presents a different kind of challenge to the professional racing driver, because he must race against novice drivers running for class wins. While the big-bore prototypes may be running 120 mph, they will have to contend with small sports cars running 65 to 70; it makes for very interesting racing, especially at night. Peter Revson expresses his views on racing at Sebring and on how not to get along with the SCCA stewards. Jackie Stewart and Keith Jackson are the hosts of this film.

NL; 21 min; 16 mm; NL; JR, HS, A; Post World War II.

GTARC

RETURN

Dramatizes the adventures of two businessmen as they leave the city for a camping trip in the rugged Canadian wilds. Presents their pleasures of canoeing on remote lakes, pitching camp, cooking fresh caught fish on a campfire, swimming in lakes, and watching a sunset. Records their hardships, also long portages and pelting rain. Displays the rugged beauty of the surroundings and provides reality by using the natural sounds of the area.

1972; 29 min; 16 mm; color; JR, HS, A; Post World War II.

UU

RETURN OF THE '66, THE

Film shows the winning of the West with the '66. See modern hunters with a '66 in Maine, Alaska, and Africa. There are excellent wildlife scenes and a shooting exhibition by Herb Parsons.

NL; 26 min; 16 mm; NL; JR, HS, A; Making of Modern Sport to Post World War II.

WINWES

REVOLUTION IN CHURCH ROAD

The 1974 Wimbledon Championship saw the overthrow of the old guard by young players Connors and Evert. Scenes include on- and off-court shots of most of the top players, especially poignant glimpses of Ken Rosewall as he nearly conquered the elusive title but failed at the final hurdle.

1974; 52 min; 16 mm; color; JR, HS, A; Post World War II.

USTEN

RHYTHMICAL GYMNASTICS

Modern rhythmic gymnastics for women are based on easily understood principles where balance, use of gravity, and the body's elasticity are the main elements. An elite group from the Gymnastic Club Elbe demonstrates some exercises in five series against changing Danish landscape backgrounds.

NL; 22 min; 16 mm; NL; JR, HS, A; Post World War II.

DANEIO

RIDE COWBOY RIDE : PARTS 1 and 2

Traces quarter horses from cow work to rodeo performance events to present-day horse show and contests.

1964; 29 min; 16 mm; color; JR, HS, A; Modern to Post World War II.

AQHA; OKSU

RIDE THE WILD SURF

Surfers pit their skills and courage against the 40-foot waves that race onto the beach at Oahu in Hawaii. Against the backdrop of the world of surfing, several young men and women come to participate in or watch one of the most exciting sports on earth.

1964; 101 min; 16 mm; color; JR, HS, A; Post World War II.

BUDGET

RIDE THE WINDS: MOODS OF HANG GLIDING

A powerful film that captures the essence of this thrilling sport. The film projects the excitement of the beginner's first flight as he slowly lifts off the ground and finds himself airborne. Many of the best hang glider pilots are shown soaring the beach ridges or flying thousands of feet in the air over rugged mountains. Set against dramatic backdrops, cameras mounted on the wing during takeoff, flight, and landing directly involve the audience in the thrill of the sport.

NL; 24 min; 16 mm, VHS, U-Matic, Beta; color; JR, HS, A; Post World War II.

CRYSP

RIGHT ON!

The fun of archery is explored in detail in this film from Fred Bear. There are more U. S. archers than golfers, and the film tells why. Not only is it a sport for everyone—young and old—it's easy to learn. A brief sequence prepares the viewer for his first archery experience.

NL; 14 min; 16 mm; color; JR, HS, A; Post World War II.

CCCD

ROAD BACK, THE

A piercing look at the fate of Jocelyn Lovell, three times gold medalist at the Commonwealth Games and winner of more than 50 national and international cycling championships. Dragged by a truck in the summer of 1983, Lovell, now a quadriplegic, underwent months of excruciating therapy to relearn such simple daily tasks as eating and brushing his teeth. Interviews with Lovell and his wife reveal the sobering extent to which their lives have been altered and illustrate the former cyclist's tremendous courage.

NL; 29 min; VHS; color; HS, A; Post World War II.

CANBC

ROAD TO ADVENTURE

Travel the *Road to Adventure* with American youth hostelers from all over the nation as they explore the American and European countryside on bicycles. It shows how boys and girls partake in bicycle hikes throughout the countryside, relaxing, exercising, and enjoying themselves in an organized atmosphere. Hosteling activities are also highlighted as Americans meet European members of youth hostels on bike trips through Europe.

NL; 30 min; 16 mm; NL; JR, HS, A; Post World War II.

ASF

ROAD TO THE SUPER BOWL

A review of the spectacular plays, great games, and terrific teams of the 1984-85 season. The road to

the Super Bowl was paved by such successes as coach Sam Wyche, the indomitable Dan Marino, running heroes Walter Payton and Eric Dickerson, all-time reception leader Charlie Joiner, as well as the soaring spirits of the Cardinals, Bears, Broncos, Dolphins, and, of course, the 49ers, who won it all.

1985; 48 min; 16 mm, VHS, U-Matic; color; JR, HS, A; Post World War II.

NFL; TMA

ROARING WHEELS

See the most famous racing drivers of the 1920s to 1940s compete in speed chases across dirt and wooden tracks, sandy beaches, snow-covered mountains, and even icy lakes to see who can come closest to violent death without crossing the thin line.

NL; 10 min; 16 mm; BW; JR, HS, A; Golden Age, Depression Era and World War II.

FILMIC

ROBERTO CLEMENTE: A TOUCH OF ROYALTY

NL; 26 min; 16 mm; color; JR, HS, A; Post World War II.

NBHF

ROCKNE OF NOTRE DAME

The life, personality, and coaching methods of Knute Rockne. His contributions to the sport of football and to the art and science of coaching are shown on the field, in "talk sessions" with fellow coaches, and in the locker room with the players.

1958; 26 min; 16 mm; BW; JR, HS, A; Depression Era.

CBS; FI; UILL

ROCKY BLEIER

A man whose career was a hymn to the values of courage and hard work. After being wounded in Vietnam, Bleier returned to the Steelers and, after 2 years of painful rehabilitation, he fought his way into the starting lineup of a world championship team. A most dramatic and inspiring story that proves that with belief in oneself, anything is possible!

1985; 9 min; VHS, U-Matic; color; JR, HS, A; Post World War II.

NFL; TMA

ROCKY MOUNTAINS, THE

Describes the origin, terrain, and environment of the Canadian Rocky Mountains and examines various plant and animal life found in the mountain areas. Thousands of tourists flock each year to witness the spectacle of rugged snowcapped peaks, alpine lakes, lush evergreens, and a fantastic array of moose, wapiti, bighorn sheep, mountain goats, bison, mountain lions, and hundreds of smaller animals and birds. However, these same tourists are threatening the continued existence of the natural environment, and establishing and maintaining the parks in their natural state is becoming more and more difficult. National parks shown include Banff, Waterton, Yoho, Kootenay, and Jasper.

1970; 28 min; 16 mm; color; JR, HS, A; Post World War II.

FI; UILL

RODEO

Shows both behind-the-scenes and close-up views of a United States rodeo. Captures the danger and loneliness that a cowboy experiences in rodeo competition, particularly in the slow-motion segments.

1969; 19 min; 16 mm; color; JR, HS, A; Post World War II.

OKSU; PHENIX

RODEO COWBOY

Cheyenne Frontier Days attract the top cowboys to such traditional events as steer riding, bronco riding, calf roping, bulldogging, and the wild horse race. The filming of these events, coupled with interviews with participants, gives the viewer an understanding of the motivation of the individuals, a glimpse into the tightly knit fraternity of the rodeo cowboy, the excitement of winning, and the dejection of losing.

1975; 21 min; 16 mm; color; JR, HS, A; Post World War II.

UILL

ROGER STAUBACH: THE ALL-AMERICAN HERO

A retrospective showing star quarterback Staubach at his best, on and off the field.

1979; 13 min; 16 mm, VHS, U-Matic; color, JR, HS, A; Post World War II.

NFL; TMA

ROGER STAUBACH: THE GALAHAD OF THE GRIDIRON

It takes courage to thrive in the moment of crisis, and there has never been a better example of courage than Roger Staubach (Quarterback, Dallas Cowboys 1969-79, Hall of Fame, 1985). The man they called "Captain Comeback" was the consummate pressure player, and he proved it time after time by leading the Cowboys to thrilling last-second victories. No player was more widely respected or better liked by his peers. Said teammate Charlie Waters, "Roger was a

man you trusted instinctively, whose reputation you would fight for, and whose friend you longed to be." This is a story of a true sports hero—an inspiration for all.

1985; 8 min; VHS, U-Matic; color; JR, HS, A; Post World War II.

NFL; TMA

ROLLER SKATE FEVER

This exhilarating look at a popular sport was filmed by a cameraman on skates, following super-skaters down Venice, California's colorful and crowded boardwalk, careening at high speeds ahead of expert racers, and gliding side by side with graceful windskaters. Jumps and stunts, races and elegant maneuvers are all synchronized to an original score.

NL; 9 min; 16 mm; color; JR, HS, A; Post World War II.

PYRAMID

ROOKIE OF THE YEAR

The story of 11-year-old Sharon Lee's attempt to play baseball in an all-boy's league. Well acted to convey anxiety, excitement, good times, and some of the heartbreaks of adolescent boys and girls competing in a world of prejudice, not of their making.

1975; 47 min; 16 mm; color; JR, HS, A; Post World War II.

OSU; TIMLIF; UILL

ROSEY GRIER: THE COURAGE TO BE ME

Inspiring profile of Rosey Grier, who overcame painful shyness, rejection, and failure and managed to achieve success in professional football, politics, entertainment, and helping young people cope with drug abuse.

1978; 23 min; 16 mm; color; JR, HS, A; Post World War II.

CF; UCB

ROUNDUP IN OKLAHOMA

A western film, showing a roundup in the early 1900s. Silent.

1907; 11 min; 16 mm; BW; JR, HS, A; Modern Sport.

OKSU

ROW!

The raw power and rhythmic poetry of crew racing come alive in this testimony to the racer's skill. Pulling together, men and women demonstrate dedication and teamwork, the hallmarks of the successful racing crew.

NL; 15 min; 16 mm; color; JR, HS, A; Post World War II.

PYRAMID

ROY CAMPANELLA

Interviews Roy Campanella, one of the greatest catchers in baseball history. Includes film footage of Campy, Jackie Robinson, Gil Hodges, and other Brooklyn Dodger players. Covers the career of this Hall Of Fame member during the Dodger's great years in New York.

NL; 20 min; 16 mm; color; JR, HS, A; Post World War II.

COUNFI; USC

RUDOLFO GAONA

Rare footage of his last fight in the old bullring in Mexico City over 60 years ago. Silent film.

NL; 14 min; 16 mm; BW; JR, HS, A; Golden Age.

BUDGET

RUGBY

The film provides highlights of three Rugby matches in a country where sport is almost a way of life. Three levels of play are depicted: international, national, and provincial. In the national match, where North Island plays South Island and the game is virtually brother against brother, feelings and standards of play rise to an apex. Rumanian and French versions available.

1976; 16 min; 16 mm; NL; JR, HS, A; Post World War II.

NFU

RUGBY ROUSES ME

The game of Rugby Union football, from the 16-year-old boy through the ambitious peak of every Australian player: an international match. This film explores the game at many levels and includes scenes from a contest between Australia and New Zealand.

1981; 27 min; 16 mm; color; JR, HS, A; Post World War II.

FLMAUS

RUN, APPALOOSA, RUN: PARTS 1 and 2

Presents the story of an Indian girl and her love for an Appaloosa colt. Together they bring honor and glory to the Nez Perce Indian Nation of the Northwest. Shows rodeo action along with the challenge of strength and endurance for both man and horse in the suicide race of the annual Hell's Mountain Relay.

1966; 48 min; 16 mm; color; E, JR, HS, A; Post World War II.

DISNEY; OKSU

RUN FOR YOUR LIFE

Filmmaker Nicholas Stiliadis, a running enthusiast, closely examines why millions of North Americans have taken up jogging as a viable alternative to competitive sports. Photographed amid the beauty of Toronto in autumn, this documentary examines the reasons runners of all ages have opted for this truly personalized form of exercise. Interviews with joggers and physicians point out the psychological and medical benefits of running and stress the importance of cardiovascular health in today's urban, sedentary life-style. From the enthusiast's viewpoint, we examine the amazing popularity of running, from whole families jogging together for pleasure to the solitary agony of marathon races.

1979; 17 min; 16 mm; color; HS, A; Post World War II.

CORF; UWISC

RUN DICK, RUN JANE

Presents Dr. Kenneth Cooper discussing and demonstrating the concept of aerobics. Explains how a program of walking and running can strengthen the heart, lungs, and circulatory system. Details the need for programs of fitness in all walks of society.

1971; 20 min; 16 mm; color; JR, HS, A; Post World War II.

BYU; UU

RUNNER

This close-up study of Bruce Kidd, a young long-distance runner, provides some insight into the qualities that are required of a track star. The viewer sees the runner caught up in the race, concentrating on his timing as he spends his strength. There is an excellent jazz score and poetic commentary by W. H. Auden.

1962; 11 min; 16 mm; BW; JR, HS, A; Post World War II.

NFBC

RUNNING FOR LIFE

Shows faculty members of University of Wisconsin who participated in experiment sponsored by the U. S. Office of Public Health to determine the effects of exercise on the middle-aged and to see if it can reduce the chance of heart disease. Shows professors jogging, doing other exercises, and reporting on their experiences. Doctors who supervised the project comment on the results.

1969; 28 min; 16 mm; NL; HS, A; Post World War II.

UCB

RUNNING HARD, BREATHING EASY: THE JEANETTE BOLDEN STORY

An inspirational program showing how Jeanette Bolden, a young California woman, overcame asthma to become a world-class sprinter in track and a member of the 1980 U.S. Olympic Team.

NL; 13 min; 16 mm, U-Matic; color, JR, HS, A; Post World War II.

CCCD

RUN SUNWARD

The oceans of the world are the battleground for a rugged breed of men known as ocean power racers. Follow them as they battle each other and the elements from Italy to England and points beyond.

NL; 24 min; 16 mm; NL; JR, HS, A; Post World War II.

TELEFILM

RURAL ROUTE ONE

Hunter Fred Bear acts as guide, demonstrating the manufacture of bows and arrows. He shows how archery instruments are used for both competition and hunting and how they are skillfully created and handcrafted.

NL; 27 min; 16 mm; NL; JR, HS, A; Post World War II.

MTPS

SADDLEMAKER

An adolescent girl masquerades as a boy to earn a saddle for her horse. The fine handwork and craftsmanship that go into making a saddle as well as expert horsemanship scenes are featured.

1961; 16 min; 16 mm; color; E, JR, HS, A; Post World War II.

MGHT; OKSU

SAFARI IN UGANDA

Describes hunting safari in Uganda organized by Uganda Wildlife Development, Ltd. Takes the viewer around the country's most exciting hunting areas, where hunters bag large elephants, zebras, lions, leopards, buffalo, rhino, and other game species.

NL; 25 min; 16 mm; NL; JR, HS, A; Post World War II.

EMBUGA

SAFARI NORTH

Two weeks of stone sheep and mountain goat hunting near Moddy Lake in northern British Co-

lumbia. With John Amber, Editor of *Gun Digest,* Fred T. Hunting, and Raymond G. Speer. Filmed and narrated by Gordon Eastman.

NL; 24 min; 16 mm; NL; JR, HS, A; Post World War II.

RCBS

SAILING (1)

Paul Elvstrom is shown sailing three different types of boats while explaining why sailing is such an important part of his life.

NL; 12 min; 16 mm; NL; JR, HS, A; Post World War II.

IU

SAILING (2)

A symphonic poem dedicated to wind and water and to the sport of yachting. The opening chords are like a largo in the early morning stillness of the water; the bustle and activity as the boats are made ready are like an andante, which is then followed by the allegro of the sunny spectacle of summer yachting. The rising storm comes up like a tempestuoso, and the yachtsmen need all their skill to reach a safe harbor. Finally, there is the largo e tranquillo of the evening over waters that are calm once again.

NL; 13 min; 16 mm; NL; JR, HS, A; Post World War II.

RNE

SAILING ABOVE THE ALPS

Documents how, up among the Alpine peaks of Switzerland, a group of hang gliding enthusiasts has achieved the ultimate in the sport. Shows Swiss Tony Wyss and his friends as they jump off the 9,000-foot Schilhorn peak and gently swoop among the other snowcapped peaks with the pine forests and alpine villages far below. A sequence showing photographer Eric Jones receiving elementary hang-gliding lessons from Wyss heightens awareness of the skill and experience necessary to soar above the Alps.

1981; 28 min; 16 mm, VHS; color; JR, HS, A; Post World War II.

IU

SAILING WITH CLOUDS

Portrays the visual, emotional, and lyrical experience of soaring through the cloud-filled sky in a sailplane. The viewer captures the sense of freedom and graceful, effortless motion through space. The journey through fleecy clouds is accompanied by an original choral score.

1974; 8 min; 16 mm; color; JR, HS, A; Post World War II.
LSU

SAIL-PLANING

The training of glider flyers, beginning with the building of model planes by boys 10-14, followed by large-scale building, and concluding with a flight over the Swiss Alps. German and English sound versions available.
1966; 19 min; 16 mm; NL; JR, HS, A; Post World War II.
MTPS

SAME OLD STEELERS, THE

Hilarious account of the most inept pro team of the 1950s.
NL; 9 min; VHS, U-Matic; NL; JR, HS, A; Post World War II.
NFL; TMA

SAM SNEAD

Tells how Sam Snead came to the game as a barefoot caddy and played golf competitively on the pro circuit for years. Features Snead reviewing more than half a century of golf.
NL; 20 min; 16 mm; color; JR, HS, A; Post World War II.
COUNFI; USC

SAM WYCHE

In his nine seasons in the NFL, quarterback Sam Wyche got by on intellect rather than talent. Wyche is miked for sound in his very first game as head coach on September 2, 1984. A revealing insight into the pressure-packed occupation of coaching pro football.
1985; 7 min; VHS, U-Matic; color; JR, HS, A; Post World War II.
NFL; TMA

SAN JUAN SPECTACULAR

Highlights of the fifth American zone championships of the Federation Internationale des Quilleurs, 1969, in San Juan, Puerto Rico. U. S. stars from ABC and WIBC tournaments battle the best from ten other nations, with some surprising results.
NL: 26 min; 16 mm; NL; JR, HS, A; Post World War II.
ABC

SAPPORO '72

Highlights winter sports in the Japanese wonderland of Sapporo. Includes ski jumping, speed skating, figure skating, bobsledding, luge, alpine and nordic skiing, and ice hockey.
NL; 26 min; 16 mm; color; JR, HS, A; Post World War II.
USOC

SATURDAY'S HERO

A dramatic, behind-the-scenes story of a young man caught up in the pressure of college football. John Derek is the top high school athlete who jumps at the offer to play football for a prestigious college in the East. Once there, the youngsters finds himself caught between his struggle to meet the grueling demands of college football and getting a decent education.
1951; 111 min; NL; JR, HS, A; Post World War II.
BUDGET

SAY IT WITH SPILLS

In the rodeo, you'll see cowboys match muscle with rambunctious livestock in steer wrestling and bull riding. Hostile horses throw their weight around in more ways than one in the bronc-riding contests. In the ring, boxers demonstrate an incredible variety of ways to fall when hit by a dynamite punch. The crashing, bashing world of auto racing ends the picture, with stock cars roaring around the track, smashing into one another.
NL; 10 min; 16 mm; NL; JR, HS, A; Post World War II.
FILMIC

SCHOOLYARD DREAMS

The first 35 years of the NBA. Athletes and coaches describe the growth of a league which began playing in high school gyms. Features team dynasties and individual superstars.
NL; 30 min; VHS, U-Matic, 16 mm; NL; HS, A; Post World War II.
KAROL

SCHEFFERVILLE 4TH ARCTIC WINTER GAMES

An exciting view of the Arctic Winter Games held in Schefferville, northern Quebec, in 1976. The events range from table-tennis to curling and include six indigenous arctic sports. The games spanned seven days of hard competition, as well as a week of sharing common northern experiences and goodwill. And, despite temperatures of -30 degrees, the participants' enthusiasm created an atmosphere of great warmth.
1976; 27 min; 16 mm; color; JR, HS, A; Post World War II.
NFBC

SCORE

Like American gridiron, rugby football is fast and bone-crushing, but its players wear little protective clothing. It can be dangerous, and it's certainly one of the fastest-growing body-contact sports. Shot during a New Zealand tour by the French international team, *Score* offers a completely new version of rugby—a study in slow motion, set to Tchaikovsky's *Manfred* symphony. It contains fine examples of the hard and driving play which characterize the game, and its images of powerful men in action give brilliant insight into the very nature of the sport.

1979; 19 min; 16 mm; NL; JR, HS, A; Post World War II.

NFU

SCRAMBLED LEGS

Unusual clips from different wrestling matches, including a four-man tag match, youngsters practicing for their chance, a man and woman in full dress suits, and a wrestler versus a boxer.

NL; 10 min; 16 mm; NL; JR, HS, A; Post World War II.

BUDGET

SEAFLIGHT

In this spectacular view of modern surfing, brilliant water photography is edited to an upbeat score, capturing the exuberant spirit of the sport and the allure of the surfing life-style.

1982; 12 min; 16 mm; color; JR, HS, A; Post World War II.

BUDGET; PYRAMID

SEA SAFARI

The target of this sea hunt is the terrifying manta ray, but many more denizens of the deep are encountered along the way.

NL; 28 min; 16 mm; NL; JR, HS, A; Post World War II.

CINES

SEBASTIAN COE: BORN TO RUN

This program examines how Coe became a world champion, probing deep into the isolation and constant pain that are an intrinsic part of his mental and physical preparation for each race. The program presents footage, not only of Coe's greatest races, but also of his training runs. It explores the relationship between an athlete and his coach. Coe and his coach (his father) talk about his training program, racing strategy, and motivation. Runners and coaches will learn not only techniques but also about the responsibility of both coach and runner in accepting success or failure in racing.

NL; 52 min; VHS, U-Matic, Beta; NL; HS, A; Post World War II.

FOTH

SECONDS TO PLAY

In a behind-the-scenes look at television production, this film follows the ABC broadcast of a collegiate football game at Los Angeles Memorial Coliseum between UCLA and Ohio State. Three days before the game, five trucks and a fifty-man television crew arrive at the Coliseum. The three-hour broadcast will require some two million dollars in equipment and several thousand hours of labor. There will be eight cameras in use: four in the stands, three on the sidelines, and one in the Goodyear blimp, 2,000 feet above the stadium. The film cuts back and forth between the frantic work in the control center and the actual broadcast seen on national television. Time between plays is filled with shots of the cheerleaders and crowd, coaches and instant replays, and commercials are inserted at irregular intervals during pauses in the action. In the end, all this work turns a college football game into a commercial television entertainment spectacular.

1976; 29 min; 16 mm; color; HS, A; Post World War II.

FI; OSU; UILL

SECRETARIAT: BIG RED'S LAST RACE

In October, 1973, Secretariat, called by some the "horse of the century," was entered into his last race—the Canadian International Championship at Woodbine. This film is the chronicle of that race and a fitting testimonial to the horse that gave horse racing its finest expression. Beautifully photographed and edited.

1975; 25 min; 16 mm; color; JR, HS, A; Post World War II.

UCB; UILL; WOMBAT

SEE HOW THEY RUN

Features comments and analyses by medical specialists, sports personalities, coaches, team doctors, and young competitors in exploring the role and control of drug administration in injured player situations, the conflicting attitudes on the status of drugs among amateur and professional sports authorities, and the future role of drugs in sports.

NL; 26 min; VHS, U-Matic; color; JR, HS, A; Post World War II.

ARFO

SEINE INSANITY

A tongue-in-cheek look at the Six Hours of Paris, one of the wildest boat races held anywhere. Top drivers not only battle each other but also barge traffic and bridges as they roar up and down the Seine River in the heart of Paris.

NL; 10 min; 16 mm; NL; JR, HS, A; Post World War II.

TELEFILM

SELF-DEFENSE FOR WOMEN: A POSITIVE APPROACH

Karate experts Kim Fritz and George A. Dillman teach a class of female students how to defend themselves successfully. Stresses the importance of a positive self-image and positive body language to destroy the "helpless woman" image and discourage potential attack.

1979; 13 min; 16 mm; color; JR, HS, A; Post World War II.

USC

SENSATIONAL SIXTIES

Pro football's Golden Decade: When America made pro football "king" for a Sunday afternoon . . . When Jim Brown set virtually every rushing record in the league . . . When Gale Sayers rapidly became one of the most exciting players in the history of the game . . . When Johnny Unitas and Ray Berry developed the forward pass to perfection . . . When Vince Lombardi's Packers made Green Bay, Wisconsin, "Titletown" . . . When Joe Namath led the Jets to victory in Super Bowl III.

NL; 24 min; 16 mm, VHS, U-Matic; NL; JR, HS, A; Post World War II.

NFL; TMA

SENSEI

Examines the Karate Kata, using a simple story to emphasize the development of the spirit through rigorous physical training.

1966; 12 min; 16 mm; color; JR, HS, A; Post World War II.

USC

SENSE OF PURPOSE, A

Basketball superstar Hector Bloom, indifferent to the forms and rhetoric of success, contemplates his future with little expectation of finding happiness and meaning. Hector views cynically the professional sports world which is eager to embrace him upon graduation. Having decided nothing about what he will do after graduation, he is left wondering where life will take him. Edited from the feature film *Drive, He Said.*

1972; 14 min; 16 mm; color; JR, HS, A; Post World War II.

COLU; LCOA; UTEX

SENTINEL: THE WEST FACE

Suspenseful documentary of two climbers scaling Sentinel Rock in Yosemite. Includes overnight bivouac on vertical surface.

1969; 28 min; 16 mm; color; JR, HS, A; Post World War II.

PYRAMID; UILL

SERVE A PURPOSE, TO

Stresses that recreation is an essential human need and examines the therapeutic value of recreation for the handicapped. Defines therapeutic recreation and shows a variety of handicapped people of all ages enjoying an assortment of recreational activities. Provides comments by professors and practitioners in the field of therapeutic recreation.

NL; 13 min; 16 mm; color; HS, A: Post World War II.

IU

SET FOR THE GOLD

An action-packed glimpse of the gold and silver medal U.S.A. men's and women's volleyball teams in their push for the 1988 Olympic gold. Footage from top international matches, up-close interviews with Olympic hopefuls, strategy sessions with the coaches.

NL; 14 min; VHS; NL; JR, HS, A; Post World War II.

MTPS

SEVEN WONDERS OF THE DIVING WORLD

A fast-paced and beautiful compilation of some of the greatest diving locations that even the most discriminating of travel diving connoisseurs would want to visit. The Red Sea, Truk Lagoon, California, Florida, the Bahamas/Caribbean, the Sea of Cortez, and Australia are highlighted as seven of the most popular diving destinations.

NL; 27 min; 16 mm; color; JR, HS, A; Post World War II.

MTPS

SHADOWS OF THE SEA

Man pits skill and experience against the death-dealing shark.

NL; 28 min; 16 mm; NL; JR, HS, A; Post World War II.

CINES

SHAPING THE ACROBAT

The daily life of a 16-year-old Chinese girl acrobat who lives in Shanghai; rehearsals, relaxation, and TV appearance.

1982; 25 min; 16 mm; color; JR, HS, A; Post World War II.
CORF; PSU

SHARK HUNT

A hardy group of Irish fishermen brave the open ocean and pounding surf in outboard-powered boats to hunt the giant basking sharks off the coast of Ireland.
NL; 10 min; 16 mm; NL; JR, HS, A; Post World War II.
TELEFILM

SHEER SPORT

Climbing a nearly perpendicular wall of rock 65 meters high takes cool nerve, even though it's not in the Alps or the Rockies. The Precambrian rock of the Laurentian mountains north of Montreal attract climbers of Le Club de Montagne Canadien. Mini-transmitters carried by the climbers, and daring camerawork, follow two men and a woman who grope and pull and inch their way upward.
1969; 49.5 min; NL; NL; HS, A; Post World War II.
NFBC

SHOOT FOR THE STARS: THE 25-YEAR OLD HISTORY OF THE DALLAS COWBOYS

A concise history of the Cowboys from their days as a ragtag 1960 expansion team to the powerhouse teams of the 1970s and 1980s. Includes a 15-minute segment never seen on television. The most memorable games and top players are profiled.
NL; 40 min; 16 mm, VHS, U-Matic; NL; JR, HS, A; Post World War II.
NFL; TMA

SHOOTING STARS

This dramatization celebrates the Edmonton Grads women's basketball team, formed in 1915 and disbanded in 1940. During that time the team was Canadian Champion (1922-1940), North American Champion (1923-1940), and World Champion (1924-1940). Their phenomenal record of 502 wins and 20 losses remains unrivalled by any team in any sport.
1987; 49.5 min; 16 mm; color; JR, HS, A; Modern Sport to Post World War II.
NFBC

SHORT DISTANCE RUNNER

Dramatizes the story of a high school student whose increased dependency on alcohol affects his schoolwork and athletic pursuits.

1978; 21 min; 16 mm; color; JR, HS, A; Post World War II.
MARTC; SIGPRS

SHOW JUMPING

Grand Prix horse jumping is one of the most exciting, suspenseful, and beautiful sporting events in the world. This program shows Leslie Burr, a member of the 1984 U.S. Olympic gold medal equestrian team on the Grand Prix circuit, culminating at Madison Square Garden, where the champions of champions compete. Superb close-up footage of thoroughbreds and riders.
NL; 10 min; 16 mm; color; JR, HS, A; Post World War II.
MTPS

SHOWMAN SHOOTER

The spectacular rifle and shotgun marksmanship of the late Herb Parsons, world-renowned Western exhibition shooter. From clay pigeons to tossed coins, he performs one rapid-fire feat after another, with many repeated in slow motion. Ted Husing narrates.
NL; 27 min; 16 mm; NL; JR, HS, A; Post World War II.
WINWES

SHOWTIME FOR SADDLEBREDS

The place is the Kentucky State Fair, where the pride of the stallions appear annually for gold medal awards. A good film for horse fans. The pride of the stallions are shown galloping, trotting, and training with harnesses. Morning exercises are also demonstrated.
NL; 20 min; 16 mm; color; JR, HS, A; Post World War II.
BUDGET

SIDEWINDER ONE

Wealthy business tycoon Alex Cord has a love for motorcycles; he also has the bucks to indulge in his favorite passion and get what he wants. He wants a local winner to ride his cycles in the various cycle motorcross races. When Cord's sister, Susan Howard, meets the new member of Cord's firm (he has been given 49 percent of the business) who just happens to be the one that will ride Cord's bikes, things start to glow. An accident causes a breakup of the couple, but love eventually wins out in a film whose main strength is eye-grabbing footage shot of several races.
1977; 97 min; 16 mm; color; JR, HS, A; Post World War II.
BUDGET

SINGLEHANDERS

Alone on the open sea, two Canadians, Bob Lush and Mike Birch, took cameras aboard their yachts during the 1980 Observer Singlehanded Transatlantic Race. The result is more than a record of this prestigious international sailing event. The sport of ocean racing becomes the starting point for an epic of challenge and determination.

1982; 49.5 min; 16 mm; VHS, HS, A; Post World War II.

NFBC

6,000,000 SKIERS

Warren Miller production illustrating the value of the USSA and its divisions.

NL; 24 min; 16 mm; NL; HS, A; Post World War II.

ESA

60 CYCLES

Subjective views show the 11th Annual St. Laurent Bicycle Race through the Province of Quebec, in which participants from thirteen countries cover 1500 miles of countryside in twelve days. Opening with a slow-motion sequence in which the film's only narration, consisting of a spoken introduction, is presented, the camera pursues the contestants from a variety of angles. Spinning wheels and crouched figures streaking past farms and through villages, cheered on by spectators, form a colorful montage. Captures all the excitement and drama of a grueling sports event where the challenge seems more personal than competitive.

1965; 17 min; 16 mm; color; JR, HS, A; Post World War II.

FI; NFBC; UILL

SKATEBOARD SAFETY

Points out that skateboarding is a sport that requires skill, training, and experience. Suggests that many injuries can be avoided by wearing shoes, safety helmets, and clothes with protective padding at the knees, hips, spine, elbows, and shoulders. Also, the skateboard should be checked for proper wheel tension and condition. Commentary by experienced and beginning skateboard enthusiasts and a lively musical score further enhance this educational and topical film.

1976; 12 min; 16 mm; color; E, JR, HS, A; Post World War II.

PYRAMID; UILL

SKATEBOARDING TO SAFETY

Skateboarding, as a sport that uses areas designed primarily for other uses, presents special dangers and requires special safety precautions. Recommended by this film are proper preparation, including inspection of surfaces; protective dress; knowledge of, and respect for, the law; knowledge of the limitations, and awareness of the problems.

1978; 10 min; 16 mm; color; E, JR, HS, A; Post World War II.

UILL

SKATEDATER

An Oscar-winning short about a group of preteen boys who ride around on skateboards. One of them falls in love with a pretty 10-year-old and must decide whether to skate with the crowd or roll off in his own direction. The film is beautifully done, without dialogue, and with a nice upbeat musical score orchestrating the youngsters' actions. Particularly recommended for upper elementary and middle school use.

1966; 20 min; 16 mm; color; E, JR; Post World War II.

PYRAMID

SKATING RINK, THE

A teenage boy, lacking in self-confidence and handicapped by an awkward stammer, has great problems relating to friends and family until he discovers an aptitude for ice skating which opens the way to new relationships and personal fulfillment. Based on the novel by Mildred Lee.

1975; 27 min; 16 mm; color; JR, HS, A; Post World War II.

LCOA; OSU

SKI ANYWHERE, ANYTIME

Until quite recently, skiing was a sport requiring wide open spaces and lots of snow. In response to an evergrowing demand, artificial ski-tracks have been built in several Belgian cities. Equipped with ski-lifts, the artificial slopes allow beginners to train for a sport which could otherwise only be practiced for a few days each winter. In winter the towns of Spa, Francorchamps, and Malmedy offer some very fine natural slopes in a beautiful setting that is appreciated by many foreign visitors as well. A French language film

1975; 13 min; 16 mm; color; JR, HS, A; Post World War II.

BELGIUM

SKI BOOM

A look at the world of skiing and snow that demonstrates the fun, beauty, and special magic that captures the enthusiasm of millions of skiers every year. From recreation to competition, the joy of skiing is captured on film. Some of the top names in skiing, such as Jean-Claude Killey and Susie Chafee, make appearances at odd points during the proceedings, but the show is the beauty of the snowcapped landscape and the world of the skiers.

1971; 25 min; 16 mm; color; JR, HS, A; Post World War II.
BUDGET

SKI CHAMPS GO TO AUSTRALIA

All the pageantry and the thrills as the world's top water skiers compete in the 9th World Water Ski Championships at Surfer's Paradise Gardens in Australia.

NL; 27 min; 16 mm; NL; JR, HS, A; Post World War II.
TELEFILM

SKI FEVER

Fast-paced boating action introduces the thrills and glamor of water-skiing. Much of the action was filmed at Cypress Gardens and includes slalom and trick skiing and kite flying, with a sequence for the beginning skier.

NL; 14 min; 16 mm; NL; JR, HS, A; Post World War II.
SOLANA

SKI FEVER

Skiing is beauty, sport, and folly. The scenes in this delightful nonverbal film include ski jumping by children, after ski "swimming" on skis, slalom racing, tracking in deep powder, and even a small avalanche.

1971; 9 min; 16 mm; color; E, JR, HS, A; Post World War II.
BUDGET

SKI FINESSE

Sten Erikson, winner of the 1952 Olympic gold medal in the giant slalom, as well as a silver medal in the slalom, is recognized as one of the great skiers of all time. Here, the viewer is given the chance to observe Erikson's beautiful style, as well as hear him discuss his method of ski instruction.

NL; 30 min; 16 mm; color; JR, HS, A; Post World War II.
BUDGET

SKI FLYING

Shows, using slow-motion photography and no narration, the various aspects of a ski-jumping competition. Focuses on the tension before the jump, the attention to proper "flying" attitude during the jump,

and the danger that adds both to the tension and beauty of the event.

1975; 6 min; 16 mm; color; JR, HS, A; Post World War II.
EBEC; LSU

SKIING

The history of skiing from its early beginnings to the present day. German and English sound versions available.

1960; 10 min; 16 mm; BW; JR, HS, A; Modern to Post World War II.
MTPS

SKIING IS BELIEVING

The world-famous Tommy Bartlett water skiers perform their precision routines.

NL; 14 min; 16 mm; NL; E, JR, HS, A; Post World War II.
TELEFILM

SKI ON THE WILD SIDE

The world of skiing is the subject of this excellent documentary that journeys around the world (a la the surfing classic *Endless Summer*). America, Switzerland, Russia, Yugoslavia, New Zealand, France, and Japan are among the countries visited as the camera focuses on footage of ski competitions, ski-jumping, and other moments (such as the World Falling Contest). Various names in the world of international skiing, such as Jean-Claude Killy, Sue Chaffee, Roger Staub, and Miereille Goitschel, are seen in action.

1967; 104 min; 16 mm; color; JR, HS, A; Post World War II.
BUDGET

SKI THE OUTER LIMITS

Man's quest to extend the outer limits of his ability is seen in the skills of professional skiers. Beautiful slow-motion and natural speed footage illustrate the disciplined technique and daring involved in downhill racing, the slalom, and giant slalom, and the grace and inventiveness of ski dancing and acrobatics. A final sequence shows that man on skis has almost realized his ambition to fly.

1969; 28 min; 16 mm; color; JR, HS, A; Post World War II.
LSU; PYRAMID

SKI TOTAL

The real face of competition skiing, shown by French champions, including 1966 Olympic Champion Jean Vuarnet, from early training to the final run. For the first time, a film of this kind has been shot by the skiers themselves, using cameras fitted into helmets to record every moment, from the agonizing second before the start right through to the finish.

NL; 16 min; 16 mm; color; JR, HS, A; Post World War II.

FACSEA

SKI WHIZ!

Jumps, somersaults, and spills are all part of this film on snow sports: skiing, ice skating, boating, bobsledding, and tobogganing. Sequences show skiers hiking up a mountain carrying skis, side-stepping down a steep hill, descending on a rope; two persons on one pair of skis; graceful skiers appearing to dance.

1972; 8 min; 16 mm; color; JR, HS, A; Post World War II.

PYRAMID; UILL

SKY CAPERS

Shows, without narration, the training, skill, and hazards of sky divers. Conveys the freedom and satisfaction of the sport with shots of the jumpers frolicking in mid-air.

NL; 16 min; 16 mm; color; JR, HS, A; Post World War II.

PYRAMID; LSU

SKY DIVE

Breathtaking sky circus created by a group of men and women as they glide in free fall and then form geometric configurations before opening their parachutes.

1979; 15 min; 16 mm; color; JR, HS, A; Post World War II.

PYRAMID; OSU

SKY DIVERS

One of the most spectacular films ever made of the popular sport of sky diving. Here is the U. S. Navy Sky Diving team, "The Shooting Stars," in a diving exhibition at Pt. Magu, California. Divers film free-fall dives of other members of the team, who jump from 10,000 feet at 120 miles per hour and open their chutes at 2,500 feet.

NL; 15 min; 16 mm; color; JR, HS, A; Post World War II.

BUDGET

SKY DIVING

Presents sky diving as a thrilling game and competitive sport enjoyed by more than 25,000 Americans. Pictures free-fall and precision work, and shows

the competitive jumper being judged on skills in free-fall maneuvers (style) and control of the chute (accuracy) in the required "International Series During Free Fall."

1970; 14 min; 16 mm; color; E, JR, HS, A; Post World War II.

TREP; UILL

SKY HIGH

Compares various aspects of flying. Includes aerobatics, sky diving, hang gliding, and the history of flying.

NL; NL; VHS, U-Matic; color; JR, HS, A; Modern to Post World War II.

ALTI

SKY SURFERS

Traces the history of flight and demonstrates the sport of hang gliding.

1975; 25 min; 16 mm; color; Making of Modern Sport to Post World War II.

FIARTS

SNO-TWISTER

A look at the planning and development of Mercur's first snowmobile race sled, the Sno-Twister. Includes exciting action on the track.

NL; 12 min; 16 mm; NL; JR, HS, A; Post World War II.

TELEFILM

SNOWMOBILE GRAND PRIX: THE RICHEST RACE

Filmed at the Snowmobile Grand Prix, better known as the King's Castle Inn at Lake Tahoe, Nevada, this competition draws entrants from all over the world, including many celebrities. Interviews of the contestants help add to the atmosphere of this most unusual and challenging sport.

NL; 27 min; 16 mm; color; JR, HS, A; Post World War II.

BUDGET

SOCCER SCENE GERMANY (1)

Soccer portrait of Berlin.

1978; 29 min; 16 mm; color; JR, HS, A; Post World War II.

CGFRG

SOCCER SCENE GERMANY (2)

This film is about Stuttgart—a city of contrasts——a city with a character all its own. Its football and its industry are dynamic, exciting, gripping.

1979; 29 min; 16 mm; color; JR, HS, A; Post World War II.
CGFRG

SOCCER SCENE GERMANY (3)

The "Vfl Borussia" Moenchengladbach club has been prominent in the German First Division soccer for many years. It was champion in five of the twelve years it belonged to the top league, and cup winner of one.
1978; 27 min; 16 mm; color; JR, HS, A; Post World War II.
CGFRG

SOCCER SCENE GERMANY (4)

Arminia Bielefeld isn't a club that can boast of international successes; for years it has been going up and down between the Bundesiga, the National League, and the Second Division. Scenes from games, training, and life within the club show that Arminia Bielefeld is a provincial team.
1979; 28 min; 16 mm; color; JR, HS, A; Post World War II.
CGFRG

SOCCER SCENE GERMANY (5)

The Hamburg Sports Club had to wait almost twenty years before winning the German Soccer Championship again. HSV, as the club is known, is just as much a part of the city of Hamburg as the world-famous port. Uwe Seeler, one of Germany's greatest soccer players, accompanies us through the soccer and city scene of Hamburg.
1979; 28 min; 16 mm; color; JR, HS, A; Post World War II.
CGFRG

SOCCER SCENE GERMANY (6)

There were five players from the FC Kaiserslautern club in the West German team that won the world football championship in 1954. These five players included team captain Fritz Walter. Twenty-five years later, the club was still one of the best in the country.
1979; 28 min; 16 mm; color; JR, HS, A; Post World War II.
CGFRG

SOCCER SCENE GERMANY (7)

FC Nuremberg, the club, as its fan call it, is the most successful German soccer club. It has won the German championship nine times, which is a record. But that is history—today the club is going up and down between the Bundesliga, the national league, and the second division. For the people of Nueremberg, the club is also part of the city's history—a living part.
1979; 29 min; 16 mm; color; JR, HS, A; Post World War II.
CGFRG

SOCCER SCENE GERMANY (8)

A billy goat and the world-renowned cathedral are the symbols in the emblem of "First FC Cologne," one of the most successful soccer clubs in Germany. The film shows training scenes, the social life on the periphery of the club, and excerpts of interesting national league matches.
1978; 27 min; 16 mm; color; JR, HS, A; Post World War II.
CGFRG

SOLO

Portrays the pleasure and dangers of mountain climbing, as a lone hiker ascends, the chimes of his hammer and piton being the only human sounds. Presents three aspects of mountain climbing—the driving rhythm of sustained physical effort, the discovery of scenes and weather unknown to others, and the commitment to challenges which must be met alone.
1972; 15 min; 16 mm; color; JR, HS, A; Post World War II.
PYRAMID; UU

SOLO: BEHIND THE SCENES

Discusses some of the cinematic problems and climbing difficulties encountered during the making of *Solo*. Explores man's relationship with himself and with nature.
1973; 11 min; 16 mm; color; JR, HS, A; Post World War II.
UWASH

SOMEONE'S IN THE KITCHEN

Sherman High's baseball star pitcher, Jamie Clark, will have to quit the team and find a job if his mother loses her position as the home economics teacher. Jamie solves the problem by having his team sign up for her class, which displeases the coach, a traditionalist who thinks cooking is "sissy stuff."
1982; 25 min; 16 mm; color; JR, HS; Post World War II.
LCOA; UU

SOMETHING EXTRA

With the departure of Joe Kapp—Bob Lee, Gary Cuozzo, and company struggled for the 1971 championship, only to lose out in the playoff. However, the film proves that the Vikings are a team comprised of "something extra." 1971 Vikings Highlights Film.

1971; NL; 16 mm; NL; JR, HS, A; Post World War II.

HAMMS

SON OF FOOTBALL FOLLIES

The ridiculous plays, absurd situations, crazy collisions, and hilarious player antics of the NFL. Bugs Bunny, Sylvester the Cat, Yosemite Sam, and other cartoon characters narrate.

NL; 22 min; VHS; NL; E, JR, HS, A; Post World War II.

KAROL

SOUTHERN "500," THE

The Southern "500" auto race is one of the most exciting spectacles in the entire world of motor sports. In addition to a wild, competitive, crash-filled race, this film also tells the history of each of the top drivers. See, in flashback, the victories and defeats of men like Bobby Allison, Buddy Baker, Richard Petty, Cale Yarborough, and David Pearson, as well as the amazing battle in which Cale Yarborough nudged another car, lost control, and found himself sailing out of the track, all four wheels clearing the guardrail at better than 140 miles an hour. Yarborough walked away.

NL; 28 min; 16 mm, VHS; color; JR, HS, A; Post World War II.

SF

SOUTHWESTERN ATHLETIC CONFERENCE FOOTBALL

These powerhouse football players sweep the viewer into the action during 1971 games played in cities like New York, Chicago, and Los Angeles. Meet the coaches and presidents of these primarily black colleges and universities, and see the impressive facilities. Bands, cheerleaders, and rock musical score.

NL; 29 min; 16 mm; NL; JR, HS, A; Post World War II.

MTPS

SO YOU WANT TO BE . . . ON THE TEAM

Personal comments interspersed with action shots of such famous athletes as Ferguson Jenkins, Randy Hundley, Bob Boozer, and Gayle Sayers, along with the narration, offer information regarding the means of entering, obtaining training, and length of performing years for the sports of baseball, football, and basketball. Emphasis is placed upon the role of the school in furnishing the means of becoming a professional player. Jack Brickhouse, sports commentator, summarizes the typical procedure that is followed by those who achieve athletic stardom.

1968; 11 min; 16 mm; color; JR, HS, A; Post World War II.

UILL

SOUTH-EAST NUBA, THE

Analyzes the Nuba, who live in a very remote part of Africa near the center of the Sudan. Shows that they have their own flamboyant culture which includes body painting and the sport of bracelet fighting.

1982; 60 min; 16 mm, VHS, U-Matic; color; JR, HS, A; Post World War II.

BBC; FI

SPACE AGE BASEBALL

Highlights of the Houston Astros' 1965 season and a tour of the Astrodome.

NL; 28 min; 16 mm; NL; JR, HS, A; Post World War II.

CINES

SPANISH RIDING SCHOOL OF VIENNA, THE

The famous white Lipizzan Stallions, guided by their riders, perform the elegant movement of haute ecole at its purest.

NL; 16 min; 16 mm; BW or color; JR, HS, A; Post World War II.

AUSINS

SPECIAL GIFT, A

A 14-year-old boy can't decide if he should yield to his father's insistence to give up his ballet training and concentrate on the acceptable "male" sport of basketball or if he should disobey his dad and risk ridicule and ostracism at school by admitting his commitment to dance.

1979; 47 min; 16 mm, VHS, U-Matic; color; JR, HS, A; Post World War II.

TAHSEM; TIMLIF

SPEED-A-WAY

This game for boys and girls is a combination of the elements of soccer, basketball, speedball, field ball, and hockey with an opportunity for players to run with the ball.

1952; 10 min; 16 mm; BW; JR, HS, A; Post World War II.

UILL

SPIRIT

Spirit has great appeal to groups interested in skiing, sports, dance, and the art of human movement. It is the story of a young man who decides to break away from his rut in the city and return to the world of skiing. *Spirit* is the visualization of a youth living out his fantasies. Follow him across America, then to Europe, and back again to experience the most exotic skiing locations and contests. Downhill racing, slalom, hotdogging, ski dancing, and comic acrobatics make up the visual poetry that is enhanced by an intriguing contemporary music score. The climax of the film occurs in a slow-motion sequence of "fire-jumpers" who literally light themselves on fire and are seen floating through space like giant falling comets.

NL; 39 min; 16 mm; color; JR, HS, A; Post World War II.
BUDGET

SPIRIT OF COMPETITION, THE

Presents the excitement and drama of the Milrose Games, one of America's favorite amateur track and field competitions. Shows the commitment and dedication young athletes bring to their sport.

NL; 28 min; VHS; color; JR, HS, A; Post World War II.
KAROL

SPIRIT OF ECSTASY

In 1913, the *Spirit of Ecstasy* demolished all competition in the Austrian Alpine trial. In 1973, the same *Spirit of Ecstasy,* now 60 years old, again thunders through the Austrian Alps in a reenactment of the 1913 race, against cars from around the world (including many that had participated in the original race). Relax and take a ride through the beautiful Alps as a passenger aboard one of these noble resurrected autos. Highlights of the tortuous 1650 miles are captured. The autos and scenery combine to provide an exciting visual travel brochure of the way things were in the past.

1974; 28 min; 16 mm; color; JR, HS, A; Modern to Post World War II.
BUDGET

SPIRIT OF THE KATA

Five women, all of them black belts in karate, are examples of how this ancient martial art can transform lives. They demonstrate how it can generate a whole range of physical, psychological, and spiritual benefits. To these women, karate means much more than self-defence; its lessons of discipline and harmony can be applied to situations on the street or in the boardroom.

1985; 27.5 min; 16 mm; NL; HS, A; Post World War II.
NFBC

SPIRIT OF THE WIND

The place of the horse in Indian life and culture. Events and stories are recounted in the context of the rodeo arena and the lives of Indians that are part of rodeo world. The horse as an important part of the lives of Indians.

1976; 27 min; U-Matic; color; JR, HS, A; Post World War II.
WSU

SPIRIT OF THE WIND

A study of spinnaker-carrying sailboats, including filming of the Yacht Club Centennial Regatta at Lake Geneva, Wisconsin.

1974; 26 min; 16 mm; color; JR, HS, A; Post World War II.
UILL

SPORT HOCHSCHULE KOLN

A college for college coaches; the famous sport school of Cologne.

1964; 29 min; 16 mm; BW; HS, A; Post World War II.
MTPS

SPORTING IN BRITAIN

Water sports, aerobatics, gliding, auto racing, golf, fishing, horseracing and riding, sky diving, carnivals and fairs, darts, fox hunting, cricket, tennis, rallys, regattas, the Highland Games, mountain climbing, skiing. Britain has them all neatly packaged into an exciting new film.

NL; 23 min; 16 mm; NL; E, JR, HS, A; Post World War II.
AUDPLAN

SPORT OF ORIENTEERING, THE

Depicts Swedish sportsmen in a cross-country orienteering race using a map and compass to find their way through unknown territory.

NL; 24 min; 16 mm, VHS; color; JR, HS, A; Post World War II.
IFB

SPORTS

Discusses ways in which sports reflect the values, biases, and structure of American society.

NL; 30 min; VHS, U-Matic; color; JR, HS, A; Post World War II.
DALCCD

SPORTS ALL SORTS

Motorcycling at Le Mans, the steeplechase and the horse show in Paris, bullfighting featuring one of the best toreros, fencing, and a judo champion are all featured.

NL; 23 min VHS, U-Matic; color; JR, HS, A; Post World War II.

FACSEA

SPORTS AS A HUMANISTIC ACTIVITY (LONG VERSION)

A panel discussion with Robert Weaver, moderator and associate professor of English at Pennsylvania State University; Heywood Hale Broun, former CBS sports commentator; Aaron Druckman, associate professor of philosophy at Penn State; Eleanor Metheny, professor emerita of Southern California; Mike Reid, former defensive tackle for Penn State and the Cincinnati Bengals; and Joe Paterno, Penn State head football coach.

1975; 59 min (also available in 29 min); VHS, color; HS, A; Post World War II.

PENNST

SPORTS BEYOND WINNING

Produced to encourage and inspire young women to participate in sports activities as a means to more fully develop their self-esteem, this film uses high school women as role models. They demonstrate and talk about the benefits of sports beyond a strong healthy body: leadership skills, flexibility, discipline, decision making, self-confidence, friendship, and self-esteem.

NL; 19 min; 16 mm, VHS; color; JR, HS, A; Post World War II.

LEVI; MTPS

SPORTS FOR EVERY TASTE

Traditional sports reunite Frenchmen every Sunday. Boxing, French style, is becoming popular again. Men and women fly through the air high over Chamonix in the French Alps. And finally, rugby is the most popular sport in southwestern France.

1977; 26 min; 16 mm; NL; JR, HS, A; Post World War II.

FACSEA

SPORTS FOR ONE

Discusses the value of exercise for physical health, release from frustration, and the development of self-reliance and self-discipline. Describes how team sports help people function with others.

1975; 22 min; 16 mm; color; JR, HS, A; Post World War II.

BYU; UWISC

SPORTS FOR THE YOUNG

Although the film centers on the sport of soccer, it is not limited to training routines, rules, and soccer competition. It relates this sport to community life and pedagogical problems. The main part of the film describes the training at the sports academy at Henner. German and English sound versions available.

1956; 40 min; 16 mm; NL; JR, HS, A; Post World War II.

MTPS

SPORT'S GOLDEN AGE

Emphasizes America's propensity for sports of all kinds. Shows several generations of champions in action: Knute Rockne, Red Grange, Helen Wills, Johnny Weissmuller, Jack Dempsey, Joe Louis, Bob Feller, Joe DiMaggio, and many others. Shows the making of sports equipment and Americans enjoying a wide variety of sports from swimming to skiing.

1949; 15 min; 16 mm; BW; JR, HS, A; Golden Age to Post World War II.

UILL

SPORTS HIGHLIGHTS, 1955

Rex Mays' 100-mile memorial classic speedrace; Baseball's All-Star game in Milwaukee; Miller High Life Open golf tournament; December skiing in Aspen, Colorado; World Championship football with the Los Angeles Rams and Cleveland Browns.

NL; 20-30 min; 16 mm; color; JR, HS, A; Post World War II.

BUDGET; MILLER

SPORTS HIGHLIGHTS, 1956

National Ski Jumping Championships in Ishpeming, Michigan; 23rd Annual All-Star Baseball Championship game; Sam Snead at the Miller High-Life Open golf tournament; 250-mile National Big Car Championship; pro football with the Chicago Bears and New York Giants.

NL; 20-30 min; 16 mm; color; JR, HS, A; Post World War II.

BUDGET

SPORTS HIGHLIGHTS, 1961

National Hockey League's Stanley Cup Playoffs; Kentucky Derby's 87th Annual Horse Race; baseball's Warren Spahn wins 300th major league victory; football's 12th annual All-Star Pro-Bowl Classic.

NL; 20-30 min; 16 mm; color; JR, HS, A; Post World War II.

BUDGET

SPORTS IMMORTALS

One of Movietone's great sports compilations showing highlights in the careers of such sports greats as Red Grange (football), Suzanne Lenglen and Helen Wills (tennis), Barney Oldfield (auto racing), Babe Ruth and Grover Cleveland Alexander (baseball), Knute Rockne (football coach), Man o' War (race horse), Gertrude Ederle (channel swimmer), Paavo Nurmi (track), Sonja Henie (ice skating).

NL; 11 min; 16 mm; BW; JR, HS, A; Golden Age and Depression Era.

BUDGET; UILL

SPORTS IN SPAIN

A presentation of all sports that can be practiced in Spain.

NL; 20 min; 16 mm; NL; JR, HS, A; Post World War II.

ASF

SPORTS LEGENDS: JESSE OWENS

Presents an interview with track star Jesse Owens, hosted by Paul Hornung. Recalls Owens' comments. Shows Owens making appearances, promoting youth athletes, youth cooperation in the home, and family teamwork.

1976; 22 min; 16 mm; color; JR, HS, A; Depression Era and World War II.

COUNFI; UWISC

SPORTSMAN

An excellent film for the young hunter. The story revolves around a teenager spending a day afield with his uncle and deals with many issues of hunting ethics.

NL; 23 min; 16 mm; color; JR, HS, A; Post World War II.

PSU

SPORTS ODYSSEY, A

This entertainment film is a montage of thrills and comedy featuring surfing, water skiing, hang gliding, and skateboarding. Old-time sports classics are included. Minimal narration with musical accompaniment. Some sequences in slow-motion.

1976; 26 min; 16 mm; color; JR, HS, A; Post World War II.

UILL

SPORTS PANORAMA

World Series; PBA National Bowling Tourney; star college quarterbacks; breezy airplane; fly casting; Adolph Rupp's Kentucky Wildcats.

NL: NL: 16 mm; NL; JR, HS, A; Post World War II.

MILLER

SPORTS PROFILE

Artie Wilson began his career as a member of the Birmingham (Alabama) Black Barons team. He tours his old Birmingham neighborhood to visit the playing field and to reminisce with his cousin. Reenactments of scenes with the athletes' childhoods and careers throughout the program, along with photographs from their private collections. Alice Coachman, a high jumper and sprinter, trained for eight years before competing at the 1948 Olympics. In winning the gold medal for the high jump, she became the first black woman to win a medal after the war.

1982; 29 min; 16 mm; color; JR, HS, A; Golden Age to Post World War II.

BCNFL; NGUZO; PSU

SPORTS PSYCHOLOGY FOR YOUTH COACHES

Designed to examine the role of the coach as a communicator and motivator, to provide a basic understanding of the communication and motivation process, and to outline a number of coaching-related principles to achieve these goals.

1982; 20 min; 16 mm; color; HS, A; Post World War II.

UWISC

SPORTS SCHOLARSHIPS, PART I: ADVANTAGES

Joe Paterno, athletic director at Penn State University, and Eric Zemper, research coordinator at the National Collegiate Athletic Association, on the advantages of sports scholarships.

NL; 25 min; VHS, U-Matic; color; JR, HS, A; Post World War II.

SIRS

SPORTS SCHOLARSHIPS, PART II: DISADVANTAGES

Continues discussion with Joe Paterno and Eric Zemper on sports scholarships, this time touching on the disadvantages.

NL; 25 min; VHS, U-Matic; color; JR, HS, A; Post World War II.

SIRS

SPORTS SHOW

Features a high school tennis player whose goal is to win Wimbledon. Shows weight control programs for young people, handicapped horseback riding, how

roller skates are made, and activities of the Argonauts scuba diving club.
1982; 24 min; VHS, U-Matic; color; JR, HS, A; Post World War II.
WCCOTV

SPORTS, SOCIETY, AND SELF

Games are played and watched in every culture. The Tarahumara are excellent endurance runners; physical training is important to the Japanese; and Africa's Baoule people enjoy a fast-paced game of mental skill called Aweie.
1983; 15 min; VHS, U-Matic; color; JR, HS, A; Post World War II.
AITECH; POSIMP

SPORTS SPECTACULAR

A tennis training course high in the mountains; the Roland Garros Tennis Internationals in Paris; land yachting on the beaches of northern France; pole vaulting, the star event of French athletes.
12 min; 1980; VHS, U-Matic; color; JR, HS, A; Post World War II.
FACSEA

SPORTS SPECTRUM (1)

Key 1969 college grid games; U.S. Open tennis; profile of golfer Charlie Sifford; Marquette's defense snares NIT basketball crown; ordeal of an NHL goalie; dune buggy daring-do.
NL; NL; 16 mm; NL; JR, HS, A; Post World War II.
MILLER

SPORTS SPECTRUM (2)

Fencing; Philippe Boisse, cycling the Paris "Six Day" event; karate: Sophie Berger; a look at the new catamarans before the big races; the French junior show jumping team.
1984; 24 min; 16 mm; color; JR, HS, A; Post World War II.
FACSEA

SPORTS SUITE, A

Youthful participants demonstrate the exuberance and joy they find in physical education and team sports. A girl gymnast performs on the bars; volleyball players on a rooftop; swimmers race in a competition pool. Due to some ingenious new camera techniques, a soccer game becomes a participation experience for the viewer.
1977; 8 min; 16 mm; color; JR, HS, A; Post World War II.
PYRAMID; UILL

SPORTS THAT SET THE STYLES

How the nature of different sports influenced what the women players wore, and how what they wore on the playing field or beaches eventually found its way into society.
NL; 28 min; 16 mm; color; JR, HS, A; Making of Modern Sport to Post World War II.
SEARS; WSU

SPORTS: THE PROGRAMMED GLADIATORS

Explores the growing commercialization of sports and the resulting pressures on athletes. Discusses the increasing emphasis on professional sports and the decline of amateurism, and the crucial role of TV in today's business-dominated sports industries. Professional basketball star Bill Bradley comments on the problems facing young athletes and the distortion of competition caused by fans.
1971; 22 min; 16 mm; color; HS, A; Post World War II.
DOCA; UCB

SPORTS THRILLS FROM 1962

Basketball's Boston Celtics vs. Philadelphia Warriors; 88th running of the Kentucky Derby; NFL championship game with the New York Giants and Green Bay Packers.
NL; 20-30 min; 16 mm; color; JR, HS, A; Post World War II.
BUDGET

SPORTS THRILLS OF 1956

1956 NFL championship game, New York vs. Chicago; '56 Miller High Life Open, ski jumping in Upper Michigan; auto racing in Milwaukee.
1957; NL; 16 mm; NL; JR, HS, A; Post World War II.
MILLER

SPORTS THRILLS OF 1957

Water skiing in Cypress Gardens, Florida; baseball's 24th Annual All-Star Classic; 3rd Miller High-Life Open golf tournament; NFL championship game with the Detroit Lions and Cleveland Browns.
NL; 20-30 min; 16 mm; color; JR, HS, A; Post World War II.
BUDGET

SPORTS THRILLS OF 1957

1957 NFL championship game, Detroit vs. Cleveland; All-Star Baseball Game; '57 Miller High Life Open; auto racing at Milwaukee; Florida water skiers.

1958; NL; 16 mm; NL; JR, HS, A; Post World War II.
MILLER

SPORTS THRILLS OF 1958

Cheyenne Frontier Days Rodeo; 1959 Pro-Bowl game; 1958 Miller High Life Open; Southern 500 stock car race; President's Cup hydroplane regatta.
1959; NL; 16 mm; NL; JR, HS, A; Post World War II.
MILLER

SPORTS THRILLS OF 1959

Speed boat racing at the Gold Cup Regatta Championships; Los Angeles Dodgers and Milwaukee Braves compete for the pennant; National Big Car championship race in Wisconsin; football's Pro-Bowl Game at the Los Angeles Coliseum.
1960; 20-30 min; 16 mm; color; JR, HS, A; Post World War II.
BUDGET; MILLER

SPORTS THRILLS OF 1960

National Basketball Association's All-Star game; Indianapolis 500; Jersey Derby horse race; 9th annual *Milwaukee Journal*'s Indoor Sport Events Championship; 11th annual Pro-Bowl Classic.
1961; 20-30 min; 16 mm; color; JR, HS, A; Post World War II.
BUDGET; MILLER

SPORTS THRILLS OF 1961

Indianapolis 500; Stanley Cup Hockey, Chicago vs. Detroit; 87th Kentucky Derby; 1962 Pro Bowl game; Warren Spahn's 300th mound victory.
1962; 16 mm; NL; JR, HS, A; Post World War II.
MILLER

SPORTS UNLIMITED, 1967

Philadelphia wins 1967 NBA Crown; Cheyenne Rodeo; North American bobsledding championships; Indianapolis 500; skiing; NCAA swimming, diving championships.
NL; NL; 16 mm; NL; JR, HS, A; Post World War II.
MILLER

SPORTS UNLIMITED, 1967

National Bobsled Championships, North America Alpine Championship game; NBA action with the Philadelphia 76ers vs. the Boston Celtics; Cheyenne, Wyoming's annual rodeo.

NL; 20-30 min; 16 mm; color; JR, HS, A; Post World War II.
BUDGET

SPORTS UNLIMITED, 1969

The NHL Minnesota North Stars vs. Montreal Canadiens; Charlie Sifford at the Los Angeles PGA Open; College basketball at Marquette; dune buggies in Florida; salute to college football's centennial year.
NL; 20-30 min; 16 mm; color; JR, HS, A; Post World War II.
BUDGET

SPOTLIGHT ON SPORTS

College basketball; Kentucky Derby and Preakness; Peggy Fleming on Olympic ice; NCAA gymnastics; Navy's Blue Angels flying team.
NL; NL; 16 mm; NL; JR, HS, A; Post World II.
MILLER

SQUARES

Austin Ruth is a rodeo cowboy moving from rodeo to rodeo, hoping to win big, but always losing. Chase Lawrence is an attractive college dropout from a rich family, running away from her stifling world and her family's life-style. The two meet when the girl nearly runs the cowboy down in her Cadillac, then gives him a ride. From then on it is an odyssey of discovery, both of self and each other, with the personalities of the two companions clashing and the attraction developing from initial mutual distrust to love, as one realizes she must live her own life, while the other finally breaks from his mold of being a loser.
1972; 92 min; 16 mm; color; JR, HS, A; Post World War II.
BUDGET

ST. ANDREWS, CRADLE OF GOLF

Beautiful scenes of the historic town of St. Andrews in Scotland and its Old Course, with unusual interior scenes of the Royal and Ancient Golf Club.
1959; 14 min; 16 mm; color; JR, HS, A; Post World War II.
USGA

STANLEY CUP HIGHLIGHTS OF 1972

Hockey action highlights of the games between the New York Rangers, Montreal Canadiens, Chicago Blackhawks, and Boston Bruins. The Boston Bruins were the winners over the New York Rangers.
NL; 25 min; 16 mm; color; JR, HS, A; Post World War II.
BUDGET

STAR CLASS, THE

Revives the history of the Star Class of sailboat from its development through the 1981 world competition at Marblehead.

1981; 28 min; 16 mm, VHS, U-Matic; color; JR, HS, A.

OFFSHR

STARS AND WATERCARRIERS : GIRO d'ITALIA RACE

Stars and Watercarriers is a concise, colorful chronicle of the Giro d'Italia's (Tour of Italy) extended madness, a tableau of rivalries and loyalty, established reputations and ascending careers, according to Josh Lehman, *Bicycling Magazine*. This film recreates the magic of the moment and brings the Giro's thrills and disappointments home to every viewer.

NL; 90 min; VHS; NL; JR, HS, A; Post World War II.

GRADY

STARS OF TOMORROW

Two of the three films on this cassette feature Canadian athletes in boxing and gymnastics who are striving for world-class perfection. The third film focusses on Soviet coaches and athletes now living in Canada, who compare the sports systems in the two countries. Contains "Fighting Back," "Almost Giants," and "East Comes West."

1964; 73.5 min; VHS; NL; HS, A; Post World War II.

NFBC

STATE GAMES: BEGINNING A TRADITION

Officials of the U. S. Olympic Committee and President's Council on Physical Fitness and Sports took one look at the Empire State Games and decided to go national with it. That's how the State Games movement began, and this is the film story of it all. Camera crews have documented not only several of the 22 State Games competitions, but also the Orlando seminar, the governors' opening announcements, and the delightful public rallies that bring athletes and public together with a torch run, fireworks, and parade of athletes.

NL; 15 min; 16 mm, VHS, U-Matic; color; JR, HS, A; Post World War II.

KLEINW

STEEL CURTAIN, THE

The sound and the fury of "Mean Joe," "Hollywood Bags," "Mad Dog," and "Arrowhead". . . a hu-morous feature on the bizarre bullies of the finest—and fiercest—defensive line of the 1970s.

NL; 8 min; VHS, U-Matic; color; JR, HS, A; Post World War II.

NFL; TMA

STEROIDS AND SPORTS

The effect of steroids on athletic performance and the considerable risk of steroid-induced cancer, heart disease, and infertility; the use of growth hormone to correct stunted growth; guidelines on when and under what conditions the administration of hormones and steroids is medically indicated.

NL; 19 min; VHS, color; JR, HS, A; Post World War II.

FOTH

STICKY MY FINGERS, FLEET MY FEET

With pathos and humor, this film deflates one of the classic American myths: the middle-aged male who clings to a youthful standard of physical prowess and he-man virility. Norman, a fortyish executive, is addicted to Sunday orgies of touch football in Central Park, where he engages in a ritual combat with his puffing, huffing, flabby contemporaries. Their dreams of glory turn to dust when they permit a 15-year-old-boy to join their sport, and his flashing performance leaves them dazed and a little older, wiser, and sadder. Adapted from a short story by Gene Williams.

1970; 23 min; 16 mm; color; HS, A; Post World War II.

MICHMED; TIMLIF

STOCK CAR 500 CHALLENGE

The famous Darlington Southern 500-mile car race—the action, the danger, the thrills.

NL; 10 min; 16 mm; BW; JR, HS, A; Post World War II.

BUDGET

STORY OF A HARNESS RACE DRIVER, THE

One of the nationally televised "Story of . . . " series, giving an excellent portrayal of harness racing through the story of champion driver Billy Haughton.

NL; 26 min; 16 mm; BW; JR, HS, A; Post World War II.

USTA

STRANGE BUT TRUE NFL STORIES

Vincent Price unearths the strange plays and bizarre players of the NFL's past 50 years: the one-eyed quarterback who led the NFL in passing one year; the player who ate blood and raw meat; weird team rituals; the strangest games; and more.

NL: 45 min; VHS; NL; JR, HS, A; Depression Era to Post World War II.

KAROL

STRASBOURG-PARIS: A PIED

Each year a group of men walk the 500 kilometers from Strasbourg to Paris. This film, sometimes funny, sometimes tragic and emotional, shows this event. Good photography. Very little dialogue, in French.

1975; 15 min; 16 mm; color; JR, HS, A; Post World War II.

FACSEA

STRATTON STORY, THE

Presents the heartwarming story of one of America's greatest baseball pitchers, Monte Stratton. Shows his rise to fame and his rehabilitation after his unfortunate accident. Shows how much rehabilitation depends upon the individual and what a man can do if he really wants to.

1953; 31 min; 16 mm; BW; JR, HS, A; Post World War II.

UGA; UTEX

STRENGTH, BULK AND BALANCE: THE WORLD OF SUMO

This film is an introduction to the popular Japanese sport of sumo wrestling. It traces the history and shows the daily routines of a number of young wrestlers training for the sumo championships.

1977; 28 min; 16 mm; color; JR, HS, A; Ancient to Post World War II.

FLSU

STRIP PITS: LAKES FOR THE FUTURE?

Don Gapen and his brother Joe visited a little-known fishing paradise in southern Indiana, a large plot of reclaimed stripping area given to Indiana by the Peabody Coal Company. In addition to the scenery and fishing sequences, emphasis is on reclamation. Strip mine lakes have great value as recreation outlets for local communities and can be used for irrigation, as well as a watering source for livestock operations.

1977; 14 min; 16 mm; color; HS, A; Post World War II.

UILL

STRUGGLE AND THE TRIUMPH, THE

A look at Olympism and the work of the U.S. Olympic Committee to put the Olympic dream within the grasp of the nation's youth as shown through the experiences of past gold medal winners. Included are appearances and commentary by Olympic greats Eric Heiden, Jesse Owens, John Naber, Terry Place, and others.

NL; 25 min; 16 mm, VHS; color; JR, HS, A; Post World War II.

CCCD; USOC

STUDY OF GRACE, A

Training of gymnastics teachers at the Medau Institute at Hohenfels Palace in Coburg, where Heinrich Medau and his wife originated modern German rhythmical gymnastics and breathing techniques.

1959; 10 min; 16 mm; NL; JR, HS, A; Post World War II.

MTPS

STYLES THAT MADE A SPLASH

A historical and whimsical look at women's bathing suits in America, from the time of Martha Washington to the bikini.

NL; 23 min; 16 mm; color; JR, HS, A; Premodern to Post World War II.

SEARS; WSU

SUGAR BOWL FILMS

1945 Duke 29, Alabama 26
1946 Oklahoma A & M 33, St. Mary's 13
1947 Georgia 20, North Carolina 10
1948 Texas 27, Alabama 7
1949 Oklahoma 14, North Carolina 6
1950 Oklahoma 35, LSU 0
1951 Kentucky 13, Oklahoma 7
1952 Maryland 28, Tennessee 13
1953 Georgia Tech 24, Ole Miss 7
1954 Georgia Tech 42, West Virginia 19
1955 Navy 21, Ole Miss 0
1956 Georgia Tech 7, Pittsburgh 0
1957 Baylor 13, Tennessee 7
1958 Ole Miss 39, Texas 7
1959 LSU 7, Clemson 0
1960 Ole Miss 21, LSU 0
1961 Ole Miss 14, Rice 6
1962 Alabama 10, Arkansas 3
1963 Ole Miss 17, Arkansas 13
1964 Alabama 12, Ole Miss 7
1965 LSU 13, Syracuse 10
1966 Missouri 20, Florida 18
1967 Alabama 34, Nebraska 7
1968 LSU 20, Wyoming 13
1969 Arkansas 16, Georgia 2
1970 Ole Miss 27, Arkansas 22
1971 Tennessee 34, Air Force 13
1972 Oklahoma 40, Auburn 22
1973 Oklahoma 14, Penn State 0

1974 Notre Dame 24, Alabama 23
1975 Nebraska 13, Florida 10
NL; 20-30 mins each. 16 mm; NL; JR, HS, A; Post World War II.
NOMWSA

SULKIES AND SILKS

Harness racing, shot at Goshen, New York; Pompano, Florida; Lexington, Kentucky; and Du Quoin, Illinois. The film depicts early beginnings of the sport and shows modern race scenes in paramutuel, fair, and Grand Circuit settings.
NL; 10 min; 16 mm; color; JR, HS, A; Post World War II.
USTA

SILKS—SULKIES—SPEED

Reviews harness racing's historic role in the United States, along with the modern-day careers of trainer-drivers Joe O'Brien and Kevin Tisher. This film reviews the first 100 years of harness racing's traveling major league and also traces the history of the sport back to the Revolutionary War.
1971; 25 min; 16 mm; NL; JR, HS, A; Pre-Modern to Post World War II.
USTA

SUMMER FEVER

Narrated by Dick Van Dyke, this film shows Little League action in Hawaii, the Pacific Northwest, in the desert country of the Southwest, and in New York and New England, culminating in exciting action at the Little League World Series.
NL; 12 min; 16 mm; NL; E, JR, HS, A; Post World War II.
LLBI

SUMMER RENDEZVOUS

Using the poetic aspects of a track and field meet, this film makes some important—although unspoken—observations about the nature of human endeavor and achievement.
1970; 30 min; 16 mm; color; HS, A; Post World War II.
OSU; UEVA

SUNDAY IN HELL, A: PARIS-ROUBLAIX RACE

Once a year, the Paris-Roubaux road race taxes the energy of Europe's best riders. Eddie Merckx, De Vlaminck, Francesco Moser, Freddy Maertens, etc. Probably the finest cycling film ever made.

NL; 110 min; VHS, NL; JR, HS, A; Post World War II.
GRADY

SUNSHINE AND GOOD SNOW

This filmshows many ways to use a pair of skis to have fun. There is alpine skiing on packed powder, alpine racing with some excellent racing footage featuring America's Cindy Nelson, and a cross-country outing in beautiful Yellowstone National Park.
NL; 22 min; 16 mm; color; JR, HS, A; Post World War II.
FACSEA

SUPER BOWL I

Vince Lombardi's Packers scuttle the AFC's upstart Kansas City Chiefs in the premiere of America's favorite sports event. January 15, 1967, Green Bay Packers 35, Kansas City Chiefs 10.
1967; 24 min; 16 mm, VHS, U-Matic; color; JR, HS, A; Post World War II.
NFL; TMA

SUPER BOWL II

The awesome Green Bay team repeats as World Champions, as they send the Oakland Raiders packing. January 14, 1968, Green Bay Packers 33, Oakland Raiders 14.
1968; 24 min; 16 mm, VHS, U-Matic; color; JR, HS, A; Post World War II.
NFL; TMA

SUPER BOWL III

Joe Namath leads his Jets to a stunning upset over the heavily favored Baltimore Colts. January 12, 1969, New York Jets 16, Baltimore Colts 7.
1969; 24 min; 16 mm, VHS, U-Matic; color; JR, HS, A; Post World War II.
NFL; TMA

SUPER BOWL IV

The AFC makes it two in a row as Kansas City Chiefs' coach Hank Stram (wired for sound) employs a wide-open offense that buries the Minnesota Vikings. January 11, 1970, Kansas City Chiefs 23, Minnesota Vikings 7.
1970; 24 min; 16 mm, VHS, U-Matic; color; JR, HS, A; Post World War II.
NFL; TMA

SUPER BOWL V

The "Blooper Bowl." Wacky plays and crazy bobbles by both the Dallas Cowboys and Baltimore Colts are offset by a heart-thumping finish. January 17, 1971, Baltimore Colts 16, Dallas Cowboys 13.

1971; 24 min; 16 mm, VHS, U-Matic; color; JR, HS, A; Post World War II.

NFL; TMA

SUPER BOWL VI (1)

The Dallas Cowboys avenge the previous year's loss by drowning the Miami Dolphins in a sea of defense. January 16, 1972, Dallas Cowboys 24, Miami Dolphins 3.

1972; 24 min; 16 mm, VHS, U-Matic; color; JR, HS, A; Post World War II.

NFL; TMA

SUPER BOWL VI (2)

Dallas Cowboys roar to triumph in highlights from the world championship pro football game. Details of the crushing defeat (24-3) of the Miami Dolphins. Some slow-motion shots.

NL; 29 min; 16 mm; color; JR, HS, A; Post World War II.

MTPS

SUPER BOWL VII (1)

The Miami Dolphins put the crowning touch on a perfect 17-0 season as they ride roughshod over the Washington Redskins. January 14, 1973, Miami Dolphins 14, Washington Redskins 7.

1973; 24 min; 16 mm, VHS, U-Matic; color; JR, HS, A; Post World War II.

NFL; TMA

SUPER BOWL VII (2)

Highlights of the Miami win over Washington in the Super Bowl in Los Angeles.

NL; 27 min; 16 mm; NL; JR, HS, A; Post World War II.

MTPS

SUPER BOWL VIII

The Miami Dolphins make it two in a row as they dismantle the Minnesota Vikings. January 13, 1974, Miami Dolphins 24, Minnesota Vikins 7.

1974; 24 min; 16 mm, VHS, U-Matic; color; JR, HS, A; Post World War II.

NFL; TMA

SUPER BOWL IX

The Pittsburgh Steelers win their first championship in forty years, and the Minnesota Vikings are disappointed a third time. January 12, 1975, Pittsburgh 16, Minnesota Vikings 6.

1975; 24 min; 16 mm, VHS, U-Matic; color; JR, HS, A; Post World War II.

NFL; TMA

SUPER BOWL X

The Steelers do it again. In this game, Bradshaw's Battalions and Franco's Army have too much firepower for the Dallas Cowboys. January 18, 1976, Pittsburgh 21, Dallas Cowboys 17.

1976; 24 min; 16 mm, VHS, U-Matic; color; JR, HS, A; Post World War II.

NFL; TMA

SUPER BOWL XI

The Oakland Raiders reign supreme as Kenny "The Snake" Stabler is pure poison for the Minnesota Vikings. January 9, 1977, Oakland Raiders 32, Minnesota Vikings 14.

1977; 24 min; 16 mm, VHS, U-Matic; color; JR, HS, A; Post World War II.

NFL; TMA

SUPER BOWL XII

It's "Doomsday" for Denver in the Superdome. Dallas wins their second Super Bowl. January 15, 1978, Dallas Cowboys 27, Denver Broncos 10.

1978; 24 min; 16 mm, VHS, U-Matic; color; JR, HS, A; Post World War II.

NFL; TMA

SUPER BOWL XIII

The highest-scoring Super Bowl game to date. The Steelers and Cowboys light up the scoreboard while each tries to become the first three-time winner. January 21, 1979, Pittsburgh Steelers 35, Dallas Cowboys 31.

1979; 24 min; 16 mm, VHS, U-Matic; color; JR, HS, A; Post World War II.

NFL; TMA

SUPER BOWL XIV

The Pittsburgh Steelers carry home an unprecedented fourth Super Bowl trophy, with a surprisingly hard-fought win over the courageous Los Angeles Rams. January 20, 1980, Pittsburgh Steelers 31, Los Angeles Rams 19.

1980; 24 min; 16 mm, VHS, U-Matic; color; JR, HS, A; Post World War II.

NFL; TMA

SUPER BOWL XV

The "Cinderella Super Bowl." The Oakland Raiders, predicted to finish at the bottom of their division, became the first wild card team to win the Super

Bowl. January 25, 1981, Oakland Raiders 27, Philadelphia Eagles 10.

1981; 24 min; 16 mm, VHS, U-Matic; color; JR, HS, A; Post World War II.

NFL; TMA

SUPER BOWL XVI

The brilliant strategy of the 49ers' head coach Bill Walsh is revealed with his unbalanced line, flea-flicker plays, and two new defensive alignments. January 24, 1982, San Francisco 49ers 26, Cincinnati Bengals 21.

1982; 24 min; 16 mm, VHS, U-Matic; color; JR, HS, A; Post World War II.

NFL; TMA

SUPER BOWL XVII

It's a "Hog Day Afternoon." Washington's great offensive line, "The Hogs," turn Super Sunday at the Rose Bowl into a day of Swine and Roses as they clear the way for a record-setting performance by John Riggins and a victory for the Washington Redskins. January 30, 1983, Washington Redskins 27, Miami Dolphins 17.

1983; 24 min; 16 mm, VHS, U-Matic; color; JR, HS, A; Post World War II.

NFL; TMA

SUPER BOWL XVIII

A blocked punt recovered for a touchdown, a touchdown interception, and Marcus Allen's 74-yard touchdown run paced Los Angeles to the most lopsided win in Super Bowl history. January 22, 1984, Los Angeles Raiders 38, Washington Redskins 9.

1984; 24 min; 16 mm, VHS, U-Matic; color; JR, HS, A; Post World War II.

NFL; TMA

SUPER BOWL XIX

Roger Craig scored 3 touchdowns, Joe Montana led the offense to a record 542 yards, and the 49ers tough defense effectively shut down the record-setting Dolphins passing attack. January 20, 1985, San Francisco 49ers 38, Miami Dolphins 16.

1985; 24 min; 16 mm, VHS, U-Matic; color; JR, HS, A; Post World War II.

NFL; TMA

SUPERCHARGED: THE GRAND PRIX CAR

In 1924, a British Sunbeam team defeated the speed restrictions set by Grand Prix regulations by supercharging the engine. This was the beginning of one of the greatest eras in the history of motor racing.

Bugatti, Alfa Romeo, Maserati, and Mercedes-Benz all appeared in a series of dramatic and sometimes dangerous races. Using unique film and restored cars road-tested by Grand Prix driver John Watson, this program recreates the Golden Age of motor racing. In 1934, the International Formula which regulated the rules governing Grand Prix racing cars was changed in an attempt to arrest the rapid rise in speeds of existing cars—which had reached 140 mph. Under normal circumstances this would have worked: the cars built to the rule were slower than before. But Germany was now returning to racing. Hitler underwrote (for political reasons) the construction and racing costs of two Grand Prix teams—Auto Union and Mercedes-Benz.

1985; 50 min; VHS, U-Matic; color; JR, HS, A; Golden Age and Depression Era.

BBC; FI

SUPERGRANDPA

Tells a story (in American Sign Language with verbal narration) about a bicycle race 1100 miles long that was won by a man 66 years old. Uses split screen with the storyteller on the left and the photographs of the race on the right. The winner was thought to be too old to enter, but he rode 1100 miles in seven days and finished 24 hours before the next-closest contestant. Signed by Howard Busy with verbal narration by Louie J. Fant, Jr.

NL; 16 min; 16 mm; color; JR, HS, A; Post World War II.

IU; JOYCE

SUPERJOCK

Jim Weatherbee is a hefty, middle-aged ex-athlete who over the years has become a sports spectator and a heavy smoker. He thinks himself a cautious man, but his son, who excels in math, points out to him that he is a heavy gambler when it comes to counting the odds of having a heart attack. In contrast to Jim, his co-worker Vic, who had never been an athlete, has taken a stress test and been convinced to begin an exercise and weight reduction program. Jim comes to realize the risk he is taking and follows his doctor's prescription to quit smoking, slim down, cut down on sugar and fat, and to begin regular exercise.

1977; 16 min; 16 mm; color; JR, HS, A; Post World War II.

UILL

SUPERMILERS, THE: THE 4-MINUTE BARRIER AND BEYOND

It has been over 30 years since Roger Bannister became the first runner to break the four-minute mile. Ten runners have held the world mile record since that time, in addition to Bannister himself, are featured in this special program. These are the greatest milers of all—eleven men from vastly different backgrounds with one thing in common: the distinction of having run the mile faster than anyone before. Each has taken a unique talent and fused it with discipline, sacrifice, and a ruthless determination to succeed; each has learned to live with and train through a mental barrier to break into the unknown. The program features footage of the world record-breaking races of each of the runners, as well as interviews with them. The featured runners are Roger Bannister, John Landy, Derek Ibbotson, Herb Elliot, Peter Snell, Michel Jazy, Jim Ryan, Filbert Bayi, John Walker, Sebastian Coe, and Steve Ovett.

NL; 64 min; VHS, U-Matic, Beta; color; JR, HS, A; Post World War II.

FOTH

SUPER 70s

During the 1970s, pro football emerged as America's new national pastime. Relive that decade's most memorable moments . . . the most thrilling runs and catches, the most exhilarating wins, the most crushing defeats. It's a story of teams: the machined precision of the Miami Dolphins, the wide-open excitement of the Dallas Cowboys, the unparalleled excellence of the Pittsburgh Steelers. It's a story of glory days and unforgettable plays: Tom Dempsey's incredible 63-yard field goal, the "Hail Mary," the "Immaculate Reception," the "Holy Roller" and "Big Ben." It's a story of legendary men: the record-breaking performances of Fran Tarkenton, the journeys of Walter Payton, Earl Campbell, and Larry Brown, the gallant greatness of O. J. Simpson. Ten years of pro football at its entertaining best.

NL; 49 min; VHS, 16 mm, U-Matic; color; JR, HS, A; Post World War II.

NFL; TMA

SUPER STARS OF THE SUPER BOWLS

This show presents the stories of the men who gave great performances in the first nineteen Super Bowls. The profiles include each game's MVP as well as outstanding performances of other players. The spotlight also hits those players who were memorable for their failings and not their successes in Super Bowl games.

1985; 51 min; VHS, U-Matic; color; JR, HS, A; Post World War II.

NFL; TMA

SURER, SWIFTER, STRONGER

Women have shattered records. They are beacons at every starting block and finish line. Today's female athletes are surer, swifter and stronger. Upbeat music and quick shots of past and present female athletes participating in a variety of sports make this a truly inspirational video.

NL; 6 min; VHS, U-Matic; color; JR, HS, A; Post World War II.

WSF

SURFERS, THE

An extraordinary color documentary telling the complete story of surfers and surfing, from California to Hawaii, from summer sun to the freezing fog of winter. It shows how a surfer begins, why he surfs, how and where he finally ends . . . in the thirty-foot surf of Hawaii.

NL; 24 min; 16 mm; color; JR, HS, A; Post World War II.

BUDGET

SURFING

Two surfing veterans of the heyday of surfing, Fred Hemmings and Paul Stroue, talk about their sport, give some instruction and hints, give some history of the sport, and show themselves in action riding the big waves in Hawaii.

1968; 30 min; 16 mm; color; JR, HS, A; Post World War II.

BUDGET

SURFSAIL

Three students tackle one of the trickiest challenges in the world, battling the severe currents and changing winds of Cook Strait on fragile windsurfers.

1978; 18 min; 16 mm; NL; JR, HS, A; Post World War II.

NFU

SURVIVAL RUN

Inspiring study of determination and trust as a blind runner, guided only by the voice and ready arm of his sighted partner, confronts and conquers one of America's most rugged and dangerous long-distance running courses.

1981; 12 min; 16 mm; color; JR, HS, A; Post World War II.

PYRAMID; UCB

SWEATER, THE

An animated version of a short story by Quebec author Roch Carrier, set in the rural Quebec of his boyhood. Carrier recalls the passion for playing hockey, which he shared with the other boys of his community. It was the time of Rocket Richard, the Canadiens' greatest star. A funny, poignant story that evokes the period of the late 1940s.

1980; 10.5 min; 16 mm; color; JR, HS, A; Post World War II.
NFBC

SWEETHEART OF THE RODEO

The rodeo success of Dee Watt, the British Columbian champion of barrel racing, is featured in this film.
NL; 24 min; 16 mm; color; JR, HS, A; Post World War II.
BCDA

SWEETWATER CANNIBAL

The muskellunge is considered by most fishermen to be the toughest, most sought-after, and most evasive fighting fish in fresh water. Bill Cullerton leads viewers on this search.
NL; 26 min; 16 mm; NL; JR, HS, A; Post World War II.
SOLANA

SWIM PARADE, THE

See the development of swimwear (beginning in 1905) from bloomer-type suits of grandma's day, right up to the French bathing suit which was just making explosive impact! Rare footage shows many famous figures in the water world. Johnny Weissmuller (years before he swung as Tarzan), Gertrude Ederle, swimming-star Ann Curtis, and divers Jo Ann Olsen and Vickie Graves. Everything is tied together with a mass diving montage, capped by prime examples of comedy diving at its nuttiest.
NL; 10 min; 16 mm; BW; E, JR, HS, A; Golden Age to Post World War II.
FILMIC

SWORDSMANSHIP

A man's honor used to be saved or destroyed by his skill with a gun or sword. Today, the sport of swordsmanship is considered one of the most exacting on the mind as well as the body. The blood and loss of life has been eliminated, but the thrills and excitement still remain. Members of the U.S. Olympic fencing team demonstrate all the movements and basic fundamentals in detail.
1956; 17 min; 16 mm; BW; JR, HS, A; Post World War II.
ALTANA; UILL

SYMBIOSIS

An inspiring original poem in which the game of football talks to the boys and men who have played with the strength and dedication that makes football

the most popular American game. It is a thoughtful message with a poignant close . . . "And I think in the end I made you a better man, no matter what your name. And I know in the end that made me a bigger and better game."
NL; 3 min; 16 mm, VHS, U-Matic; color; JR, HS, A; Post World War II.
NFL; TMA

T'AI CHI CH'UAN: A SERIES

Presents T'ai Chi Ch'uan, a sport which originated several hundred years ago in China. Features Marshal Ho'O, professor of Chinese history at the California Institute of the Arts, instructing the fundamentals of T'ai Chi performance and history. Programs 1 through 26.
NL; NL; NL; color; JR, HS, A; Ancient to Post World War II.
KCET; PUBTEL

TABLE TENNIS

Table tennis experts are shown in singles and doubles. After an explanation of the grip, the players demonstrate push shots, service, spin shot and return, forehand and backhand shots, and footwork.
1936; 9 min; 16 mm; BW; JR, HS, A; Depression Era.
UILL

TAKE OFF

A ten-minute nonnarrated version of the classic ski film, *Ski the Outer-Limits*. This film has become a classic of the short film. Photographed at Vail, Jackson Hole, Taos, Chamonix, Kitzbuhel, in both slow motion and natural speed, it shows the style, control, and balance required to push toward the outer limits of one's ability. Downhill racing, slalom and giant slalom, ski dancing, and acrobatics are some of the limit-pushing directions the skiers take.
1969; 10 min; 16 mm; color; JR, HS, A; Post World War II.
BUDGET

TAKE THE TIME

Shows how different women use various forms of exercise and sports, such as racquetball, walking briskly, running, dancing, or cross-country skiing, along with good nutrition, to improve and maintain their physical fitness and health.
1980; 18 min; 16 mm; color; HS, A; Post World War II.
IOWA

TALKING ATC SAFETY

Viewers ride with the Patterson family as they take off on their Honda ATC three-wheelers for a treasure hunt. Against the beautiful background of Coos Bay we meet Manny, the animated spokesperson, who tells us how to ride the ATC, as illustrated by the Pattersons, for maximum fun and safety.

NL; 20 min; 16 mm, VHS, U-Matic; color; JR, HS, A; Post World War II.

HONDA; MTPS

TALL SHIPS ARE COMING, THE

Shows crews training and sailing in European waters during the summer of 1975 as preparation for Operation Sail 1976. Views the celebration of the 700th birthday of the city of Amsterdam and a sailing spectacle in London called the London Festival of Sail.

1975; 28 min; 16 mm; color; JR, HS, A; Post World War II.

DREWAS

TALL SHIPS RACE (MAGPIE), THE

Takes viewers through the Bay of Biscay to Portsmouth on Britain's only fully square-rigged sailing ship, the *T.S. Royalist,* for the Tall Ships' Race. A crew of sea cadets, along with the narrator, show how life on this reproduction of the original is not too different from what it was a hundred years ago. Even with modern conveniences (such as engines) the daily routine of swabbing decks and repairing sails must go on. The beauty of the sea and the camaraderie it brings to the men on board carry them through problems with the wind and lack of provisions.

1976; 28 min; 16 mm; color; JR, HS, A; Post World War II.

UILL

TASTE OF VICTORY

Racing film. Excellent introduction to young racers, giving them a flavor of the United States Ski Team.

NL; 25 min; 16 mm; NL; JR, HS, A; Post World War II.

ESA

TEACHER, TAKE US ORIENTEERING

A group of school children learn the basics of a sport which is an exciting and practical combination of physical and mental skills. After being introduced in the classroom to map symbols and the color key, they move outdoors to a series of exercises which prepare them to run a course: control markers, Silva-type compasses, and regulating and measuring paces. As a group competes, shots of individuals reveal the benefits of orienteering—high level of physical activity, serious application of map and compass-reading skills, and sheer enjoyment.

NL; 14 min; 16 mm, VHS; color; JR, HS, A; Post World War II.

IFB

TEACHING SPORTS SKILLS TO YOUNG ATHLETES

What happens when a young athlete learns a new skill? What factors affect the learning abilities of young athletes? What is the most effective way to introduce a new sport? This film will give coaches some guidelines for planning and conducting effective practices and effectively teaching specific sports skills.

1982; 20 min; 16 mm; color; A; Post World War II.

UWISC

TEAMWORK

Shows how commitment to a team can make the difference between success and failure in sports and business. Narrated by Jack Whitaker.

NL; 8 min; VHS, U-Matic; color; JR, HS, A; Post World War II.

SFTI

TELL IT TO THE GIRLS

Describes the Women's International Bowling Congress's services and briefly explains its purposes and origin.

NL; 22 min; 16 mm; NL; JR, HS, A; Post World War II.

WIBC

TEMBO

The late Howard Hill was long known as "the world's greatest archer" and was always called on to do trick bow and arrow shooting for the movies. Howard did the shooting for Errol Flynn in *Robin Hood* and made countless short subjects on bow hunting for Warner Brothers Studios in the 1940s. In 1952 he went on a safari to Africa and produced the only feature film featuring his artistry. This is a very unique documentary of hunting. With bow and arrow, Howard Hill shoots many big-game animals, including a wild bull elephant.

1952; 80 min; 16 mm; color; JR, HS, A; Post World War II.

BUDGET

TEN FOR GOLD

Motivational film on Bruce Jenner.

NL; 30 min; 16 mm; color; E, JR, HS, A; Post World War II.
GEMILL

TENNIS

Through the spectators and the players, this film reflects the atmosphere of a great tennis tournament. It shows us some of the world champions in action, such as Manuel Orantes, as well as more inexperienced players, some of whom may become champions.
1972; 12 min; 16 mm; color; JR, HS, A; Post World War II.
BELGIUM

TENNIS BALLS

This is a brief, entertaining, but educational film of how tennis balls are made. Designed for the elementary and intermediate school child, it features Jonathan Winters, JoAnne Worley, and Woody Allen interviewing children and their impressions of how tennis balls are made, and also shows the actual industrial process involved in producing tennis balls, from the initial rubber to the finished felt-covered ball.
NL; 4 min; 16 mm; color; E, JR; Post World War II.
USTEN

TENNIS CLUB

Everyone knows what tennis is, but just how did that racquet begin? This lighthearted look at the history of the sport begins in the Stone Age and speeds on through the Roman Empire and medieval times right up to today's sophisticated action. With ample touches of satire, Bozzetto examines styles of dress, play, and sportsmanship—or lack of it!
NL; 10 min; 16 mm, VHS; color—animation; JR, HS, A; Ancient to Post World War II.
DIST16

TENNIS EVERYONE

Showing both young and old Americans taking lessons at clubs and camps, this film includes shots of great players of the 70s, particularly John Newcombe, who acts as a guide throughout the film.
1974; 26 min; 16 mm; color; JR, HS, A; Post World War II.
USTEN

TENNIS LESSON, THE

Deals with the issue of the increasing human dependence on technology by telling a story about a woman and a tennis ball machine.

1977; 9 min; 16 mm, VHS, U-Matic; color; Post World War II.
PHENIX

TENNIS MATCH, THE

This dramatic short subject benignly spoofs the current tennis phenomenon. It demonstrates how four grown men regress to squabbling children during a doubles match and portrays the consequences of taking the game too seriously.
1977; 16 min; 16 mm; color; JR, HS, A; Post World War II.
USTEN

TENNIS MOTHERS

For some, tennis is more than just a national rage, it is a path to fame and fortune. Guiding the young players to these goals is the tennis mother, who dreams that her son or daughter will be the Jimmy Connors or Chris Evert of the future. A perceptive and humorous view of parental pressure. We are shown a typical day in the life of Hyse Wilpon, a 12-year-old girl whose mother is a self-appointed tennis coach.
1975; 14 min; 16 mm; color; HS, A; Post World War II.
CAROUF; CBS; MICHMED; USTEN

TENNIS RACQUET

This animated Disney cartoon stars Goofy playing a game of lawn tennis as it has never before been played. Goofy takes it all in stride and keeps his concentration in spite of many distractions, including a Goofy gardener planting grass seed and mowing the court.
1977; 7 min; 16 mm; color; E, JR; Post World War II.
USTEN

TENPIN SHOWCASE

Highlights behind-the-scenes activity of an ABC tournament. Action on the lanes; windup of the thrilling Masters and its first 300 game; the intercollegiate tournament. Viewers will see what makes a tournament tick and how it comes into being.
NL; 19 min; 16 mm; NL; JR, HS, A; Post World War II.
ABC

TENTH INTERNATIONAL GAMES OF THE DEAF

Shows the strength and skill of deaf contestants participating in an Olympic sports spectacle.

1965; 40 min; 16 mm; color; JR, HS, A; Post World War II.

MONUMT

TETON TRAILS

The wildlife and scenic beauties of the 6500-foot-high valley of Jackson Hole and Grand Teton National Park. Interest in these natural wonders is climaxed by a party of mountain climbers scaling 13,766-foot Grand Teton Peak.

NL; 27 min; 16 mm; NL; JR, HS, A; Post World War II.

CHEVRON

T FORMATION (OPEN PLAYS)

Shows open plays, trick plays, and pass plays of T-formation football.

1947; 10 min; 16 mm; color; JR, HS, A; Post World War II.

UILL

THAT'S WHAT LIVING'S ABOUT

Lively, philosophical look at leisure: what it means, how it affects our lives now, and how it may affect them in the future. Explores the uses and misuses of leisure in our society. Presents the vital balance between work and leisure and examines the relationship between leisure and retirement. Shows more than 150 residents of Torrance, California, involved in a wide variety of active and inactive leisure pursuits, alone and with families, friends, and groups.

1973; 18 min; 16 mm; color; HS, A; Post World War II.

UCB

THEIR GAME WAS GOLF

Golfing for ladies is not new, but they are outnumbered. The Ladies Professional Golf Association has succeeded in promoting the sport to national popularity and recognition, and St. Lucie proves a favorite site for tournaments. The ladies are offered tips for stylish, comfortable, and well-equipped playing.

NL; 28 min; 16 mm; NL; JR, HS, A; Post World War II.

FLADC

"THERE WAS ALWAYS SUN SHINING SOMEPLACE": LIFE IN THE NEGRO BASEBALL LEAGUES

Chronicles the history of the black baseball leagues that flourished before Jackie Robinson integrated the major leagues in 1947. Rare historical footage shows the ball players as they traveled the back roads of America, the Caribbean, Mexico, and Latin America. Features interviews with Satchel Paige, James "Cool Papa" Bell, Buck Leonard, Judy Johnson, and Monte Irvin. Narrated by James Earl Jones.

1983; 58 min; 16 mm; BW; JR, HS, A; Golden Age, Depression Era, Post World War II.

PENNST

THEY GROW UP SO FAST

Shows the need for and the importance of the physical education program, and particularly how the proper guidance and encouragement was needed by a 10-year-old boy before he was able to handle himself physically. Depicts how, through the efforts of the school principal, the PTA, and the physical education instructor, the school board is convinced of its need for a consultant for the elementary school. Points out the benefits derived by children in rhythmic and self-testing activities, along with gymnastics and swimming, for present health and later life.

1955; 25 min; 16 mm; color; A; Post World War II.

AAHPER; UILL

THEY SAID IT COULDN'T BE DONE

The pursuit of goals sometimes causes a certain amount of skepticism. Many react by saying, "You'll never do that," but not everyone shares such sentiment. This program chronicles the trials, errors, and eventual triumph of former Minnesota Vikings' quarterback Fran Tarkenton, Buffalo Bills' superstar O. J. Simpson, and John McKay's Tampa Bay Buccaneers. Each overcame doubt and setbacks to accomplish something that was generally considered impossible.

NL; 13 min; 16 mm, VHS, U-Matic; Post World War II.

NFL; TMA

THEY'RE OFF

For fans of horse racing, *They're Off* presents excitement, thrills, and mishaps . . . thrown jockeys, spills, rambunctious winners, and moments from many great races (Sea Biscuit vs. War Admiral, Sir Barton vs. Man O' War vs. Whirlaway), the Hambletonian (with horse-drawn sulkys), the Preakness, and several moments from the Kentucky Derby (including its Diamond Jubilee in 1948) are shown. Everything is topped off with the Grand National Steeplechase, where horses and riders fly through the air in thrilling jumps . . . or chilling spills!

NL; 10 min; 16 mm; NL; JR, HS, A; Depression Era to Post World War II.

FILMIC

THINK BIG . . . AIM HIGH!

Designed to provide academic motivation for young student athletes. Penn State head football coach Joe Paterno, quarterback Todd Blackledge, tailback Curt Warner, and athletic academic adviser Don Ferrell discuss the importance of education, controlling one's own future, learning to budget time, and developing study skills.

1984; 13 min; 16 mm; color; JR, HS, A; Post World War II.

PENNST

THIS IS HARNESS RACING

This basic film on the popular sport of harness racing deals with those who train, drive, and look after the horses. Explains in detail the difference between pacers and trotters, using slow-motion technique to describe each gait. Shows how the horses are trained on the track, in water, behind the starting gate, and in qualifying races. Concludes with an exciting sequence of night harness racing.

1975; 15 min; 16 mm; color; JR, HS, A; Post World War II.

UILL; USTA

THIS IS NASTAR

1970 winners in the NASTAR giant slalom skiing competition for recreational skiers.

NL; 28 min; 16 mm; NL; JR, HS, A; Post World War II.

CINES

THIS IS SKIING

Spills, thrills, and hot-dogging accent this film as we view the lighter side of snow skiing and tobogganing.

NL; 1 min; 16 mm; color; JR, HS, A; Post World War II.

BUDGET

THIS SPORTING LIFE

An intensive character study of a professional rugby player who has elevated himself from the coal mines of England through the sheer brutality and aggressiveness demanded by this violent sport. This film was named as one of the Ten Best of the Year by the New York *Herald Tribune*. It is the story of one man, what he must do to succeed, and how he comes to terms with failure. Viewers see him on the playing field, at posh London parties thrown for sports celebrities, in his attempts to win the love of the embittered widow he loves, and totally alone in the barren room.

1963; 126 min; 16 mm; NL; JR, HS, A; Post World War II.

BUDGET

THOROUGHBRED

At a horse farm in winter, a foal is born into the warmth of a hay stall while the father energetically runs in the snow-covered fields outside. In spring, the young colt is seen as he prances and frolics through green pastures, and as autumn approaches, the yearling is taken to the auction. Once sold, patient training and exercise prepare the thoroughbred for life at the track. During his first race, depicted in slow motion, everything he has been taught is synthesized into one valiant effort.

1972; 22 min; 16 mm; color; E, JR, HS, A; Post World War II.

PYRAMID; UILL

THREE FOR ADVENTURE

Three men battle the Atlantic to become the first to cross the ocean in an outboard boat.

NL; 35 min; 16 mm; NL; JR, HS, A; Post World War II.

SOLANA

THREE IN EUROPE

European BSA Motocross team.

NL; 25 min; 16 mm; NL; JR, HS, A; Post World War II.

NORTRIC

THUNDERBIRDS IN CHINA

Young Vancouver hockey players, the University of British Columbia Thunderbirds, show their skills to the teams of China. It is a journey that takes them far into that vast country and to an understanding of East and West. Hockey in China still has far to go, but this film leaves no doubt that the Chinese players and fans are alive to the challenge.

NL; 58 min; 16 mm; color; JR, HS, A; Post World War II.

CCS

TICONDEROGA: A CLASSIC UNDER SAIL

Documents the history, launching, and racing records of the classic sailboat *Ticonderoga*.

1977; 13 min; 16 mm; color; JR, HS, A.

PICNIC

TIMBER CARNIVAL

Sports competition between the most rugged men alive, the lumberjacks. This exciting film includes such events as tree climbing, topping, sawing, axe throwing, log rolling, and the joust while rolling logs. Filmed in the lumber country of Oregon, Washington, and Canada.

NL; 20 min; 16 mm; color; JR, HS, A; Post World War II.

BUDGET

TIMELESS GAME, THE

Presents an almost poetic explanation of cricket, a nearly unexplainable game: its rituals, customs, and history emphasize its timeless nature. Historical reenactments in costume of this "ballet of bat and ball." Comments include reasons for rule changes and scorekeeping, the influences of gambling, commercially sponsored players, and gentlemen players. Newsreels and historic film footage of Victorian and international flavor are combined with topical music and scenes depicting the important role of spectators of the games.

NL; 28 min; color; JR, HS, A; Pre-Modern to Post World War II.

UILL

TIME OF YOUR LIFE, THE

Coach George Allen, of the President's Council for Physical Fitness and Sports, kicks off this motivational movie about senior citizens keeping in shape. Viewers watch one senior couple as they visit many of America's most appealing tourist cities and attractions. They enjoy fitness facilities of hotels large and small, keeping up the effective regimen on the road that succeeded at home. Eddie Albert is the host.

NL; 30 min; 16 mm, VHS, U-Matic; color; JR, HS, A; Post World War II.

KLEINW

TITLE DRIVE

The challenge of world outboard racing highlighted by the film leads up to the championships by covering four well-known events: the Gold Coast; Marathon; Miami, Florida; the Elsinore "500" in California; and six other contests. The high point of the competition is at Lake Havasu.

NL; 20 min; 16 mm; NL; JR, HS, A; Post World War II.

SOLANA

TO BE THE BEST: THE GARY PLAYER STORY

Golfer, rancher, devoted father of six, fitness fanatic, religious zealot, and egotist are terms for Gary Player, who combines natural ability with an intense dedication to winning. He is seen on the golf course and at his ranch as he discusses his all-consuming desire to be the best.

1977; 26 min; 16 mm; color; JR, HS, A; Post World War II.

UCOLO

TO BUILD A HOCKEY DYNASTY

One of the best hockey players ever Gordie Howe, is back on the ice, this time joined by his two sons. Howe is part of a complex mythology of heroes. The question now is whether his adoring fans will stay with him or turn their attention to the exploits of young Marty and Mark. The film takes a close look at sports hero-worship.

1976; 17 min; 16 mm; color; HS, A; Post World War II.

DOCA; OKSU

TO CLIMB A MOUNTAIN

Follows a young man and woman, both of whom are blind, as they join several sighted friends to scale a particularly rugged peak in the Sierra Nevadas. Shows their determination and enthusiasm and records their feelings about the adventure. As one of them says: "Blind people climb mountains every day." Warm, inspiring production.

1975; 15 min; 16 mm; color; JR, HS, A; Post World War II.

UCB

TO GLORY

Dramatizes the first America's Cup Race and traces the history of the winning sailing vessel, the *America*.

1977; 50 min; 16 mm; color; JR, HS, A; Making of Modern Sport.

COUNFI

TO HALT MAN'S PHYSICAL COLLAPSE

Discussions by physiologist Dr. Robert Goode, Ernest Jokl, president of UNESCO'S Council of Sport and Physical Education, and George Plimpton, author and sports writer. Addresses the subject of the modern person's state of fitness. Although modern people spend billions of dollars on spectator sports, they probably make up the most unfit generation of any age. The situation and its inherent problems are presented, with the necessary remedies.

NL; 20 min; 16 mm; color; HS, A; NL; Post World War II.

OKSU

TOKYO OLYMPIAD

A philosophical documentary of the 18th Olympiad, filmed in Tokyo. Captures, in the young athletes and the crowd, a spirit of international unity, and asks, "Is it then enough for us, this infrequent, created peace?"

1964; 33 min; 16 mm; color; HS, A; Post World War II.

PYRAMID; UILL

TO LIVE AGAIN

The film explores a new concept in the treatment of alcoholism through a conventional hospital program combined with a special Outward Bound program. The Outward Bound experience is a viable adjunct therapy as patients undergo a rigorous test of physical stamina and experience new psychological and social activities. The film explores how a holistic approach strengthens personal development, interpersonal effectiveness, environmental awareness, and redefines personal values.

NL; 25 min; 16 mm, VHS, U-Matic, Beta; color; HS, A; Post World War II.

CRYSP

TOLLER

Both a figure skater and an accomplished painter, Canadian Toller Cranston was a versatile talent. He held a world figure skating championship, gained not only by technical mastery, but an innovative approach incorporating acting, ballet, and a concern for detail. His paintings show the same characteristics.

1976; 27 min; 16 mm; color; JR, HS, A; Post World War II.

UILL

TOM DEMPSEY

Despite a deformed foot and hand, Tom Dempsey enjoyed a successful ten-year career as a place kicker for six different teams. His greatest moment came in 1970, when he kicked a 63-yard field goal, the longest in NFL history. Dempsey's inspiring story is that of a man who overcame obstacles through his relentless pursuit of excellence and his burning desire to succeed. A good motivational story.

1985; 6 min; VHS, U-Matic; color; JR, HS, A; Post World War II.

NFL; TMA

TOM LANDRY

More than a compendium of statistics, this show gives the viewer an insight into the character of Thomas Wade Landry, the man under the hat. His legacy to professional football is remarkable, both as a coach and as a man.

NL; 17 min; 16 mm, VHS, U-Matic; color; JR, HS, A; Post World War II.

NFL; TMA

TOMORROW: MEXICO (JUTRO MEKSYK)

A conflict between an ambitious coach and a diver whom he had led to the championship. A Polish language film.

NL; 100 min; 16 mm; BW; JR, HS, A; Post World War II.

POLEMB

TOO MUCH SPEED

Witness racing car and motorcycle maniacs, and even fearless fanatics on bicycles, obsessed with speed. Features one of the most spectacular, nerve-shattering mass smash-ups on film—taken at a Daytona Beach race.

NL; 10 min; 16 mm; NL; JR, HS, A; Post World War II.

FILMIC

TO RUN

A demanding sport, cross-country ski racing is gaining popularity. A graphic split-screen effect reveals the physical and mental stresses on the competitor.

1971; 10 min; 16 mm; color; JR, HS, A; Post World War II.

FLMAUS

TOTAL FITNESS IN 30 MINUTES A WEEK

Dr. Laurence Morehouse demonstrates how to stay fit with a minimum of effort in this filmed adaptation of his best-selling book. He teaches how to develop a personal fitness program, regardless of age, weight, sex, occupation, or present physical condition. Visually memorable techniques emphasize the three pulse-rated exercises and the five-point program that can lead to total physical fitness in just 10 minutes a day a three days a week. Dispels common myths about exercise.

1976; 31 min; 16 mm; color; JR, HS, A; Post World War II.

PYRAMID; UILL

TOUR MAGNIFIQUE

Professional racing cyclists tackle the world's most spectacular road, the trans Southern Alps highway to Milford Sound. Special camera mounts convey the thrill of the ride through untamed country.

1981; 17 min; 16 mm; NL; JR, HS, A; Post World War II.

NFU

TOURNAMENT

A documentary on the grace and grit of modern tennis through a gripping study of the anatomy of the

1971 U.S. Open Tennis Championships at Forest Hills. Against a modern music background, slow-motion techniques are used to show the players in competitive action as a narrator reports on the games. Slow-motion and excellent photography highlight the play of Pancho Gonzales, Chris Evert, Stan Smith, and Billie Jean King.

1971; 27 min; 16 mm; color; JR, HS, A; Post World War II.
UILL

TOURNAMENT GOLF WITH THE LADIES

When prize money is involved, America's pros swing sweetly and accurately.

NL; NL; 16 mm; NL; JR, HS, A; Post World War II.
MILLER

TOURNAMENT OF CHAMPIONS

Tournament of Champions refers to the top eliminators in many classes of the fastest-growing spectator sport in the world, drag racing. It portrays the immensity of the number of participants, the huge purse offered, and the crowds at the National Drag Race. There are literally hundreds of run-off events in a three-day period. Street machines, stockers, altereds, funny cars, and the biggest brutes of the rail, or fuel-burning dragster.

NL; 30 min; 16 mm; color; JR, HS, A; Post World War II.
BUDGET

TO WIN AT ALL COSTS: THE STORY OF THE AMERICA'S CUP

Tells the story of the America Cup races from 1851 to 1983, when Australia brought an end to one of the longest winning streaks in history.

1983; 56 min; VHS; color; JR, HS, A; Making of Modern Sport to Post World War II.
MYSTIC; OFFSHR

TOWN AND COUNTRY RECREATION

Shows what happens to a sleepy town when a recreation program comes to life though voluntary leadership and grows into a year-round public-supported program. Explains basic recreation planning and organization, financing, building of facilities, utilization of local resources, development of enthusiasm, and group action. Shows where to get help and how to utilize it.

1957; 22 min; 16 mm; color; HS, A; Post World War II.
UILL

TRAINING THE TOREADOR

A vintage bull-fighting short in which men, women, and even children face the bull and prepare for thrills in the arena.

1946; 10 min; 16 mm; NL; JR, HS, A; Post World War II.
BUDGET

TRIBUTE TO AMERICA'S WOMEN ATHLETES, A

This program acknowledges the accomplishments of all women in athletics and recognizes their importance as role modes for today's young athletes. The Women's Sports Foundation has created an award for the Greatest American Woman Athlete for the last 25 years. A great inspirational and exciting program.

NL; 8 min; VHS, U-Matic; color; JR, HS, A; Post World War II.
CCCD

TRIBUTE TO LOMBARDI

This program depicts how Vince Lombardi's character and will to win made him such an outstanding coach. It portrays how he inspired the Green Bay Packers to three championships and how he motivated his team with love, loyalty, and teamwork.

NL; 4 min; 16 mm, VHS, U-Matic; color; JR, HS, A; Post World War II.
NFL; TMA

TROBRIAND CRICKET: AN INGENIOUS RESPONSE TO COLONIALISM

Documents ethnographically the modifications made by residents of the Trobriand islands in Papua, New Guinea, to the traditional British game of cricket. Shows all the ritualistic changes incorporated by the islanders, including the magnificent costumes, songs, and dances made up for their version of the game. Discusses how, in response to colonialism, the islanders changed the game into an outlet for mock warfare, community interchange, tribal rivalry, sexual innuendo, and a lot of fun.

1976; 53 min; 16 mm; color; HS, A; Post World War II.
MICHMED

TROT TOWN, USA

Narrated by Bud Palmer. Film depicts the cultural heritage of harness racing in Goshen, New York, and includes highlights of the Hall of Fame of the Trotter, Historic Track, and the harness horse tradition and background of Goshen itself.

NL; 12 min; 16 mm; JR, HS, A; Post World War II.
USTA

TROUT AT COLOMBIA'S LAKE TOTA

NL; 5 min; 16 mm; NL; JR, HS, A; Post World War II.
BRANIFF

TROUT FLY, THE

To illustrate how the trout fly imitates the insect life that makes up the basic diet of the trout, a complex, precise, stylized, colorful trout fly is reconstructed in closely photographed scenes that reveal the materials and tools required to devise this artificial insect. The film ends with a fisherman selecting a logical spot in the stream to cast the fly with success, hooking a glossy trout.
1967; 14 min; 16 mm; color; JR, HS, A; Post World War II.
UILL

TUKTA AND THE MAGIC BOW

The Inuit used the bow and arrow for hunting. We see a bow being made and how the Inuit practice their shooting skill by aiming arrows at snow men and snow bears. Tuktu's father proves himself the best at this test of hunting skill.
1968; 14 min; 16 mm, U-Matic; NL; E, JR, HS, A; Ancient to Post World War II.
NFBC; FI

TUKTA AND THE MAGIC SPEAR

Tuktu accompanies his family, fishing through the ice during the long, cold winter. He also sees his father catch fish with a spear during the summer, and he longs to grow up and spear fish, too.
1967; 14 min; 16 mm, U-Matic; NL; E, JR, HS, A; Ancient to Post World War II.
FI; NFBC

TUKTU AND THE SNOW PLACE

After going on a trek to new hunting grounds, Tuktu's family and a friends build igloos, in particular a giant igloo where feasting, dancing, and games take place.
1967; 14 min; 16 mm, U-Matic; NL; E, JR, HS, A; Ancient to Post World War II.
FI; NFBC

TUKTU AND THE TEN THOUSAND FISHES

Tuktu is taken on a fishing trip to the ancient stone weir. He sees his father and other hunters spear fish in great numbers, and watches his father and his uncle make fire with an Inuit fire drill.
1976; 14 min; 16 mm, U-Matic; NL; E, JR, HS, A; Ancient to Post World War II.
FI; NFBC

TUKTU AND THE TRIALS OF STRENGTH

Strong and hardy Inuit hunters demonstrate and test their strength in Inuit boxing, tug-of-war, and other strenuous activities. We see and hear the drum dance, a demonstration of Inuit poetry and rhythm.
1967; 14 min; 16 mm, U-Matic; NL; E, JR, HS, A; Ancient to Post World War II.
FI; NFBC

TUMBLES, MUMBLES, AND BUMBLES

Memorable bloopers are followed by inspiring successes in this sports-action film designed to show that anyone, even a superstar, can make and overcome mistakes. It's packed with dynamic sports scenes featuring famous athletes and ordinary sports enthusiasts.
NL; 13 min; 16 mm; color; JR, HS, A; Post World War II.
PYRAMID

TURN LEFT AT CHARLOTTE

Features Richard Petty, the most successful race driver in NASCAR Grand National racing history, and his father, Lee, explaining the philosophy behind the Petty family racing effort. Includes films of Richard's crash at Darlington Raceway.
NL; 21 min; 16 mm; color; JR, HS, A; Post World War II.
GTARC

TURN OF THE CENTURY

Explores the effects of the massive influx of immigrants at the turn of the century, what we learned from the invasion of Cuba, and the feelings and attitudes reflected in American sports, politics, and business.
NL; 24 min; 16 mm; color; NL; Modern Sport.
REAF

TURN OF THE WHEEL, THE

Success as a motor racing driver depends on skill and chance. Formula Pacific champion Dave MacMillan became New Zealand champion partly due to the collision of another driver. Then, as the series leader in America, he was put out of the running by a near-fatal accident. What qualities does one need to endure as a driver in this most dangerous of sports? How much of the success of the public heroes depends on the work of unseen mechanics? *Turn of the Wheel* captures one of the most spectacular accidents to occur in New Zealand's motor racing history.

1981; 25 min; 16 mm; NL; JR, HS, A; Post World War II.

NFU

TURNED ON!

A quick-cut montage of dune buggies, speedboats, skiers, snowmobiles, and motorcycles, against a background of synchronized music. The possibilities of the human body in motion, whether sailing, surfing, or skiing, appear to be the greatest "turn-on" of all.

1969; 7 min; 16 mm; color; JR, HS, A; Post World War II.

MICHMED; PYRAMID

TWENTY-FIVE YEARS: THE NBA STORY

Traces the history of the NBA, beginning with the reign of the Minneapolis Lakers in the late 1940s and early 1950s, when they won 5 championships in 6 years. The creation of the 24-second rule in 1954 revolutionized the game, and 3 years later the Boston Celtics began a dynasty using speed, great rebounding, and intimidating defense to win 9 world championships in a 10-year period.

NL; 25 min; 16 mm; NL; JR, HS, A; Post World War II.

WSTGLC

TWENTY-FOUR HEURES DU MANS

Suit up with Jim Busby and live his experience behind the wheel of a B. F. Goodrich Comp T/A-Equipped Porsche Carrera Turbo. Feel the ambience around Le Mans: crew, drivers, and cars are tested to the maximum. Exciting contrasts . . . from crowds to loneliness, dazzling lights to utter darkness.

1982; 19 min; 16 mm; color; JR, HS, A; Post World War II.

MTPS

TWENTY-FOUR HOURS AT FRANCORCHAMPS

Motor racing, a sport that calls for courage, daring, caution, and prudence, is extremely popular in Belgium. The twenty-four hour race at Francorchamps is one of the best-known events in the racing world. It is open to Formula I cars, and drivers have to cover 4,000 kilometers. The first motor race took place in 1922, and the actual "twenty-four hours" came into existence in 1925. Reorganized in 1964, the contest now takes place over a circuit with every safety precaution devised, both for the drivers and for the crowds of people who come to watch the great race every year.

1966; 10 min; 16 mm; color; JR, HS, A; Golden Age to Post World War II.

BELGIUM

TWENTY-FOUR HOURS OF DAYTONA

Featuring such famous drivers as Paul Newman, Jacky Ickx, and others, this film highlights endurance road racing at Daytona International Speedway in Florida. Competition in specially prepared grand touring cars illustrates not only the ultimate in engine durability and suspension engineering, but the grueling and exhausting test for the drivers.

NL; 18 min; 16 mm; color; JR, HS, A; Post World War II.

MTPS

TWENTY-SIX TIMES IN A ROW

In 1954, the mile was run in four minutes for the first time in history. In 1976, it was run in four minutes 26 times in a row! Waldemar Cierpinski won the gold medal at the XXI Olympic Games in Montreal for this record-breaking performance in the marathon. The camera follows Cierpinski as he runs, while his voice tells of his feelings of disappointment when, thinking he had another lap to run, he missed the final sprint.

NL; 24 min; 16 mm, VHS, U-Matic; color; JR, HS, A; Post World War II.

NFBC; PMI

TWO BALL GAMES

Compares and contrasts Little League and sandlot baseball. Provides insight into the role of play, competition, skill acquisition, and parental involvement in child development. Provides a step-by-step comparison, with the use of careful film editing, of the similarities and differences in organized and neighborhood baseball. Filmed in Auburn and Ithaca, New York.

1975; 29 min; 16 mm; color; HS, A; Post World War II.

UWASH

TWO BOLTS OF LIGHTNING

Highlighting cutter and chariot racing, this film gives an inside look at one of AQHA's most exciting events. Racing scenes were filmed during the World Championship Cutter and Chariot Racing Finals at Pocatello, Idaho.

NL; 15 min; 16 mm; color; JR, HS, A; Post World War II.

AQHA

TWO HUNDRED TWENTY BLUES

Questions the value of integration in a system that is run by whites. Tells the story of Sonny, a black high school athlete who is looking forward to an athletic scholarship to sponsor his education in architecture and shows how Larry, a new black militant student, challenges Sonny's security in a white system. Describes how Sonny's integrated life is now torn between black and white.

1970; 18 min; 16 mm, VHS, U-Matic; color; JR, HS, A; Post World War II.

KINGBC; PHENIX

TWO, THREE, FASTEN YOUR SKI

This award-winning film about a hospital rehabilitation program for amputee skiers portrays the fun and excitement from the skier's point of view. As one of the skiers says, "They shouldn't admire us because we ski with one leg. We like to think of three-track skiing as a separate and unique sport." Another says, "I always used to say that I can't, even before I tried things: but now I'm finding out that I can do things like that."

NL; 17 min; 16 mm, VHS, U-Matic, Beta; color; JR, HS, A; Post World War II.

CRYSP

TWO-WHEELER

This is a highly sophisticated film about bicycle racing. Its opening shots are romantic, soft-focused shots of the spoke and wheel of a bicycle turning very slowly, with the click of the ball bearings as accompaniment. *Two-Wheeler* is an altogether delightful experience, in tune with the sport and the reality of bicycle riding.

NL; 17 min; 16 mm, VHS, U-Matic, Beta; color; JR, HS, A; Post World War II.

CRYSP

ULTIMATE CHALLENGE

There's no racecourse in the world tougher to beat, more difficult, more demanding, more challenging than that at Nurburgring, Germany. Twenty-four punishing hours over a 14.1 mile course high in the Eifel Mountains. This feature shows B. F. Goodrich off-the-shelf street Radial T/A tires meeting the ultimate challenge for a handling tire.

NL; 23 min; 16 mm; color; JR, HS, A; post World War II.

MTPS

UNICYCLE: LOOKING AT MY WORLD

In a delightful display of cycling skill, Tony travels from friend to friend, home to school, and job to job on a unicycle. As he goes about his day, he shares his many thoughts and feelings about himself, older people, and life in general.

1976; 15 min; 16 mm; color; JR, HS, A; Post World War II.

UILL

UNOFFICIAL BASEBALL HANDBOOK

NL; 30 min; 16 mm; color; JR, HS, A; Post World War II.

NBHF

UN VELO

This film shows the pleasure and health benefits derived from bicycling. At the annual meeting of the "Tourist Cyclists," a group of young and not-so-young people are off for a cross-country sight-seeing tour.

1976; 17 min; 16 mm; NL; JR, HS, A; Post World War II.

FACSEA

U.S. OPEN 1975

Filmed at Forest Hills, all of the excitement of the semifinal match between Orantes and Vilas is captured in flashbacks to match points. There is also good coverage of the final rounds: Evert vs. Goolagong and Connors vs. Orantes.

1975; 24 min; 16 mm; color; JR, HS, A; Post World War II.

USTEN

USTA: THE FIRST HUNDRED YEARS

In salute to the 100th anniversary of the United States Tennis Association, this film presents an overview of the organization today and its involvement in every aspect of the game of tennis. The film surveys a player on one of the satellite circuits who is hoping to feed into a major championship event, looks at young developing players, and reminisces with the seniors as they all enjoy the "sport for a lifetime."

1981; 28 min; 16 mm; color; JR, HS, A; Modern to Post World War II.

USTEN

UTAH, A WINNING TRADITION

Presents the University of Utah's basketball teams through past years and their accomplishments in establishing a winning tradition. Features many of the great stars and coaches of University of Utah basketball history. Introduces coach Bill Foster and lists his contributions to Utah basketball. Shows the University of Utah campus and the advantages of the Salt Lake Valley. Contains some highlights of the 1971-72 Utah basketball season.

1973; 15 min; 16 mm; color; HS, A; Post World War II.
UU

UTAH'S NATIONAL PARKS AND RECREATION

Describes Utah as a place with picturesque scenery and diverse recreational opportunities. Deals specifically with recreational opportunities available through national parks, national recreation areas, national monuments, and national forests within the state of Utah. Visits, through spectacular photography, areas such as Zion National Park, Bryce Canyon, Lake Powell, Arches National Park and Canyonlands. Discusses the weather and geological processes that helped form these areas. Explores with interviews, the premise that the National Park Service has betrayed the people of San Juan County; another interview explains the National Park Services' point of view.
1981; 30 min; VHS, U-Matic; color; HS, A; Post World War II.
UU

UTAH'S STATE PARKS AND PRIVATE RECREATION

Describes the various state, local, and private, cultural, and recreational areas in the state of Utah. Describes, through the use of on-location photography, many of the state's recreational areas. Visits such striking areas as Dead Horse Point, Snow Canyon, Newspaper Rock, and Iron Missouri for their scenic, cultural, and historic value. Discusses the importance of tourism and the economic value the ski industry has for the state of Utah. Stresses that these scenic, cultural, and historic areas are important to the state of Utah, and advises preserving these areas.
1981; 30 min; VHS, U-Matic; color; HS, A; Post World War II.
UU

VASA SKI RACE, THE

Held in memory of Gustavus Vasa, who fled from the Danes in 1521, this race takes place every year, the first Sunday in March. In 1966, six thousand competitors entered the race. The film shows the impressive sight of all of them taking off together at the start, glimpses of the race, and the atmosphere of folk festival that surrounds this unique event. The material has been intermixed with scenes from an early silent movie dramatization of the life of Gustavus Vasa, who was to become one of the most colorful kings in Swedish history.

1966; 29 min; 16 mm; NL; JR, HS, A; Post World War II.
MTPS

VENEZUELAN ADVENTURE

General James H. Doolittle guides a fishing trip to the Caribbean, where tarpon, marlin, tuna, and dolphin abound, and into the rivers of Venezuela, teeming with peacock, bass, pavone, and ferocious piranah. See a jaguar hunt and an almost legendary region that has the world's highest waterfall.
NL; 30 min; 16 mm; NL; A; Post World War II.
MCDO

VIOLENCE: JUST FOR FUN

With weapons, armor, and gladiators trained to fight each other, Roman spectators applaud the destruction of human lives for entertainment, easily accepting violence as an enjoyable aspect of "civilized" life. The battles are savage and vicious—gladiators fall into pits of fire, get stabbed, beaten, eaten by lions, and run over with chariots.
1972; 14 min; 16 mm; color; JR, HS, A; Ancient Sport.
LCOA; SYRA; UNH

VISIONS OF EIGHT

Presents eight aspects of the 1972 Olympic Games in Munich, Germany. Looks at the pole-vault, decathlon, 100-meter dash, losing athletes, marathon runners, women contestants, weightlifters, and the tension before the starting gun.
1973; 105 min; 16 mm; color; JR, HS, A; Post World War II.
CINEMV; WOLPER

VISIONS OF GLORY

A history and update of the Olympic movement in the United States. This film features footage from the 1984 summer and winter games and the Olympic Festival. Viewers journey through the Olympic training center in Colorado Springs to discover how sports medicine and science are helping tomorrow's Olympic heroes train today.
NL; 24 min; 16 mm, VHS; color; Post World War II.
MTPS; USOC

VISIT WITH AN EQUESTRIAN

A visit with Josef Neckermann in his office during his daily practice session with his horse Asbach, and at the 1960 Olympics in Rome, where he won the bronze medal for Germany.

1960; 17 min; 16 mm; BW; JR, HS, A; Post World War II.
MTPS

VIVA OLYMPIC VITALITY

The story of the 1968 Summer Olympics in Mexico City.

NL; 28 min; 16 mm; color; JR, HS, A; Post World War II.
USOC

VIVE LE TOUR!

Follow the excitement and struggle of some of the world's fastest cyclists in the annual Tour de France cycling race. *Vive le Tour!* captures the reality of the race—the speed, collisions, roar of the crowd, and the exploitation.

1976; 19 min; 16 mm; color; JR, HS, A; Post World War II.
NYFILMS; OSU

VOLLEYBALL: A SPORT COME OF AGE

Traces volleyball's evolution from a Sunday-afternoon pastime for tired businessmen to an exciting, competitive sport that now attracts 150 million players around the world. The viewer is taken to an Olympic game, where United States team member Larry Rundle describes the growth of the sport. Manhattan Beach in Southern California provides a fast-paced look at the world of beach volleyball. The reason this sport has skyrocketed in popularity is discussed by skilled players.

1975; 22 min; 16 mm; color; JR, HS, A; Post World War II.
OXFORD; UILL

VOM ALPENSTOCK ZUM KANDAHAR

The history of skiing in Austria, from the earliest beginnings to the Winter Olympics in Aspen, Colorado, 1952.

NL; 15 min; 16 mm; BW; JR, HS, A; Making of Modern Sport to Post World War II.
AUSINS

VOYAGE OF ODYSSEUS

Highly original and imaginative retelling of Odysseus' voyage home from the Trojan War. Figures on Greek vases come to life, and the gods speak. Narrated by Julie Harris.

1982; 27 min; 16 mm; color; JR, HS, A; Ancient Sport.
CF; OSU

VROOM!

A variety of cinematic devices, including stop-action, slow-motion, and split-screen techniques, are used to convey some of the fun and excitement of drag racing competition. A history of the sport, from its organization of street hot-rodders in the 1950s to the present-day ultrasophisticated machines. Interviews with racers and spectators provide a running commentary on the ever-present hazards of fire and crashes, speed of the machines, women dragsters, and why people want to become drag racers.

1974; 17 min; 16 mm; color; JR, HS, A; Post World War II.
PYRAMID; UILL

WAKE UP THE ECHOES

Wake Up the Echoes is the first documentary movie to explore the muscle and mystique that is Notre Dame football. From the Gipper to the Golden Boy, the stirring saga of the Fighting Irish is told with never-before-seen footage, eyewitness interviews, and on-the-spot authentic live sound.

NL; 52 min; 16 mm; VHS, U-Matic; color; JR, HS, A; Golden Age to Post World War II.
NFL; TMA

WALK! AMERICA!

A compelling account of one man's year-long walk through all 50 states to demonstrate to Americans the importance of cardiovascular health through exercise, proper nutrition, and other life-style modifications. The film presents interesting medical facts on the benefits of walking.

24 min; 16 mm, VHS, U-Matic; color; JR, HS, A; Post World War II.
MTPS

WALKER CUP HIGHLIGHTS

Historic events in golf's oldest team competition between Great Britain and the United States. Robert T. Jones, Jr., Francis Ouimet, and other great players are shown. First half, black and white; second half, color sequences of the 1959 match at Muirfield, Scotland.

1959; 16 min; 16 mm; BW and color; JR, HS, A; Golden Age to Post World War II.
USGA

WALT GARRISON

Walt Garrison was a cowboy on and off the field. His cowboy background made him one of the funniest and most colorful members of the NFL. A fascinating story of true grit, honesty, and courage.

1985; 8 min; VHS, U-matic; color; JR, HS, A; Post World War II.

NFL; TMA

WAR WITHOUT WEAPONS

A behind-the-scenes look at Australian rules football, a tough, fast game that is played only in Australia.

1980; 27 min; 16 mm; color; JR, HS, A; Post World War II.

FLMAUS

WATERPROOFING AMERICA: OR DIFFERENT STROKES FOR DIFFERENT FOLKS

Consists of historical footage featuring the activities and people who have made Red Cross National Aquatic and First Aid Schools a tradition over the last 50 years.

1972; 9 min; 16 mm; BW; JR, HS, A; Golden Age to Post World War II.

AMRC

WAY THEY WERE, THE: THE NEW YORK JETS—THEIR FIRST 25 YEARS

Highlights include a look at original New York Titans' owner Harry Wismer, a colorful and memorable eccentric, the Jets' 1968 World Championship season, and a look to the team's future. Top Jets are profiled including Joe Namath, John Riggins, Don Maynard, Gerry Philbin, Mark Gastineau, and Wesley Walker.

1985; 23 min; 16 mm, VHS, U-Matic; NL; JR, HS, A; Post World War II.

NFL; TMA

WAY OF THE TROUT, THE

An angler holding a six-pound trout reflects on the life-and-death struggle of the fish, considered by some to be the most beautiful freshwater fish in the world. The film covers the birth of this trout, its difficult fight for survival, the hazards it encounters from above and below the surface of the stream, and finally as it reaches adult stage.

NL; 35 min; 16 mm; NL; JR, HS, A; Post World War II.

DOALL

WEEKEND ATHLETES

"If you only exercise on the weekend . . . you're going to die on the weekend." This statement well summarizes a basic thesis of the film's content. Jules Bergman, ABC Science Editor, is the host/narrator, and other participants include many medical and sports authorities. Cutaway models of the human body, computers, and other advanced measuring machines are used to analyze the effects of exercise on the bones, muscles, tendons, and heart, as well as to suggest some solutions. Bergman concludes by saying "You don't play sports to get into shape; you get into shape to play sports."

1976; 49 min; 16 mm; color; HS, A; Post World War II.

ABC; BEST; UILL

WEIGHT TRAINING

Animated diagrams show how muscles work and how weight training greatly improves athletic performance. Live demonstrations illustrate the correct execution of the basic weight-training exercises performed in Olympic competition.

1963; 16 min; 16 mm; BW; JR, HS, A; Post World War II.

UILL

WEIGHT TRAINING

Follows the development of a systematic weight-training program for a high-school shotput candidate, to show how weight training exercises can be used to increase an athlete's strength and endurance. Identifies the key muscles used in each of the various track and field events and demonstrates how to develop these muscles.

1963; 16 min; 16 mm; BW; JR, HS, A; Post World War II.

UILL

WE ONLY GET PAID TO WIN

Looks at Mark Donohue and Roger Penske, one of the most successful teams in the history of automobile racing.

NL; 21 min; 16 mm; color; JR, HS, A; Post World War II.

GTARC

WET AND WILD

In rapid succession, one big wave after another swells, curls, and thunders onto the shore in this montage of surfing's most dangerous beaches. Filmed on location in Hawaii and California.

1967; 15 min; 16 mm; color; E, JR, HS, A; Post World War II.

PYRAMID

WHAT MAKES HIM RUN

Footage of major races at prominent tracks across the country comprise this look at quarter horse racing.

NL; 25 min; VHS; color; JR, HS, A; Post World War II.
    AQHA

WHAT MAKES JACKY ICKX RACE?

Follow the career of Jacky Ickx, a conscientious and careful workman who is fully aware of the risks of his profession. He also knows that those risks are fewer than the dangers an average driver is likely to meet on a road full of weekend drivers. Ickx chose this career because he was raised in a motor-racing environment. His father, his mother, and his brother were all racing drivers before him.

1971; 23 min; 16 mm, 35 mm; color; JR, HS, A; Post World War II.
    BELGIUM

WHAT MAKES SALLY RUN?

The prejudice and lack of backing that women athletes have suffered in the Unites States is recounted in this film, which also presents national and world-class women athletes in the Puget Sound area.

NL; 25 min; 16 mm; color; JR, HS, A; Post World War II.
    KINGBC

WHAT MAKES THEM RUN?

Why would thousands of people rush into the forests of Sweden clutching a map in one hand and a compass in the other? They are competing in the sport of orienteering, a healthy blend of mental and physical exercise which requires that racers find their way through unfamiliar terrain as quickly as possible. As the camaraderie and the mental and physical conditioning inspired by the sport become apparent, it is easy to understand what makes them run.

NL; 20 min; 16 mm, VHS; color; JR, HS, A; Post World War II.
    IFB

WHAT THE WELL-DRESSED HARNESS HORSE SHOULD WEAR ... AND WHY

Narrated by well-known harness trainer-driver Bill Haughton. Film carefully explains harness gear of a trotter and pacer and the difference between a jogging cart and a sulky.

NL; 10 min; 16 mm; NL; JR, HS, A; Post World War II.
    USTA

WHAT WILL THEY THINK OF NEXT?

Humorous approach to the research and development of snowmobiles. High speed and slow motion reminiscent of silent film days are used.

NL; 27 min; 16 mm; NL; JR, HS, A; Post World War II.
    MTPS

WHEELIN' STEEL

Focuses on the 25th National Wheelchair Games held June 17-21, 1981, at the University of Washington, Seattle. Some 350 athletes qualifying in seven events—track, field, swimming, weightlifting, archery, table tennis, and slalom—competed in the games. While the film is a composite experience of what transpired over the five days of competition, it focuses on six of the major athletes, showing how *Wheelin' Steel* is more than a film title. It is also a philosophy and this presentation is aimed at opening the viewers' minds and changing their attitudes about wheelchair athletics and those who compete in them.

1981; 58 min; U-Matic; color; JR, HS, A; Post World War II.
    UWASH; UWP

WHEN SNOW WAS INVENTED

This film traces the history of skiing in Switzerland from 1892, when Christopher Iselin imported three pairs of skis from Norway and made an expedition in 1893 which opened the Swiss Alps to skiing. Then celebrities took up the new sport and the Swiss issued skis to their troops. Finally royalty began to ski, sending skiing on its way to today's popularity.

NL; 14 min; 16 mm; NL; JR, HS, A; Modern Sport to Post World War II.
    SNTO; TRIBUNE

WHEN SPORTS WERE KING

In racing, football, golf, and baseball, you'll meet the greatest sportsmen and sportswomen of the century. *When Sports Were King* is a veritable Who's Who, with dozens of America's best sports stars, including Babe Ruth, Lou Gehrig, Earl Sande, Bill Johnson, Knute Rockne, Red Grange, Bill Tilden, Molla Mallory, Helen Wills, Mary Brown, Bobby Jones, and many, many others.

NL; 10 min; 16 mm; BW; JR, HS, A; Golden Age, Depression Era and World War II.
    FILMIC

WHEN YOU SKI, YOU ARE THE WIND

Three coordinate themes are presented: the enjoyment of learning to ski, the beauty of winter, and the pleasures of alpine skiing. There is no narration; communication is through imagery, music, and pithy comments from the skiers themselves. The comments of the ski school students are a cumulative affirmation of how much fun is to be had in learning to ski.

NL; 33 min; 16 mm; color; JR, HS, A; Post World War II.
MTPS

WHERE THERE'S A WHEEL THERE'S A WAY

Addresses the physical and psychological benefits obtained by the handicapped through participation in team sports.
NL; 19 min; U-Matic; color; JR, HS, A; Post World War II.
UNDMC

WHEREVER WE FIND THEM

Shows the numerous athletic opportunities available to handicapped individuals, including racketball, skiing, track, swimming, bowling, and weightlifting. Describes how exercise and participation in organized competition builds strength and confidence.
1979; 29 min; 16 mm; color; JR, HS, A; Post World War II.
USNAC; USVA

WHITE CRANE SPREADS WINGS

Demonstrates the ancient Chinese art of T'ai Chi Chuan, which aims at complete coordination of mind and body through a system of precise physical movements.
1976; 9 min; 16 mm; color; JR, HS, A; Post World War II.
CFS

WHITE SEARCH, THE

Follows one man's search for his skiing paradise (with a detour to Death Valley, thanks to a bungling chauffeur). As he continues his search, the viewer is treated to such scenic spots as Utah (the Alta Deep Powder); Mittendorf, Austria (ski flying championships); Aspen, Colorado (the Delicatessen Duel); and Portillo, Chile (downhill championships).
1972; 90 min; 16 mm; color; JR, HS, A; Post World War II.
BUDGET

WHITE WATER

In Georgia, a group of people prepare to "shoot the rapids" on the Chattooga River, celebrated in the movie *Deliverance,* starring Jon Voight, who narrates this film on white water. To the experts, the danger is minimal, for they have a healthy respect for the river and approach it with care. Life preservers are always worn; crash helmets and wet suits provide protection and warmth in case of a spill. An absolute rule is never to travel alone. These precautions pay off for the people in the film who ride the churning white water in kayak, canoe, and raft, successfully effecting a rescue operation when a canoe capsizes. An empty rubber raft bobbing on the current tells the sad tale of two boys who entered the river without telling anyone of their plans. They wore no protective clothing and had no knowledge of the hazards of the river.
1976; 25 min; 16 mm; color; JR, HS, A; Post World War II.
FI; NBC; UILL

WHITE WATER

A look at the growing sport of whitewater canoeing. Filmed during the national whitewater canoeing competition held on the Nantahala River in the Smokey Mountains of North Carolina.
1970; 11 min; 16 mm; NL; JR, HS, A; Post World War II.
AMRC

WHITE WATER RAFTING

A spectacular whitewater adventure in the Northeast. Ken Crayton rides the wild whitewater of the Upper Hudson River with Pat Cunningham, owner of the Hudson River Raft Company.
NL; 28 min; VHS; NL; JR, HS, A; Post World War II.
KAROL

WHOLE LOT PROUD

Filmed in the panoramic Ozarks, the rugged hills of South Dakota, and among the sprawling beauty of Tennessee, this is the story of park rangers. They play a year-round role in making over 400 recreation lakes more enjoyable for those who love the outdoors.
NL; 25 min; 16 mm, VHS; JR, HS, A; Post World War II.
MTPS

WHOLE NEW BALANCE, A

How an adult affects the attitudes of girls and boys playing football together.
NL; 9 min; 16 mm; color; JR, HS, A; Post World War II.
PHENIX

WHO'S KEEPING SCORE?

A film about the latest innovation in bowling—the Brunswick Automatic Scorer completely eliminates manual scorekeeping and adds more fun and excitement to the game through its computerized system.

NL; 10 min; 16 mm; NL; JR, HS, A; Post World War II.
BRNSWK

WHO'S ON FIRST?

Features Abbott and Costello and the only comedy routine in the Baseball Hall of Fame. A "normal" conversation between Abbott and Costello about the starting lineup of the St. Louis Wolves baseball team becomes a classic case of reciprocal misunderstanding while demonstrating some of the inherent problems in effective communication.

1955; 7 min; 16 mm; BW; JR, HS, A; Post World War II.
SALENG; WSU

WHY PHYSICAL EDUCATION?

Designed to show boys and girls the importance of developing and maintaining physical skills useful for both work and play. Pictures boys doing directed exercises. Animation shows how muscles develop through use. Girls are shown doing gymnastics and exercises. Other activities illustrated include synchronized swimming, modern dance, and basketball. Mentions the desirable goal "a sound mind in a sound body," and urges fitness for work, study, expression, and survival.

1963; 14 min; 16 mm; color; JR, HS; Post World War II.
UILL; WEX

WILD AND WONDERFUL WORLD OF AUTO RACING

An exciting portrayal of the second-largest sport in the Unites States. Respect for safety is the hallmark of witnessing the vicarious thrills of stock car racing in Daytona, drag racing in Dallas, and sports car racing in Watkins Glen and the Indianapolis Motor Speedway. The film culminates with the Indianapolis 500 as Bruce McLaren, Don Gurney, and champ Mario Andretti come to the fore.

NL; 28 min; 16 mm, VHS; color; JR, HS, A; Post World War II.
SF

WILDERNESS BELOW, THE

Follows one spelunker as he explores a cavern, revealing the beauty, mystery, and solitude experienced by those who enter these underground wilderness areas. Shows the caver lowering himself into the mouth of the cave, paddling a raft on a subterranean waterway, and exploring the cave's flora and fauna. Includes an original electronic music score and no narration. Filmed primarily in the Cumberland Caverns, McMinnville, Tennessee.

1973; 12 min; 16 mm; color; JR, HS, A; Post World War II.
IU

WILDERNESS NOMADS

A teacher, a parent, a dog, a cameraman, and a group of Canadian teenagers who call themselves the "Wilderness Nomads" undertake a challenging trip through the lakes and whitewater rapids of northern Canada. The students have to face many unknown and potentially dangerous or difficult situations. They also make the meals, gather unfamiliar herbs, make camp, and watch sunsets. They talk of their freedom out in the wilderness, their sense of independence, and also their sense of counting as individuals.

1974; 18 min; 16 mm; color; JR, HS, A; Post World War II.
LCOA; UILL

WILDERNESS SURVIVAL

Joyce MacDuffie, an expert on wilderness survival techniques, demonstrates the art of survival in this short film. Emphasis is placed on basics—building shelter, obtaining food, and first aid.

NL; 17 min; 16 mm; NL; JR, HS, A; Post World War II.
NRA

WILDERNESS TRAIL

Portrays an actual pack trip into the Bridger Wilderness Area in the Bridger National Forest in Wyoming. Shows how such areas are preserved in their natural state.

1961; 15 min; 16 mm; color; JR, HS, A; Post World War II.
IOWA; USDA; USNAC

WILD HERITAGE

The role of firearms in the conquest and settlement of America's frontiers and wilderness is portrayed through the eyes of some of the country's most famous illustrators who caught America as it was growing up.

NL; 30 min; VHS; NL; JR, HS, A; Premodern to Modern Sport.
KAROL

WILD RIVER

Covers an adventurous water journey from beginning to end—190 miles, 23 days—as Frank and John Craighead and their families lead a thrilling expedition down Idaho's Middle Fork and Salmon rivers, encountering and surmounting difficulties such as overturned kayaks, hidden rocks, hair-raising rapids, and food shortages. Dangers of pollution are depicted by the sight of new buildings interrupting the natural scenery and litter cluttering the riverbanks. Brief glimpses of two other rivers, the Hudson and Potomac, reveal the effects of pollution in the nation's waterways.

1969; 50 min; 16 mm; color; JR, HS, A; Post World War II.

FI; OSU; UILL

WILL OF A CHAMPION, THE

Speaking before a Jaycee audience in St. Paul, Minnesota, Bob Richards creates in the audience the "will of a champion." Reference is made to the 1964 Olympic games in Tokyo; how competition increases your desire and the need to think under pressure.

NL; 29 min; 16 mm; NL; JR, HS, A; Post World War II.

NINEFC

WILL TO WIN, THE

A dynamic and thought-provoking study of men-in-motion reaching toward the limits of their ability. High-risk sports such as hockey, skiing, football, sky diving, and auto racing are filmed to give one the feeling of being directly involved with the participant.

1970; 27 min; 16 mm; color; JR, HS, A; Post World War II.

PYRAMID; SDSU

WINDFLIGHT

Here's an exhilarating look at windsurfing. Cameras mounted on masts and helmets enable the viewer to "ride" Hawaii's sensational waves and experience sailboarding's high-performance thrills. *Windflight* is a dynamic display of physical agility and athletic artistry, featuring the first 360-degree flips ever filmed, the largest windsurfing waves ever ridden, and incredible aerial loops, jibes, and freestyle performances by some of the top names in sailboarding.

NL; 13 min; 16 mm; color; JR, HS, A; Post World War II.

PYRAMID

WINGS OF THE WIND

Joys and dangers of the sport of hang gliding are presented in picture and narration. Interviewed are a hang gliding expert, a glider engineer, and the chief of flight standards for the government.

1976; 15 min; 16 mm; color; JR, HS, A; Post World War II.

BUDGET; UILL

WINNER IS WAITING, A

Motivational film examines discipline and dedication; novice and Olympic champion swimmers train and perform.

NL; 23 min; 16 mm; NL; JR, HS, A; Post World War II.

MTPS

WINNER NEVER QUITS

Documents a high school football team, describing the peer group pressure and the role-playing experienced by the athletes, cheerleaders, and coaches.

1977; 18 min; 16 mm, VHS, U-Matic; color; JR, HS, A; Post World War II.

PHENIX; UILL

WINNERS ALL

"In the Olympics, it is not the winning but the taking part that counts." This credo serves as a motto for the thousands who participate in the Junior Olympics.

NL; 27 min; 16 mm; NL; JR, HS, A; Post World War II.

MTPS

WINNERS ALL OUR LIVES

There is a movement afoot that is giving inspiration, joy, and improved health to those past middle age. Filmed at the World Games in Puerto Rico, this film explores these new directions and shows the motivation, techniques, exhilarations, and camaraderie of these over-forty competitors. This film is about goal-setting, about using techniques to enhance emotional and physical well-being, and about the attitudes that can lead to excellence. Narrated by Dr. Denis Waitley.

1985; 18 min; 16 mm; color; A; Post World War II.

UWISC

WINNING

Mike Wallace presents this segment from "Sixty Minutes" dealing with the phenomenon of midget football. As the players on the Hollywood Hills Red Raiders and the Miramar Saints (Florida) play their big game, Wallace questions the Lombardi principle that seems to govern the adults supervising the competition: "Winning isn't everything; it's the only thing!" The coaches and the parents verbalize their own positive opinions and the opportunities that competition provides to the youngsters. The players, however, seem somewhat unclear as to the benefits and remark how playing this "game" will make them "better men."

1974; 16 min; 16 mm; color; HS, A; Post World War II.
UWASH

WINNING AND LOSING (SOME NOTES ON A HIGH SCHOOL FOOTBALL SEASON)

Follows the DuBois Area (Pennsylvania) High School football team through one bittersweet season. The program not only captures reflections of the coach and several key players on the strategies, thrills, and tears associated with high school football, it deals as well with deeper questions related to the role of sports in our society, how young athletes react to the experiences of winning and losing, and what motivates them to participate. Discussion guide included.
1982; 59 min; VHS; color; JR, HS, A; Post World War II.
PENNST

WINNING DIFFERENCE, THE

Gymnastics, a sport that requires precision in every move, takes as much motivation to insure success as it does talent. Join the action, drama, and trials of gymnasts as they enjoy "the winning difference."
NL; 28 min; VHS; color; JR, HS, A; Post World War II.
KAROL

WINNING IS EVERYTHING

Examines some of the effects of highly competitive sports on children of various ages. Also looks at the roles played by their parents and coaches. Shows actual sporting events where children are involved, such as soccer, swimming, baseball, football, and hockey. Some of the children who are participants express themselves. Discusses the implementation of some new policies related to children participating in highly competitive sports.
1978; 24 min; 16 mm; color; HS, A; Post World War II.
LUF; UWISC

WINNING ISN'T EVERYTHING

Examines the dangers of the attitudes and violence in professional sports filtering down to the college, high school, and backyard levels. Instead of making winning "the only thing," athletes are advised that it's okay to win, but not to quit playing if they lose. Visit a Boys Club, a YMCA, and a panel discussion with high school coaches. Contrasting opinions and objectives are offered by parents, coaches, and players. The problem of making partic-ipation accessible to those who are cut from the team is discussed.
1976; 23 min; 16 mm; color; JR, HS, A; Post World War II.
FI; NBC; UILL

WINNING SPIRIT, THE

The Hershey Youth Program, created in 1975, emphasizes participation and sportsmanship. It introduces children to physical fitness through track and field events which come naturally to them. Participants (ages 9-14) get instruction in track and field basics.
NL; 15 min; 16 mm; color; JR, HS, A; Post World War II.
MTPS

WINNING WAY TO GO

Sports car racing at America's most beautiful road racing and oval race courses. This action-packed program illustrates the intense competition between race teams in their quest to win motor racing's top awards in the International Motor Sports Association series.
NL; 26 min; 16 mm, VHS; JR, HS, A; Post World War II.
MTPS

WINNING WITH ASTHMA . . . ATHLETES OF THE YEAR AWARDS

NL; 15 min; 16 mm, VHS, U-Matic; JR, HS, A; Post World War II.
MTPS

WINTER CARNIVAL THEME

Features a 17-year-old athlete for all seasons, who competes in the biathlon, an event that combines cross-country skiing and sharpshooting.
1982; 24 min; VHS, U-Matic; color; JR, HS, Post World War II.
WCCOTV

WINTER MADE IN SWITZERLAND

A film about skiing, skating, tobogganing, curling, and other winter sports in Switzerland. Without narration.
NL; 18 min; 16 mm; NL; E, JR, HS, A; Post World War II.
SNTO; TRIBUNE

WINTER OLYMPICS

NL; NL; 16 mm; NL; JR, HS, A; Post World War II.
COCA

WOMAN IN SPORTS, THE, PART I: GET OUT, GET UP, GET GOING!

Dramatization about a young woman hesitant to get involved in sports. As she discovers the benefits—physical and mental—her enthusiasm grows.

NL; 30 min; 16 mm; NL; JR, HS, A; Post World War II.

KLEINW; WSF

WOMAN IN SPORTS, THE: PART II: RECORDS, REWARDS, MYTHS

This capsule history of women's sports, narrated by Donna de Varona, gives viewers the opportunity to witness the triumphs and setbacks that women have experienced during the evolution of women's sports, and debunks many of the myths inhibiting women's participation.

NL; 30 min; 16 mm; NL; JR, HS, A; Premodern to Post World War II.

KLEINW; WSF

WOMAN IN SPORTS, THE: PART III: REFLECTIONS OF THE CHAMPIONS

Accomplished athletes Cathy Rigby, Sheila Young, Janet Guthrie, Micki King Hogue, Wyomia Tyus, and others provide an inspiring view of their motivation.

NL; 30 min; 16 mm; NL; JR, HS, A; Post World War II.

KLEINW; WSF

WOMAN IN SPORTS, THE: RECORDS, REWARDS, AND HEROINES

Documents the evolution of women in sports. Shows women excelling in swimming, basketball, golf, gymnastics, skating, skiing, auto racing, tennis, and softball.

NL; 30 min; 16 mm, VHS, U-Matic; color; JR, HS, A; Ancient Sport to Post World War II.

KLEINW

WOMAN'S PLACE, A

An inspiring documentary of achievement, based in part from material gathered for the *LIFE* special report "Remarkable American Women."

NL; 25 min; 16 mm, VHS; NL; JR, HS, A; Post World War II.

CCCD; TIMLIF

WOMEN AND SPORTS: BASKETBALL

This film is the first in a series of motivational films about girls' and women's sports. It is directed primarily at junior high and high school; however, it may also be useful for college students.

NL; 11 min; 16 mm; color; JR, HS, A; Post World War II.

COCA

WOMEN AND SPORTS: GYMNASTICS

The 1977 collegiate women's gymnastics competition is presented in this film, which also includes comments from coaches, gymnastics training sessions, and slow-motion segments of performance.

NL; 15 min; 16 mm; color; JR, HS, A; Post World War II.

COCA

WOMEN AND SPORTS: VOLLEYBALL

This film highlights the the increasingly popular sport of volleyball. Segments of play are presented from the 1977 National Invitational Women's Volleyball Tournament held at the University of California, Los Angeles.

NL; 13 min; 16 mm; color; JR, HS, A; Post World War II.

COCA

WOMEN CAN HUNT, TOO

Joan Cone, an avid hunter and gourmet cook, discusses women in hunting: public attitudes, problems of the woman hunter, and practical tips for the one out of twenty American hunters who are women.

NL; 17 min; 16 mm; NL; JR, HS, A; Post World War II.

NRA

WOMEN IN MEN'S SPORTS

Why can't a 5'5" girl play on the high school team if a 5' 3" boy can? Are women to be deprived of the thrills, the lessons, and the joy of contact team sports? Does equality mean equal access to all playing fields? Beth Balsley, who won access to her high school football team in court, is joined by Phil Donahue and experts Dorothy Harris, Ph.D., board member of the Women's Sports Foundation and sports psychiatrist at Penn State, and Dr. Vern Seefeldt, director of Youth Sports at the Institute of Michigan State University, in a discussion of women in the sports arena.

NL; 28 min; VHS; scolor; JR, HS, A; Post World War II.

FOTH

WOMEN IN SPORTS

Top feminine talent in championship track and gymnastics.

NL; 28 min; 16 mm; NL; JR, HS, A; Post World War II.

CINES

WOMEN IN SPORTS

Females, young and old, are finding fun and satisfaction in strenuous, muscle-building sporting activities, which, more often than not, were men's terrain some years ago. Women are taking to marathon runs, hockey rinks, racquetball, and tennis courts in record numbers. The focus is on women in competitive sports as this new revolution is documented for viewers.

NL; 27 min; 16 mm, VHS, U-Matic; color; JR, HS, A; Post World War II.

CCCD; SEARS

WOMEN IN SPORTS

This film is a collection of interviews and action shots of everyday people enjoying sports and talking about the value of their experience.

NL; 30 min; 16 mm; NL; JR, HS, A; Post World War II.

MTPS; SEARS; WSF

WOMEN IN SPORTS

Women's sports enjoy new prominence today. In this film, James Michener reviews the history of women in sports and examines the current status of women athletes and women's athletics. Rare footage of historic firsts and fascinating conversations with pioneers of women's sports highlight the film. In addition, coaches, journalists, young athletes, and superstars like Chris Evert Lloyd, Janet Guthrie, and Nancy Lopez offer intriguing commentary on the past, present, and future role of women in sports.

NL; 26 min; NL; color; JR, HS, A; Modern Sport to Post World War II.

EMLEN

WOMEN IN SPORTS: AN INFORMAL HISTORY

With New York City's 26-mile marathon race as the backdrop, the film gives an overview of women's roles in sports, past and present. Stress is on women's true strength and stamina as opposed to the traditional role of passivity that women have been unrealistically forced to play. Well-researched capsule history and coverage of early sports stars. Highlights every possible sports arena, from skating and roller derby to tennis and horse racing, and spans ancient to contemporary periods.

1976; 28 min; 16 mm; color; JR, HS, A; Ancient to Post World War II.

MICHMED; UWISC

WOMEN IN SPORTS SERIES (FOUR PROGRAMS)

Kiki Cutter Beattie, Billie Jean King, Barbara Roquemore, Joan Weston (skiing, tennis, parachuting, roller derby).

NL; 22 min; 16 mm; color; JR, HS, A; Post World War II.

OXFORD

WOMEN'S GYMNASTICS: AN INTRODUCTION

Explains and demonstrates the four competitive events in women's gymnastics: the balance beam, the uneven parallel bars, the vault, and the floor exercise. Features demonstrations by U.S. Olympic coach Muriel Grossfield and scenes of young gymnasts in actual competition.

1968; 17 min; 16 mm; color; E, JR, HS, A; Post World War II.

UILL

WOMEN'S RIGHTS

One girl's desire to swim on the boys' team, in spite of state athletic restrictions, serves as the background for the much larger issue of women's rights. A simulated courtroom drama presents arguments for both sides. The issue is left to the viewers to decide.

1974; 22 min; 16 mm; color; JR, HS, A; Post World War II.

PHENIX; UMO

WONDERFUL WORLD OF BIKES, THE

Shows a gamut of cycling experiences, with emphasis on its wholesome enjoyment for fun and fitness by the very young, the newly independent, and the adult. Some spectacular scenery provides the backdrop for a series of Amateur Bicycle League events.

NL; 28 min; 16 mm; NL; JR, HS, A; Post World War II.

ASF

WONDERFUL WORLD OF BOWLING

NL; 20 min; 16 mm; NL; JR, HS, A; Post World War II.

MILLER

WONDERFUL WORLD OF WHEELS

The world of wheels is the subject of this film that serves as a tribute to the adventure, freedom, and feeling of escape associated with cars. Everything is on view: toy cars, go-karts, model cars, sports cars, dune buggies, drag racers, and other vehicles. Additional footage from such car events as the Indianapolis 500, the Bonneville Salt Flats runs, and footage shot at the Riverside Race Track.

1968; 32 min; 16 mm; color; JR, HS, A; Post World War II.

BUDGET

WOODLAND INDIANS OF EARLY AMERICA

Authentic reconstructions and scenes in the eastern Great Lakes regions provide settings for this study of woodland Indian life prior to European influence. The daily life of the Chippewa family is observed.

1958; 11 min; 16 mm; color; JR, HS, A; Premodern Sport.

CORF; OSU

WORLD BOWLING CHAMPIONSHIPS, THE

A dramatic full-color presentation of the 32-nation nonprofessional tournament held in Milwaukee in August, 1971. The United States men's team, led by Ed Luther, win five- and eight-man events; the triumphs of the Puerto Rico doubles team; Luther's march to the individual championships; competition in the women's division. See Hong Kong's Peter Leung and Australia's Graham Smith narrowly miss 300 games. Features superb slow-motion.

NL; 30 min; 16 mm; NL; JR, HS, A; Post World War II.

ABC

WORLD CHAMPIONSHIP OF GREAT GYMNASTS, THE

The Championship Games of Strasbourg in 1978 are beautifully photographed in this film showing the U.S., U.S.S.R., and Japan teams competing with great gymnasts such as Mukhina, Kim, Johnson, Comaneci, Andrianov, Thomas, Kenmotsu, and Deltchev.

1978; 40 min; 16 mm; color; JR, HS, A; Post World War II.

FACSEA

WORLD IS ONE, THE: 1964 OLYMPICS

Join the huge crowds in both Innsbruck and Tokyo for the 1964 Olympic Games. Many sensational performances are recorded as one world record after another is shattered. All the thrilling highlights of the summer and winter Olympic games have been captured in this film, as well as colorful scenes of life and culture in Austria and Japan.

NL; 27 min; 16 mm; color; JR, HS, A; Post World War II.

SDSU; USD

WORLD OF J'AI-ALAI

Gives a brief history of the sport of j'ai-alai, from its origins in the Basque region to the game played in the United States in the 1970s. Culminates with the first American amateur to become a professional world champion.

1979; 14 min; 16 mm; color; JR, HS, A; Post War II.

FLADC

WORLD OF KIDS, THE

In this Academy Award winner, children prove that size doesn't matter when it comes to boxing, bowling, golfing, and other major sports. Tough small frys compete in rodeo events, and a young sharpshooter makes Daddy perspire as he holds the targets. In a half-pint western, kids who can't reach the stirrups ride tall in the saddle. The Soap Box Derby shows speed-crazy toddlers as reckless as their adult counterparts, while babes on skis and diving boards sneer in the face of danger. A hidden camera captures the expressive reactions of children watching a puppet show that delights, charms, and terrifies them.

NL; 10 min; 16 mm; NL; JR, HS, A; Post World War II.

FILMIC

WORLD OF OFF-ROAD RACING, THE

This engrossing documentary that provides a look at the Grand Prix of off-road competition, the Parker Dam 400, which begins in Nevada and ends in California. It is also a look at the man behind the interest in off-road racing, Mickey Thompson, whose organization (Score International) has set the stage for a whole new world of auto thrills.

NL; 25 min; 16 mm; color; JR, HS, A; Post World War II.

BUDGET

WORLD OF SURFING, THE

For surfing fans and just about anyone who digs the sheer adventure of the breathtaking sport of surfing. Hawaii provides the skyscraper waves.

NL; 28 min; 16 mm; NL; JR, HS, A; Post World War II.

CINES

WORLD'S BIGGEST FISH BOWL

A film on the revival of sport fishing in the Great Lakes, with special emphasis on Lake Michigan. Relates the story of how salmon fishing came to the Midwest along with the revival of lake trout, steelhead, and brown trout angling in the nation's inland seas. Includes safety sequences on boating in big water.

NL; 27 min; 16 mm; NL; JR, HS, A; Post World War II.

SOLANA

WORLD SERIES HIGHLIGHTS

Separate films covering 1959 through 1974.

1959-74; NL; 16 mm; NL; JR, HS, A; Post World War II.

COCA

WORLD SERIES OF 1955

This film presents highlights of the games played during the 1955 World Series: the Brooklyn Dodgers vs. the New York Yankees.

1955; 40 min; 16 mm; BW; JR, HS, A; Post World War II.

MLBP; UWISC

WORLD SERIES OF 1956

This film presents highlights of the games played during the 1956 World Series: the New York Yankees vs. the Brooklyn Dodgers.

1956; 40 min; 16 mm; BW; JR, HS, A; Post World II.

MLBP; UWISC

WORLD SERIES OF 1957

This film presents highlights of the games played during the 1957 World Series: Milwaukee Braves vs. the New York Yankees.

1957; 40 min; 16 mm; BW; JR, HS, A; Post World II.

MLBP; UWISC

WORLD SERIES OF 1958

This film presents the highlights of the games played during the 1958 World Series: the Milwaukee Braves vs. the New York Yankees.

1958; 40 min; 16 mm; color; JR, HS, A; Post World II.

MLBP; UWISC

WORLD SERIES OF 1959

This film presents highlights of the games played during the 1959 World Series: the Los Angeles Dodgers vs. the Chicago White Sox.

1959; 40 min; 16 mm; color; JR, HS, A; Post World II.

MLBP; UWISC

WORLD SERIES OF 1961

This film presents highlight of the games played during the 1961 World Series: the New York Yankees vs. the Cincinnati Reds.

1961; 40 min; 16 mm; color; JR, HS, A; Post World II.

MLBP; UWISC

WORLD SERIES 1962

Highlights of the games between the New York Yankees and the San Francisco Giants.

1963; 45 min; 16 mm; color; JR, HS, A; Post World War II.

OSU

WORLD SERIES OF 1964

This film presents highlights of the games played during the 1964 World Series: the St. Louis Cardinals vs. the New York Yankees.

1964; 40 min; 16 mm; color; JR, HS, A; Post World II.

MLBP; UWISC

WORLD SERIES OF 1965

This film presents highlights of the games played during the 1965 World Series: the Los Angeles Dodgers vs. the Minnesota Twins.

1965; 40 min; 16 mm; color; JR, HS, A; Post World II.

MLBP; UWISC

WORLD SERIES OF 1966

This film presents highlights of the games played during the 1966 World Series: the Baltimore Orioles vs. the Los Angeles Dodgers.

1966; 40 min; 16 mm; color; JR, HS, A; Post World II.

MLBP; UWISC

WORLD SERIES OF 1967

This film presents highlights of the games played during the 1967 World Series: the St. Louis Cardinals vs. the Boston Red Sox.

1967; 40 min; 16 mm; color; JR, HS, A; Post World II.

MLBP; UWISC

WORLD SERIES 1972

The excitement of the 1972 fall classic again provided many thrills for the nations' baseball fans. Night World Series baseball made a strong impact. The teams—Cincinnati Reds and the Oakland Athletics.

1973; 40 min; 16 mm; color; JR, HS, A; Post World War II.
OSU

WORLD SERIES 1973

For the third consecutive year, the World Series is decided in a seventh game showdown. The Oakland As became the first team to win back-to-back championships in eleven years as they defeated the New York Mets. The powerful As are held in check by the talented Mets' pitching staff, but Burt Campaneris and Reggie Jackson belt decisive homeruns in the final game to subdue the tenacious New Yorkers.
1974; 40 min; 16 mm; color; JR, HS, A; Post World War II.
OSU

WORLD SERIES 1975

The Cincinnati Reds beat the Boston Red Sox in the seventh game. Called the Super Series, it is regarded as baseball at its best.
1975; 35 min; 16 mm; color; JR, HS, A; Post World War II.
OSU

WORLD SERIES 1976

Highlights of the "Red October Sweep" in which the Cincinnati Reds were victorious over the New York Yankees in the first four consecutive games of the Series. Pete Rose and Johnny Bench were outstanding players for the Reds. Narrated by Joe Garagiola.
1976; 29 min; 16 mm; color; JR, HS, A; Post World War II.
OSU

WORLD SERIES 1977

The New York Yankees were the victors, winning 4 games to the Los Angeles Dodgers' 2 wins. A phenomenal performance was given by Yankee Reggie Jackson, who hit 3 home runs in a single game, scored 10 runs, and got on base 25 times. Narrated by Curt Gowdy.
1977; 30 min; 16 mm; color; JR, HS, A; Post World War II.
OSU

WORLD SERIES 1978

As in the previous year's series, the New York Yankees were victorious over the Los Angeles Dodgers. In a fantastic comeback, the Yankees became the first team to win 4 straight series games after losing the first 2 games.

1978; 32 min; 16 mm; color; JR, HS, A; Post World War II.
OSU

WRESTLER, THE

Edward Asner stars in this drama of the world of professional wrestling. Asner is the promoter-manager who runs afoul of a rackets boss when he arranges a match between the World's Heavyweight Champion (played by real-life wrestling champ Verne Gagne) and a promising challenger. The story moves at a steady pace, with many real-life stars of the mat world, such as Harold "Oddjob" Sakata, "Superstar" Billy Graham, H. B. Haggerty, Dick the Bruiser, the Crusher, Dusty Rhodes, and Dick Murdoch popping up in various roles and supplying the action.
1975; 95 min; 16 mm; color; JR, HS, A; Post World War II.
BUDGET

WRESTLING

From the Golden Age of professional wrestling comes this rare filmed wrestling match between two greats of the era. The match took place at Madison Square Garden in New York City on June 9, 1932.
1932; 30 min; 16 mm; NL; JR, HS, A; Depression Era.
BUDGET

WRESTLING THRILLS

Wrestling action from the halcyon days of professional wrestling in the 1940s.
NL; 10 min; 16 mm; NL; JR, HS, A; Post World War II.
BUDGET

YACHTING IN GREECE

Yachts, sailboats, and motorboats are shown as well as modern marinas throughout the Greek Islands that provide repairs and supplies. Sail past the out-islands Mykonos, Naxos, and others.
NL; 18 min; 16 mm; NL; JR, HS, A; Post World War II.
ACR

YEAR IN REVIEW 1980

Presents a capsulized summary of the key events of the year. Focuses on those stories that have the greatest impact on the world. Covers those changes and milestones that have occurred in religion, politics, science and sports. Reports the events and charts the trends of a year that is a most significant one in the world's history.

NL; 28 min; VHS, U-Matic; color; JR, HS, A; Post World War II.
JOU

YEAR IN REVIEW 1982

Reviews major events of 1982 and also shows headline news in science, sports, politics, and religion.
NL; 50 min; VHS, U-Matic; color; JR, HS, A; Post World War II.
JOU

YEAR OF THE DIRTY THIRTY

Iowa State University began the 1959 football season with a team called the Dirty Thirty, because of the thirty hard-playing members. This film contains action scenes from each game of the season.
1960; 26 min; 16 mm; BW; JR, HS, A; Post World War II.
IOWA

YEARS OF GLORY ... YEAR OF PAIN: THE 25-YEAR HISTORY OF THE BUFFALO BILLS

All of the Bills' history is recounted in this entertaining show: the AFL Championship seasons, O. J. Simpson's record years, and the playoff teams in the early 1980s. The franchise's brightest stars are featured, including Jack Kemp, Frank Lewis, Elbert Dubenion, Butch Byrd, Joe Cribbs, and, of course, O. J. Simpson—"the Juice."
NL; 28 min; 16 mm, VHS, U-Matic; NL; JR, HS, A; Post World War II.
NFL; TMA

YEARS OF TRADITION—NIGHT OF PRIDE : 1972 ALL STAR BASEBALL HIGHLIGHTS

Atlanta (July 1972) and Hank Aaron, hometown hero, turns the All-Star Game and the crowd topsy-turvy. Major League stars and baseball at its best.
NL; 27 min; 16 mm; NL; JR, HS, A; Post World War II.
MTPS

YOU CAN MAKE IT IF YOU TRY

Tells how Thurman teaches the gang how to study and how the game helps Thurman learn athletic skills.
1979; 15 min; 16 mm, VHS, U-Matic; color; E, JR, HS, A; Post World War II.
UWISC

YOU CAN'T LOSE

Filmed in the Chicago area. Two young boys learn to bowl and enjoy the game thoroughly.
NL; 15 min; 16 mm; NL; E, JR, HS, A; Post World War II.
AJBC

YOU HAVE SOMETHING TO OFFER

Duane's handicap limits his sporting abilities until he finds his particular skill.
1977; 14 min; 16 mm, VHS, U-Matic; color; JR, HS, A; Post World War II.
FLMTON; MGHT

YOUNG AND JUST BEGINNING

The work of a 10-year-old gymnast is featured in this film. Her present training and her prospects as an Olympic contender are revived.
NL; 29 min; 16 mm; color; HS, A; Post World War II.
NFBC

YOUNG BULLFIGHTERS, THE

Presents the story of two young men, one Mexican and one American, who train to become toreadors. Shows how the bulls are raised and selected and also other people involved in the bullfights.
1970; 45 min; 16 mm; color; JR, HS, A; Post World War II.
SCORPO; FILCOM

YOUNG PEOPLE IN SPORTS

Describes the importance of sports for young people. Points out that sports teach about competition, about defeat as well as victory, about making decisions and living with them, about goals and aspirations, and about good relationships with family, friends, competitors, and coaches.
NL; 15 min; 16 mm; color; JR, HS, A; Post World War II.
KLEINW

YOUNG WOMEN IN SPORTS

Four exciting young athletes explore their feelings about strength, about competition, about themselves as women and as athletes, and about the benefits of participation in sports. Terri Sabol (discus), Kyle Gayner (gymnastics), Gayle Butler (track), and Shirley Babashoff (swimming) reveal the drama of competition, the satisfaction of extreme effort, and the results of concentrated training and preparation. The film gives viewers a good opportunity to see exactly what's involved in the serious pursuit of these sports.

1975; 16 min; 16 mm; color; JR, HS, A; Post World War II.

MICHMED; PHENIX

YOUR MOVE

Demonstrates the beneficial effects of athletics and exercise on everyone, especially women. Demolishes the myth that sports make females "masculine," and shows enjoyable sports activities for people of all ages.

1976; 22 min; 16 mm; color; JR, HS, A; Post World War II.

FI; NFBC; UCB

YOUTH OF THE WORLD

A rare film classic about the 1936 Winter Olympics. Flash-cutting of telescopic close-ups, compacted speeds of competition, slow motion, and revelation of athletic skill set new standards for cinema.

1936; 25 min; 16 mm; BW; JR, HS, A; Depression Era.

BUDGET

YOUTH OF THE WORLD (JUGEND DER WELT)

Carl Junghans' "lost classic" film of the 1936 Winter Olympics in Germany. Shots of Hitler and his staff viewing the skilled performances compose "an ironic elegy to the strength and daring" of the youth.

NL; 32 min; 16 mm; color; JR, HS, A; Depression Era.

PYRAMID; UILL

YOUTH SPORTS: IS WINNING EVERYTHING?

This film examines the pressures that parents and coaches can place on a child to win and the psychological and social harm that this "winning is everything" ethic can have on a child's developing self-image.

NL 28 min; 16 mm; color; HS, A; Post World War II.

NILLU

YOU'VE COME A LONG WAY, BABY!

Using the 1973 U.S. Open Championships as a backdrop, the viewer is treated to a look at the changing face of women's tennis, including dress and style of play. Special emphasis is placed on play of King, Evert, Court, and Goolagong.

1973; 25 min; 16 mm; color; JR, HS, A; Post World War II.

USTEN

ZA GOLF M DO CSSR

Golf in Czechoslovakia.

NL; NL; 16 mm; NL; JR, HS, A; Post World War II.

CZECHEM

DISTRIBUTOR INDEX

AAHPER
American Alliance for Health,
Physical Education and Recre-
ation
1201 16th St., NW
Washington, DC 20036

ABB
Astro Bluebonnet Bowl
1701 Chamber of Commerce
Building
Houston, TX 77002

ABC
American Bowling Congress
5301 South 76th St.
Greendale, WI 53129-1127
FAX (414) 421-1194

ABCS
ABC Sports
See Pyramid

ACR
AC & R Public Relations
437 Madison Ave.
New York, New York 10022

AGTOA
American Greyhound Track Op-
erators Association
1065 NE 125 St.
Suite 219
North Miami, FL 33161
(305) 893-2103

AIMS
Aims Media Inc.
6901 Woodley Ave.
Van Nuys, CA 91406-4878
(800) 367-2467

AIOS
Australian Institute of Sport
PO Box 176
Belconnen Act 2516
Australia

AITECH
Agency for Instructional Tech-
nology
Box A
Bloomington, IN 47402-0120
(800) 457-4509

AJBC
American Junior Bowling Con-
gress
See ABC

ALMI
Almi Cinema 5 Films
1900 Broadway
New York, NY 10036

ALTANA
Altana Films
155 W. 68th St.
New York, NY 10023

ALTI
Alti Corporation
3333 N. Torrey Pines Ct, Suite
320
La Jolla, CA 92037
(619) 452-7703

AMEDFL
American Educational Films
Box 8188
Nashville, TN 37207
(615) 868-2040

AMRC
American National Red Cross
Audio-Visual Loan Library
5816 Seminary Rd.
Falls Church, VA 22041

APPAL
Appalshop Films, Inc
PO Box 743
306 Madison St.
Whitesburg, KY 41858
(606) 633-0108

AQHA
American Quarter Horse Associ-
ation
PO Box 200
Amarillo, TX 79168
(806) 376-4811

ARFO
Addiction Research Foundation
of Ontario
33 Russell St.
Marketing Serv. Dept. 682
Toronto, Ontario
Canada M5S 2S1
(416) 595-6260

AS
Asia Society
725 Park Avenue
New York, NY 10021
(212) 288-6400

ASA
Amateur Softball Assoc.
2801 NE 50th
Oklahoma City, OK 73111-7203
(405) 424-5266

ASF
Association-Sterling Films
5797 New Peachtree Road
Atlanta, GA 30340

ASSOC
Association Films Inc.
866 Third Ave.
New York, NY 10022

ATHI
Athletic Institute
200 Castlewood Dr.
N. Palm Beach, FL 33408

AUDPLAN
Audience Planners Inc.
5107 Douglas Fir Rd.
Calabasas, CA 91302
(818) 884-3100

AUIS
Australian Information Services/
   Australian Consulate General
636 5th Avenue
New York, NY 10020
(212) 245-4000

AUSINS
Austrian Institute
11 East 52nd St.
New York, New York 10022
(212) 759-5165

AVATLI
Avatar Learning, Inc.
13701 Riverside Dr. 600
Sherman Oaks, CA 91423

BBC
British Broadcasting Co-TV
630 Fifth Ave.
New York, NY 10020

BBP
Bureau of Business Practice
24 Rope Ferry Rd.
Waterford, CT 06386-9985
(800) 876-9105

BCDA
British Columbia Department of
   Agriculture
Information Branch
Kelowna, BC
Canada

BCNFL
Beacon Films
PO Box 575
1250 Washington St.
Norwood, MA 02062

BELGIUM
Embassy of Belgium
3330 Garfield St. NW
Washington, DC 20008-3515
(202) 333-6900

BESTF
Best Film and Video Corp.
98 Cutter Mill Rd.
Great Neck, NY 11021
(516) 487-4515

BHAWK
Blackhawk Films Eastin-
Phelan Corp.

1235 W. 5th St.
Davenport, IA 52805

BNCHMK
Benchmark Films Inc.
145 Scarborough Rd
Briarcliff Manor, NY 10510
(914) 762-3838

BRANIFF
Braniff International
Box 612167
Dallas, TX 75261

BRNSWK
Brunswick Corp.
1 Brunswick Plaza
Skokie, IL 60077-1089
(708) 470-4700

BRNSWK
Brunswick Division Film Li-
   brary
One Brunswick Plaza
Skokie, IL 60077
(708) 470-4700

BROWN
Browning
Public Relations Department
Morgan, Utah 64050

BROWNS
Cleveland Browns
1085 W. Third St.
Cleveland, OH 44114-1097
(216) 696-3800

BUDGET
Budget Films
4590 Santa Monica Blvd
Los Angeles, CA 90029

BYU
Brigham Young University
Audo Visual Services
290 HRCB
Provo, UT 84602
(801) 378-2713

CANBC
Canadian Broadcasting Corp.
PO Box 50D
Station A
Toronto, Ontario
Canada M5W 1E6
(416) 975-3500

CANEMB
Embassy of Canada
501 Pennsylvania Ave. NW
Washington, DC 20001-2111
(202) 682-1740

CANFDC
Canadian Filmmakers Distribu-
   tion Center
Feinberg Library
Room 126
State University of NY (SUNY)
Plattsburgh, NY 12901

CAROUF
Carousel Film & Video
260 Fifth Ave.
New York, NY 10001
(212) 683-1660

CBIS
Cotton Bowl Information
   Services
Box 7185
Dallas, TX 75209

CBS
Columbia Broadcasting Syst.
383 Madison Ave.
New York, NY 10017

CCCD
Cally Curtis Company
1111 N. Las Palmas Ave.
Hollywood, CA 90038-1289
(213) 467-1101

CCG or CCS
Canadian Consulates General
Film Librarian
Copley Pl.
Boston, MA 02116

CF
Churchill Films
12210 Nebraska Ave.
Los Angeles, CA 90025
(800) 334-7830

CFDC
Campus Film Distributors Corp.
24 Depot Sq.
Tuckahoe, NY 10707
(914) 961-1900

CFOP
Columbia Forum Productions

10621 Fable Row
Columbia, MD 21043

CFS
Creative Film Society
7237 Canby Ave.
Reseda, CA 91335
(818) 885-7288

CGFRG
Consulate General of the Federal Republic of Germany
460 Park Ave.
New York, NY 10022-1906
(212) 308-8700

CHAMP
Champion Films
PO Box 315
Franklin Lakes, NJ 07417

CHEVRON
Chevron Film Library
1200 State Street
Perth Amboy, NJ 08861
(908) 738-2000

CIHIB
Bob Cihi
Carey Rd.
Sasgua Hills
East Norwalk, CT 06855

CINES
Cine Services
2317 East Capitol Drive
Milwaukee, Wisconsin 53211

CNEMAG
Cinema Guild
Division of Document Associates
1697 Broadway
Suite 802
New York, NY 10019
(212) 246-5522

COCA
Coca-Cola Co.
310 N. Ave. NW
Atlanta, GA 30303

COLU
Instructional Support Services
The Library
Teacher's College
Columbia University
525 W. 120th St.
New York, NY 10025

COMPSS
Compass Films
6444 Fountain Ave.
Hollywood, CA 90038

CORF
Coronet Instructional Films
Distributed by Simon & Schuster Film and Videos
108 Wilmot Rd.
Deefield, IL 60015
(800) 621-2131

COUNFI
Counselor Films Inc./Career Futures, Inc.
1728 Cherry St.
Philadelphia, PA 19103
(215) 568-7904

CREATW
Creative Works Inc.
625 N. Michigan Ave.
Chicago, IL 60611

CRYSP
Crystal Productions
1812 Johns Dr.
PO Box 2159
Glenview, IL 60025
(800) 255-8629

CTFL
Canadian Travel Film Library
1251 Ave. of the Americas
16th Floor
New York, NY 10019

CTV
CTV Television Network, Ltd.
48 Charles St. E.
Toronto, Ontario
Canada M4Y 1T4
(416) 924-5454

CZECHEM
Czechoslovakian Embassy
3900 Linnean Ave. NW
Washington, DC 20008

DALCCD
Dallas Community College District
4343 N. Highway 67
Mesquite, TX 75150
(214) 324-7784

DANEIO
Danish Information Office
280 Park Ave.
New York, NY 10017

DARRAH
Marlin Darrah Films
289 Mint Ave.
Eugene, OR 97404

DETLION
Detroit Lions
1200 Featherstone Rd.
Pontaic, MI 48342-1938
(313) 335-4131

DIRECT
Direct Cinema Ltd.
PO Box 69799
Los Angeles, CA 90069
(213) 396-4774

DISNEY
Walt Disney Productions
Educational Film Division
500 S. Buena Vista Ave.
Burbank, CA 91503

DIST16
Distribution 16
32 W. 40th St., #2L
New York, NY 10018

DOALL
Do-All Company
254 N. Laurel Ave.
Des Plaines, IL 60016-4389
(708) 842-1122

DOCA
Document Associates
211 E. 43rd St.
New York, NY 10017

DREWAS
Drew Assoc.
16 E. 74th St.
New York, NY 10021

DUPONT
E.I. Du Pont Nemours & Co.
Applied Technology Division
Brandywine Bldg. 1375
Wilmington, DE 19898

EBEC
Encyclopedia Britannica Educational Corporation

310 S. Michigan Ave.
Chicago, IL 60604
(800) 621-3900

EMA
Educational Media Australia
7 Martin Street
South Melbourne VIC 3205
Australia

EMBARGO
Embassy of Argentina
1600 New Hampshire Ave. NW
Washington, DC 20009-2512
(202) 939-6400

EMBIND
Embassy of India
2107 Massachusetts Ave. NW
Washington, DC 20008-2811
(202) 939-7000

EMBKUW
Embassy of Kuwait
2940 Tilden St. NW
Washington DC 20008-1193
(202) 966-0702

EMBUGA
Embassy of Uganda
5909 15th St. NW
Washington, DC 20011-2816
(202) 726-7100

EMJAP
Embassy of Japan
2514 Massachusetts Ave. NW
Washington, DC 20008

ESA
U.S. Skiing
PO Box 100
Park City, UT 84060

ESMARK
Esmark Inc.
55 E. Monroe St.
Chicago IL 60603

FACSEA
French American Cultural Exchange Services & Educational Aid
972 5th Avenue
New York, NY 10021
(212) 737-9700

FGTO
French Government Tourist Office
610 Fifth Ave.
New York, NY 10022-2493
(212) 757-1125

FI
Films Inc.
5547 N. Ravenswood Ave.
Chicago, IL 60640-1199
(800) 323-4222

FIARTS
Film Arts
461 Church Street
Toronto, Ontario
Canada M4Y 2C5
(416) 962-0182

FIESTA
Fiesta Bowl
120 S. Ash Ave.
Tempe, AZ 85008

FILCOM
Film Communicators
Dist. by MTI Film & Video
108 Wilmot Rd.
Deerfield, IL 60015
(800) 621-2131

FILMIC
Filmic Archives/Reel Images
600 Main St.
Monroe, CT 06468
(203) 261-1920

FLADC
Florida Department of Commerce Film Library
Collins Bldg
107 W. Gaines St.
Tallahassee, FL 32304

FLMAUST
Film Australia
Eton Road
Lindfield NSW 2070
Australia

FLMLIB
Filmakers Library Inc.
124 E. 40th St.
Suite 901
New York, NY 10016
(212) 808-4980

FLMTON
Filmation Studios
18107 Sherman Way
Reseda, CA 91335

FLSU
Florida State University
Film Library
Tallahassee, FL 32306

FOTH
Films for the Humanities & Sciences
PO Box 2053
Princeton, NJ 08543
(800) 257-5126

FRANCDC
Franciscan Communications Center
1229 S. Santee St.
Los Angeles, CA 90015
(800) 421-8510

GBP
Green Bay Packers
1265 Lombardi Ave.
Green Bay, WI 54303
(414) 496-5700

GEMILL
General Mills Inc.
1 General Mills Blvd.
Minneapolis, MN 54426-1348
(612) 540-2311

GFILM
Gibson Film
15 Courtenay Place
Wellington, New Zealand

GM
General Motors Corp.
Mgmt. & Organization Div.
1700 W. Third Ave.
Flint, MI 48502
(313) 762-9867

GN
GN Productions
1019 N. Cole Ave
Los Angeles, CA 90038

GRADY
Tim Grady Productions
704 Hennepin Ave.
Minneapolis, MN 55403
(612) 333-4594

GRATV
Granada TV
1221 Avenue of the Americas
New York, NY 10020

GSVP
Good Sports Video Productions
489 Harrison
Sausalito, CA 94965

GTARC
Goodyear Tire and Rubber
1144 E. Market St.
Akron, OH 44316-0001
(216)-796-2121

HAMMS
Hamm's Sport Films
1569 Selby Ave.
St. Paul, MN 55104

HEARST
Hearst Metrotone News
235 E. 45th St.
New York, NY 10017

HIGGIN
Alfred Higgins Productions, Inc.
635D Laurel Canyon Blvd.
North Hollywood, CA 91606
(818) 762-3300

HONDA
Honda North America
1919 Torrence
Torrence, CA 90504-2746

HRAW
Holt, Rinehart & Winston
383 Madison Ave.
New York, NY 10017
(212) 872-2000

IBM
IBM Film Activities
IBM Corporation
Old Orchard Rd
Armonk, NY 10504

ICARUS
Icarus Films
Suite 1319
200 Park Ave South
New York, NY 10003
(212) 674-3375

IFB
International Film Bureau, Inc.

332 S. Michigan Ave.
Chicago, IL 60604-4382
(800) 432-2241

IFF
International Film Foundation
155 W. 72nd St.
New York, NY 10023
(212) 580-1111

ILCA
International Lightning Class
   Assn.
808 High St.
Worthington, OH 43085

IOWA
Iowa State University/ISURF-
   FILM
Media Resources Center
Media Productions Unit
Exhibit Hall South
Ames, IA 50011
(515) 294-2316

IRA
International Rodeo Association
PO Box 615
Pauls Valley, OK 73075

IREFL
International Rehabilitation
   Film Review Library
20. W. 40th St.
New York, NY 10018
(212) 869-0460

ISLA
Indiana State Library Assn.
Extension Division
140 N. Senate Ave.
Indianapolis, IN 46204

IU
Indiana University
Audio-Visual Center
Bloomington, IN 47405-5901
(812) 855-8087

IVCH
Intercollegiate Video Clearing
   House
PO Drawer 33000R
Miami, FL 33133
(305) 443-3500

JOU
Journal Films Inc./Altshul
   Group
930 Pitner
Evanston, IL 60202
(800) 323-5448

JOYCE
Joyce Motion Picture Co.
8613 Yolanda
PO Box 458
Northridge, CA 91324

KAROL
Karol Media/Karol Video
22 Riverview Drive
Wayne, NJ 07470-3191
(800) 526-4773

KCCFC
Kansas City Chiefs Football
   Club
One Arrowhead Drive
Kansas City, MO 64129-1651
(816) 924-9300

KCET
KCET/Los Angeles
4401 Sunset Blvd.
Los Angeles, CA 90027
(213) 667-9425

KENJPF
Joseph P. Kennedy Jr.
   Foundation
1701 K St., NW
Washington, DC 20006

KENTSTU
Kent State University
AV Services
Kent, OH 44240

KFD
Kingsway Film Distributors
PO Box 8240
Stirling St.
Perth, WA 6000
Australia

KINGBC
King Broadcasting Company
333 Dexter Ave.
Seattle, WA 98109-5183
(206) 448-5555

KINGFT
King Features Educational Division
235 E. 45th St.
New York, NY 10017
(212) 682-5600

KINGSP
King Screen Productions
Division of King Broadcasting Co.
333 Dexter Ave.
Seattle, WA 981095183
(206) 448-5555

KITCHN
Kitchen Center for Video
512 W. 19th St.
New York, NY 10011
(212) 255-5793

KLEINW
Walter J. Klein Co., Ltd.
6311 Carmel Rd.
Box 2087
Charlotte, NC 28247-2087
(704) 542-1403

KODAK
Eastman Kodak Company
PO Box 92918
Rochester, NY 14692

KRASKER
Krasker Memorial Film Library
Boston University
565 Commonwealth Ave.
Boston, MA 02215

KRMATV
KRMA-TV
1261 Glenarm Pl
Denver, CO 80204-2100
(303) 892-6666

KTCATV
Twin Cities Public Television Inc.
1640 Como Avenue
St. Paul MN 55108
(612) 646-4611

LAWREN
Lawren Productions Inc
PO Box 666
Mendocino, CA 95460

LCOA
Learning Corporation of America/Coronet MTI
Simon & Schuster
108 Wilmot Rd.
Deerfield, IL 60015
(800) 621-2131

LEVI
Levi Strauss & Co.
1155 Battery St.
San Francisco, CA 94106

LIPTON
Thomas J. Lipton Co.
523 S. 17th St.
Harrisburg, PA 17104-2220
(717) 234-6215

LLBI
Little League Baseball Inc.
PO Box 3485
South Williamsport, PA 17701-0485
(717) 326-1921

LPGA
Ladies Professional Golf Association
2570 Vousia St., Suite B
Daytona, FL 32114

LSU
Louisiana State University
Instructional Resources Ctr
Baton Rouge, LA 70803

LUF
Lucerne Media
37 Ground Pine Rd.
Morris Plains, NJ 07950
(800) 341-2293

MARTC
Burt Martin Assoc.
315 N. Lake
PO Box 6337
Burbank, CA 91510

MCDO
McDonnell Douglas Corp.
Film and Television Comm.
3855 Lakewood Blvd.
Suite 36-16
Long Beach, CA 90846
(213) 392-5766

MCFI
Mar/Chuck Film Industries Inc.
PO Box 61
Mt. Prospect, IL 60056

MEDIAG
Media Guild
11722 Sorrento Valley Rd.
Suite E
San Diego, CA 92121
(619) 755-9191

MGHT
McGraw-Hill Films
674 Via De La Valle
PO Box 641
Del Mar, CA 92014
(714) 453-5000

MGM
MGM Films
1350 Ave. of the Americas
New York, NY 10019

MICHMED
Michigan Media
University of Michigan
Media Resources Center
400 4th Street
Ann Arbor, MI 48103-4816

MILLER
Miller Brewing Company, Film Section
Trade Relations Dept.
4000 West State Street
Milwaukee, WI 53208

MIMET
Miami-Metro Department of Public Tourism
Miami, FL

MLBP
Major League Baseball Productions
1212 Avenue of the Americas
New York, NY 10036

MOHOMV
Morris Home Video
2730 Monterey
105 Monterey Business Park
Torrance, CA 90503
(213) 533-4800

MONUMT
Monumental Films & Recordings Inc.
2160 Rockrose Ave.
Baltimore, MD 21211
(800) 821-9179

MORRALL
Helen Morrall
1980 Fairbanks Ave.
Ottawa, Ontario
Canada K1H 5Y6

MSU
Michigan State University
Instructional Media Center
East Lansing, MI 48824
(517) 353-9229

MTI
MTI Teleprograms/Coronet
   International
Distributed by Simon and
   Schuster
108 Wilmot Ave.
Deerfield, IL 60015
(800) 621-2131

MTOLP
Made-to-Order Library Prod.
345 Fullerton Parkway
Suite 1101
Chicago, IL 60614
(312) 525-7703

MTPS
Modern Talking Picture Service
5000 Park Street North
St. Petersburg, FL 33709-2200
(813) 541-7571

MULTPP
Multimedia Program
   Productions
140 W. 9th St.
Cincinnati, OH 45202
(513) 352-4047

MYSTIC
Mystic Seaport Museum
50 Greenmanville Ave.
Mystic, CT 06355-1935
(203) 572-0711

NBC
National Broadcasting
   Company, Inc
30 Rockefeller Plaza
New York, NY 10020
(212) 664-4444

NBHF
National Baseball Hall of Fame
Film Rental Library
PO Box 590-F
Cooperstown, NY 13326
(607) 547-9988

NCS
National Cinema Service
Box 43
Ho Ho Kus, NJ 07423

NET
National Educational Televi-
   sion, Inc.
WNET/Thirteen
Indiana University
Bloomington, IN 47401

NEWDAY
New Day Films
Suite 902
121 W. 27th St.
New York, NY 10001
(212) 645-8210

NYFILMS
New Yorker Films
16 West 61st Street
New York, NY 10023
(212) 247-6110

NFBC
National Film Board of Canada
1251 Avenue of the Americas
16th Floor
New York, NY 10020-1175
(212) 586-5131

NFL
NFL/AFL Films, Inc.
330 Fellowship Rd.
Mt. Laurel, NJ 08054
(609) 778-1600

NFU
Marketing Division
National Film Unit
PO Box 46-002
Lower Hutt
New Zealand

NGUZO
Nguzo Saba Films
2482 Sutter
San Francisco, CA 94115

NILLU
Northern Illinois University
Media Distribution Communica-
   tion Services
DeKalb, IL 60115
(815) 753-0171

NINEFC
Ninety-Two Hundred Film
   Center
9200 Wayzata Blvd.
Minneapolis, MN 55440

NOMWSA
New Orleans Mid-Winter Sports
   Association
Suite 510, 611 Gravier St.
New Orleans, LA 70130

NORTRIC
Norton Triumph Corporation
20334 Greenspring Drive
Timonium, MD 21093

NRA
National Rifle Association
1600 Rhode Island Ave. NW
Washington, DC 20036-3240
(202) 828-6000

NSC
National Safety Council
444 N. Michigan Avenue
Chicago, IL 60611-3991
(800) 621-7619

NZGTO
New Zealand Government
   Tourist Office
630 Fifth Avenue
New York, NY 10020

OFFSHR
Offshore Productions
617 E. Thomas Street
Seattle, WA 98102
(206) 323-3040

OKSU
Oklahoma State University
Audio Visual Center/Public In-
   formation Office

Stillwater, OK 74078-0118
(800) 654-4055

OMCL
Outboard Marine Corp.
100 Sea Horse Dr.
Waukegan, IL 60085-2195
(708) 689-6200

OSU
Ohio State University Center
    for Teaching Excellence
Columbus, OH 43210

OWENSC
Owens-Corning Fiberglas
    Corporation
Fiberglas Tower
Toledo, OH 43659-0001
(419) 248-8000

OXFORD
Oxford Films/Paramount
Distributed by Aims Media
6901 Woodley Ave.
Van Nuys, CA 91406-4878
(800) 367-2467

PANTHEON
Societe du Cinema Pantheon
53 Avenue des Champss-Elysees
Paris 8e
France

PARMT
Paramount Pictures Corp.
15 Columbus Circle
New York, NY 10023-7799
(212) 373-7000

PEACH
Peach Bowl Inc.
Box 1336
Atlanta, GA 30301

PEFC
Philadelphia Eagles Football
    Club
Veteran's Stadium
3501 S. Broad St.
Philadelphia, PA 19148-5298
(215) 463-2500

PENNST
Penn State University
Audio-Visual Services
Univ. Div. of Media & Learning
    Resources

Special Services Bldg.
University Park, PA 16802
(800) 826-0132

PERRYM
Marily Perry TV Productions,
    Inc.
677 5th Ave., 5th Floor
New York, NY 10022
(212) 308-2250

PES
Peter Eckrich and Sons Inc.
PO Box 388
Fort Wayne, IN 46801

PGA
Professional Golfers Association
100 Ave. of the Champions
Palm Beach Gardens, FL 33418
(407) 624-8400

PHENIX
Phoenix/BFA Films & Video, Inc.
468 Park Ave. South
New York, NY 10016
(212) 684-5910

PICA
Prudential Insurance Company
    of America Prudential Plaza
751 Broad St.
Prudential Plaza
Newark, NJ 07102-3777
(201) 877-6000

PICAD
Picadilly Films International Co.
Box 16255
Lapham Station
San Antonio, TX 78246

PMI
Public Media Incorporated
    /Films, Inc.
1213 Wilmette Ave.
Chicago, IL 60640
(800) 323-4222

PNTIO
Portuguese National Tourist &
    Information Office
570 Fifth Avenue
New York, NY 10036
(212) 354-4403

POLEMB
Polish Embassy

2640 16th St. NW
Washington, D.C. 20009-4202
(202) 234-3800

POSIMP
Positive Image Productions Inc.
4900 Leesburg Pike, Suite 206
Alexandria, VA 22302

PSU
Portland State University
Division of Continuing Ed.
Film Library
PO Box 1383
1633 SW Park Ave.
Portland, OR 97207

PUBTEL
Public Television Library
475 L'Enfant Plaza, SW
Washington, DC 20024

PYRAMID
Pyramid Film & Video
PO Box 1048
Santa Monica, CA 90406
(800) 421-2304

RCBS
RCBS Inc.
PO Box 1919
605 Oroville Dam Blvd.
Oroville, CA 95965
(916) 533-5191

RCPDF
RCP Destination Films
Toronto, Canada

RCSU
Resource Center Spinal Unit
Royal North Shore Hospital
Pacific Highway
St. Leonards NSW 2065
Australia

REAF
Reaction Films
Steck-Vaughn Co.
PO Box 2028
Austin, TX 78767

RMIBHF
RMI Media Productions
Blackhawk Films
5959 Triumph St
City of Commerce, CA 90040
(213) 888-2229

RNE
Netherlands Embassy
4200 Linnean Ave. NW
Washington, DC 20008
(202) 244-5304

RRFLM
Reels and Reality Film Co.
9349 S. Lafayette Ave.
Chicago, IL 60620
(312) 478-7197

RSTF
Roma Straddo Tribune Films
38 W. 32nd St
New York, NY 10001

SAFC
South Australian Film Corp.
113 Tapleys Hill Road
Hendon
South Australia 5014

SAL
Swedish American Line
636 Fifth Ave.
New York, NY 10020

SALENG
Salenger Educational Media
1635 12th St.
Santa Monica, CA 90404
(213) 450-1300

SANMRP
Sanmar Productions
365 W. 19th St.
New York, NY 10011

SARBO
Sports and Recreation Bureau
of Ontario
Toronto, Ontario
Canada

SCNDRI
John Secondari
1560 Broadway
New York, NY 10036

SCORPO
Scorpio
2240 N. Pacific St.
Seattle, WA 98103

SDSU
Audio Visual Center
South Dakota State University

Pugsley 101, Box 2218A
Brookings, SD 57007-1199

SEARS
Sears, Roebuck & Co.
Informational Program
    Production
233 S. Wacker Dr.
Sears Tower
Chicago, IL 60684-0001
(312) 875-2500

SF
Sterling Educational Films
241 E. 34th St.
New York, NY 10016
(212) 262-9433

SFTI
Sports Films & Talents Inc.
12755 State HWY 55
Minneapolis, MN 55441

SHELL
Shell Oil Company
Marketing Division
8500 N. Michigan
Indianapolis, IN 46268
(317) 872-7440

SIGPRS
Signal Press
1730 Chicago Ave.
Evanston, IL
(312) 864-1322

SIRS
Social Issues Resources Series
    Inc.
PO Box 2348
Boca Raton, FL 33427-2348
(800) 327-1513

SNTO
Swiss National Tourist Office
608 Fifth Ave.
New York, NY 10020
(212) 757-5944

SOLANA
Solana Studios
2700 Gordon Dr.
Naples, FL 33940

SOLIL
Soliloquy Corporation
1722 18th St.
Los Alamos, NM 87544

SPEER
Speer Inc.
PO Box 896
Lewiston, Idaho 83501

STATNS
Statens Filmcentral
Danish Government Film Office
27 Vestergarde, DK 1456
Copenhagen K, Denmark
(01) 13 26 86

STNFLD
Stanfield House
PO Box 3208
Santa Monica, CA 90403

STP
STP Corporation
5300 Broken Sound Blvd. NW
PO Box 3070
Boca Raton, FL 33431

STRPRO
Stryker Productions
915 Delmar Ave.
Alameda, CA 94501

SWNTO
Swedish National Tourist Office
75 Rockefeller Plaza
505 Fifth Avenue
New York, NY 10019

SYRA
Syracuse University
Film Rental Center
1455 E. Colvin St.
Syracuse, NY 13210

TAHSEM
Martin Tahse
1041 N. Formosa Ave.
Los Angeles, CA 90046

TBVS
Tennis Book Video Service
Dept. 1. 22-24
Buckingham Palace Rd.
London SW1 W0P
UK

TELEFILM
Telefilm LTD
PO Box 709
Homosassa Springs, FL 32647

TEXACO
Texaco Inc.
2000 Westchester Ave.
White Plains, NY 10604

TEXTURE
Texture Films Inc./Films Inc.
5547 N. Ravenswood Ave.
Chicago, IL 60640
(312) 878-2600

TFCP
Tasmanian Film Corp.
6 McLaren St.
North Sydney NSW 2060
Australia

TFN
Track & Field News
Box 296
Los Altos, CA 94022
(415) 948-8188

TIMLIF
Time-Life Films Inc.
100 Eisenhower Dr.
PO Box 644
Paramus, NJ 07652
(201) 843-4545

TMA
Thompson Mitchell & Assoc.
3525 Piedmont Rd. NE
Atlanta, GA 30326

TREP
Trend International Productions
PO Box 38669
Hollywood, CA 90038

TRIBUNE
Tribune Films
38 West 32nd St.
New York, NY 10001

TWYMAN
Twyman Films Inc.
329 Salem Ave.
Box 605
Dayton, OH 45401
(800) 543-9594

UCB
University of California-Berkley
Extension Media Center
2223 Fulton Ave.
Berkeley, CA 94720

UCLA
University of California at Los
   Angeles
Media Center/IML
405 Hilgard Ave.
Los Angeles, CA 90024
(213) 825-0755

UCOLO
University of Colorado
   Films/Video
Academic Media Services
Stadium 760
Boulder, CO 80303
(303) 492-7341

UCONN
University of Connecticut
UCIMT Erickson Memorial
   Film & Video Library
PO Box U-1, Room 3
249 Glenbrook Rd
Storrs, CT 06269-2001
(203) 486-2530

UEVA
Universal Education and Visual
   Arts
Div. of Univ. Studios, Inc.
100 Universal City Plaza
Universal City, CA 91608

UGA
University of Georgia
Center For Ed.
Athens, GA 30601

UILL
University of Illinois
Visual Aids Service
1325 S. Oak St.
Champaign, IL 61820
(800) 367-3456

UIOWA
UI/ISU
Audiovisual Center/Iowa Films
C-8 Seashore Hall
Iowa City, IA 52242
(319) 353-5885

UMOC
University of Missouri-Columbia
Film and Video Library
Academic Support Center
505 E Stewart Road
Columbia, MO 65211

UNDMC
University of North Dakota
Medical Center Rehabilitation
   Hospital
University Station Box 8202
Grand Forks, ND 58202

UNH
University of New Hampshire
Audio Visual Center
Durham, NH 03824
(603) 862-2240

UNIJAP
Unijapan Films
9-13 Ginza 5-Chome
Chuo-Ku
Tokyo, 104
Japan

UNL
University of Nebraska-Lincoln
Extension Division
Instructional Media Center
Lincoln, NE 68508

UPENN
University of Pennsylvania
3440 Woodland Ave.
Philadelphia, PA 19104

UPI
United Press International
1400 I St. NW
Suite 800
Washington, DC 20005-2289
(800) 777-5532

USAF
US Air Force
The Pentagon
Washington, D.C. 20330

USARMY
United States Army
Audio Visual Suport Centers:
Ft. Meade, MD 20755
Ft. McPherson, GA 30330
Ft. Sam Houston, TX 78234
Ft. Richardson, AK 98749
Presido, CA 94129
Camp McCoy, WI 54656
Ft. Shafter, HA 96823

USD
University of South Dakota
114 Service Center
Vermillion, SD 57069

USDA
U.S. Dept. of Agriculture
Motion Pictures Serv.
Room 1850
South Building
Washington, DC 20250

USGA
United States Golf Assoc.
Liberty Corner Rd.
Far Hills, NJ 07931-0000
(908) 234-2300

USNAC
US National Audiovisual Center
8700 Edgeworth Drive
Capitol Heights, MD 20743-3701
(301) 763-1896

USOC
United States Olympic
    Committee
1776 E. Boulder St.
Colorado Springs, CO 80909-
    5793
(719) 578-4500

USOIAA
US Office of Inter-American
    Affairs
2201 C St.
Washington, DC 20520

USOOE
Utah State Office of Education
250 E. 5th South
Salt Lake City, UT 84111

USRA
USRA Clearinghouse
625 Bethlehem Pike
Ambler, PA 19002

USTA
United States Trotting
    Association
750 Michigan Ave.
Columbus, OH 43215-1191
(614) 224-2291

USTEN
United States Tennis Assoc.
1212 Ave. of the Americas
12th Floor
New York, NY 10036-1694
(212) 302-3322

USVA
US Veteran's Administration
Vermont at H. St.
Washington, DC 20420

UTEX
University of Texas-Austin
Film Library
Drawer W
Austin, TX 78712

UU
University of Utah
Educ. Media Ctr.
207 Milton Bennion Hall
Salt Lake City, UT 84112

UWASH
University of Washington
Center For Educational
    Resources T-2-81
HSB 5b-56
Seattle, WA 98195
(206) 545-1186

UWFKD
United World Films
Kinetic Division
Division of Universal Studios
    Inc.
2001 S. Vermont Ave.
Los Angeles, CA 90007
(213) 731-2131

UWISC
University of Wisconsin
Video Resource Library
425 Henry Hall
Madison, WI 53706
(608) 263-3663

UWP
University of Washington Press
PO Box 50096
Seattle, WA 98145-5096
(800) 441-4115

VANTAGE
Vantage Communications
78 Main St.
PO Box 546-G
Nyack, NY 10960
(914) 358-0147

VERVE
Verve Films Inc.
733 Green Bay Road
Wilmette, IL 60091

VIACOM
Viacom International
1515 Broadway
New York, NY 10036-5794
(212) 258-6000

VIDEOC
Video Classroom
4th Floor, 437 Kilda Rd
Melbourne VIC 3004
Australia

VITT
Vitt Media International
1114 Avenue of the Americas
New York, NY 10036

WCBSTV
51 W. 52nd St.
New York, NY 10019-6101
(212) 975-4321

WCCOTV
WCCO-TV
Media Services
11th on the Mall
90th S. 11th St
Minneapolis, MN 55403

WEAL
Weal Publishing Center
Educational Development
    Center
55 Chapel St.
Newton, MA 02160

WEX
Wexler Film Productions Inc
801 N. Seward St.
Los Angeles, CA 90038
(213) 462-6671

WGBH
WGBH Educational Foundation
125 Western Ave.
Boston, MA 02134-1098
(617) 492-2777

WIBC
Women's International Bowling
    Congress
5301 S. 76th St.
Greendale, WI 53129-1191
(414) 421-9000

WINNEB
Winnebago Industries Inc.
PO Box 152

Forest City, IA 50436-0152
(515) 582-3535

WINWES
Winchester-Western
275 Winchester Ave.
New Haven, CT 06504

WNVT
North Virginia Educational
　Television
　　See LAWREN

WOLPER
Wolper Productions
8489 W. Third St.
Los Angeles, CA 90048

WOLVER
Wolverline
745 State Circle
Box 1941
Ann Arbor, MI 48106

WOMBAT
Wombat Film & Video

Altschul Group
250 W. 57th Suite 2421
Ossining, NY 10562
(914) 315-2502

WRP
William Rose Productions
955 Massachusetts Ave., Suite
　240
Cambridge, MA 02139

WSF
Women's Sports Foundation
342 Madison Ave.
New York, NY 10173

WSTGLC
West Glen Communications
1430 Broadway
New York, NY 10018-3396
(212) 921-2800

WSU
Washington State University
Film & Video Media Center
Pullman, WA 99163

WTBS
WTBS-TV
1050 Techwood Dr. NW
Atlanta, GA 30318-5604
(404) 827-1717

WWS
Weston Woods Studios
Institutional Media Institute
389 Newtown Turnpike
Weston, CT 06883
(800) 243-5020

YALEU
Yale University
Audio Visual Center
130 Wall St.
New Haven, CT 06520

ZIPPORAH
Zipporah Films
One Richdale Ave, Unit #4
Cambridge, MA 02140
(617) 576-3603

NAME INDEX

TOPIC INDEX

MILWAUKEE BUCKS
Almost Perfect

MINNESOTA VIKINGS
First 10 years, The (1970 Viking
　　Highlight Film)

MOTORCYCLING
Cross Country
Evel Knievel
Goals, Challenges and Choices
Moto Brave
On Any Sunday
Sidewinder One
Three in Europe
Too Much Speed

MOTOR SPORTS, LAND
All-Americans, The
Auto-Race-Arama
Auto Racing
Baja 1000
Baja: Off Road With BFG
Baja: Road to Manhood
Championship Challenge
Four-5-6 Plus
Gentlemen, Start Your Engines
Karting
Man Behind the Wheel
1911 Indianapolis 500-Mile Race
On Any Sunday
One Tough Texan
On the Go
Power and Wheels: The
　　Automobile in Modern Life
Race to Live
Rallye Des Neighes
Requiem for a Race Track
Roaring Wheels
Sidewinder One
Sno-Twister
Snowmobile Grand Prix: The
　　Richest Race
Southern "500," The
Spirit of Ecstasy
Sports Cars: The Rage to Race
Talking ATC Safety
Three in Europe
Too Much Speed
Tournament of Champions
Turned On!
Twenty-Four Heures Du Mans
What Makes Jacky Ickx Race?
What Will They Think of Next?
Wonderful World of Road
　　Racing, The

MOTOR SPORTS, WATER
Lunker Lore
Racing Rivers
Record Breakers
Run Sunward
Seine Insanity
Three for Adventure
Title Drive, The
Turned On!
Yachting in Greece

MOUNTAIN CLIMBING
Abimes
Abyss
All the Way Up There
Americans on Everest
Call of the Mountains, The
Challenge of Mount Everest
Challenge, The
Climb
Climb for the Top
Eieger, The
Everest Unmasked: The First
　　Ascent Without Oxygen
First Ascent
Fitzroy
From the Ocean to the Sky
Great Challenge, The
High in the Himalayas
I Always Come Back to the
　　Himalayas
Ice, Rock, and Sky
Jungfrau: Ascent on Skis
Jungfrau: First Rottal Ascent
Jungfrau: First Ascent
Le Conquerant De L' Inutile
Left Wall of Cenotaph Corner
Le Pilier De La Solitude
Lifeclimb
Lure of the Mont Blanc, The
Matterhorn
Nothing's Stopping You
Once Before I Die
Portalet
Sentinel: The West Face
Sheer Sport
Solo
Solo: Behind the Scenes
Teton Trails
To Climb a Mountain

MOVEMENT EDUCATION
Movement: To Live Is to Move
Movement Exploration: What
　　Am I?

NATIONAL SPORT
Coaches

Great Game (Soccer)
People's Game, The
Rest and Leisure in the USSR
Rugby

NATIVE AMERICANS AND
SPORT
Cree Hunters of Mistassini
Fishing at the Stone Weir,
1 and 2
Haudenosaunee: Way of the
　　Longhouse
Jigging for Lake Trout
Journey: The Quest for Self -
　　Reliance
Kashia Men's Dances: South-
　　western Pomo Indians
Lacrosse
Lacrosse: Litte Brother of War
Northern Games
Play and Cultural Continuity,
　　Part 4: Montana Indian
　　Children
Run, Appaloosa, Run: Part 1
Run, Appaloosa, Run: Part 2
Spirit of the Wind (1)
Tukta and the Magic Bow
Tukta and the Magic Spear
Tukta and the Snow Place
Tukta and the Ten Thousand
　　Fishes
Tukta and the Trials of Strength
Woodland Indians of Early
　　America

NUTRITION AND SPORT
Nutrition and Eating Disorders
　　Series

OFFICIATING
Officials, The
Referee

OLYMPIC GAMES, ANCIENT
Ancient Greece
Games and Festivals: Greece
Olympia
Olympic Cavalcade
Olympics, The

OLYMPIC GAMES, MODERN
American Athlete: The Junior
　　Olympic Way
Animal Olympians
Beginnings
Best I Can, The (2)
Best You Can Be, The
Beyond the Finish Line